AF838666

MEDIA AND COMMUNICATIONS - TECHNOLOGIES, POLICIES AND CHALLENGES

ADVANCES IN SOCIAL NETWORKING RESEARCH

MEDIA AND COMMUNICATIONS - TECHNOLOGIES, POLICIES AND CHALLENGES

Additional books in this series can be found on Nova's website under the Series tab.

Additional e-books in this series can be found on Nova's website under the e-book tab.

MEDIA AND COMMUNICATIONS - TECHNOLOGIES, POLICIES AND CHALLENGES

ADVANCES IN SOCIAL NETWORKING RESEARCH

SALVADOR REESE
EDITOR

LIBRARY OF CONGRESS
SURPLUS
DUPLICATE

nova publishers
New York

Copyright © 2016 by Nova Science Publishers, Inc.

All rights reserved. No part of this book may be reproduced, stored in a retrieval system or transmitted in any form or by any means: electronic, electrostatic, magnetic, tape, mechanical photocopying, recording or otherwise without the written permission of the Publisher.

We have partnered with Copyright Clearance Center to make it easy for you to obtain permissions to reuse content from this publication. Simply navigate to this publication's page on Nova's website and locate the "Get Permission" button below the title description. This button is linked directly to the title's permission page on copyright.com. Alternatively, you can visit copyright.com and search by title, ISBN, or ISSN.

For further questions about using the service on copyright.com, please contact:
Copyright Clearance Center
Phone: +1-(978) 750-8400 Fax: +1-(978) 750-4470 E-mail: info@copyright.com.

NOTICE TO THE READER

The Publisher has taken reasonable care in the preparation of this book, but makes no expressed or implied warranty of any kind and assumes no responsibility for any errors or omissions. No liability is assumed for incidental or consequential damages in connection with or arising out of information contained in this book. The Publisher shall not be liable for any special, consequential, or exemplary damages resulting, in whole or in part, from the readers' use of, or reliance upon, this material. Any parts of this book based on government reports are so indicated and copyright is claimed for those parts to the extent applicable to compilations of such works.

Independent verification should be sought for any data, advice or recommendations contained in this book. In addition, no responsibility is assumed by the publisher for any injury and/or damage to persons or property arising from any methods, products, instructions, ideas or otherwise contained in this publication.

This publication is designed to provide accurate and authoritative information with regard to the subject matter covered herein. It is sold with the clear understanding that the Publisher is not engaged in rendering legal or any other professional services. If legal or any other expert assistance is required, the services of a competent person should be sought. FROM A DECLARATION OF PARTICIPANTS JOINTLY ADOPTED BY A COMMITTEE OF THE AMERICAN BAR ASSOCIATION AND A COMMITTEE OF PUBLISHERS.

Additional color graphics may be available in the e-book version of this book.

Library of Congress Cataloging-in-Publication Data

Names: Reese, Salvador, editor.
Title: Advances in social networking research / editor, Salvador Reese.
Description: Hauppauge, New York : Nova Science Publishers, Inc., [2016] |
Series: Media and communications: technologies, policies and challenges | Includes bibliographical references and index.
Identifiers: LCCN 2016017077 (print) | LCCN 2016022499 (ebook) | ISBN 9781634852258 (hardcover) | ISBN 9781634852432 ()
Subjects: LCSH: Online social networks--Research. | Information technology--Research.
Classification: LCC HM742 .A38 2016 (print) | LCC HM742 (ebook) | DDC 302.30285--dc23
LC record available at https://lccn.loc.gov/2016017077

Published by Nova Science Publishers, Inc. † New York

CONTENTS

PREFACE

This book provides current research on social networking. The first chapter presents an application of network analysis to characterize the role of the Information and Communication Technologies (ICT) sector as an enabler of knowledge and innovation diffusion across the economy. Chapter Two proposes a novel algorithm for computing the similarity of users in a social network considering their characteristics. Chapter Three addresses both the modeling of information dissemination, especially via epidemics and evolutionary game theoretic techniques, as well as their control via optimal control frameworks and dual optimization techniques. Chapter Four is designed to explore socially networked spaces as an important process within teacher professional development. Social networking enables teachers to access new ideas, to collaborate and to contribute to a shared knowledge, regardless of time and place.

Chapter 1 - Traditionally studies on the sector of Information and Communication Technologies (ICT) have focused on the analysis of its economic impact, not taking into account the qualitative importance of the networked industrial structure. ICT are general purpose technologies, that is, they are characterized by a fast pace of technological progress, they are suitable for a wide variety of activities, and they enable the generation of innovations. Consequently, the importance of ICT do not rely itself on the weight of the producing sector, but on the effects of their widespread diffusion across the economy.

Recent research has applied network theory to the study of ICT. Network analysis can bring some novel insights into the potential of new technologies to facilitate knowledge flows and consequently, to generate new sources of income and wealth. This chapter then present an application of network analysis to characterize the role of the ICT sector as an enabler of knowledge and innovation diffusion across the economy.

Chapter 2 - The search for similar people is one of the most desirable aspects by users in a community, e.g., in a social network. The identification of similar people promotes the exchange of information about not only common topics, but can also lead to their participation in projects with shared interests. In marketing, it may also be useful to identify, e.g., potential customers that are similar to the customers who buy the most. It can also be used to recommend potential friends to a new user (the so-called *cold start problem*).

In this chapter, the authors propose a novel algorithm for computing the similarity of users in a social network considering their characteristics, e.g., musical and literary tastes, gender, race, among others. However, that the authors' proposal is generic in the sense that the social network analyst is free to choose the set of characteristics that will be used to establish the similarity among the users. In addition, the authors also propose an extension of the authors' algorithm to the identification of similar couples, i.e., the authors face the *cold start problem for couples*. This could be useful, e.g., when a marriage is looking for similar couples in order to develop joint activities: trips, financial projects, and social meetings.

Chapter 3 - Information dissemination is one of the most critical processes in modern societies and one of the most important reasons for the proliferation of communications networks, especially of online social networks that have enabled global information exchange at rapid scales. This chapter will focus on information dissemination models that compared to the current literature, they specifically take into account aspects related to user interest and its temporal variability in the dynamics of information spreading. The authors focus on a dissemination framework regarding solely useful information, where users of communications and online social networks are willing to accept information and potentially further propagate it to their uninformed peers, depending on the interest each user has on specific topics. This is a novel perspective to consider information user interests affect significantly the outcome and the dynamics of information propagation and impact its control process. Such models can be employed for further improving information dissemination analysis and control methodologies, and they can be exploited in various application domains, e.g., from infrastructure design and management, to marketing and advertising improvement. This chapter addresses both the modeling of information dissemination, especially via epidemics and evolutionary game theoretic techniques, as well as their control via optimal control frameworks and dual optimization techniques. dissemination under inhomogeneous mixing, since the time-varying user interests affect significantly the outcome and the dynamics of information propagation and impact its control process. Such models can be employed for further improving information dissemination analysis and control methodologies, and they can be exploited in various application domains, e.g., from infrastructure design and management, to marketing and advertising improvement. This chapter addresses both the modeling of information dissemination, especially via epidemics and evolutionary game theoretic techniques, as well as their control via optimal control frameworks and dual optimization techniques.

Chapter 4 - This chapter is designed to explore socially networked spaces as an important process within teacher professional development. Social networking enables teachers to access new ideas, to collaborate and to contribute to a shared knowledge, regardless of time and place. These factors are significant and necessary in a world where a knowledge building economy is a noteworthy indicator of economic prosperity. To live and prosper in the digital age, to understand and function successfully in online spaces and to be able to be self-directed in the authors' learning is foundational for the authors' current and future worlds. The online world has become an integral part of the physical world and with that has come the need for teachers to be fore-runners in shaping the authors' students to live and learn as a basic necessity. The rise of social networking with its inherent disposition for sharing and knowledge-producing exchanges logically suggests a merger with education to improve teaching and learning outcomes.

Teacher professional development has seen a renaissance, and a shift from training or workshops held on school sites to online environments affirming redefinitions of teacher practices to work in new ways, to work in partnership and better focus on high task complexity and continuous learning. To support this re-direction towards an online networked professional learning model, an understanding of the advantages social networking can offer teacher professional development is required.

The chapter provides an extensive literature review with illustrations of practice of both the use of social networking in pre-service and in-service teacher professional development contexts that identify relationships and patterns of understanding in each place. What is presented in the chapter are new understandings of the components of effective online professional development in these spaces including critical points for consideration and the dilemmas that can occur around implementation. A final elaboration of what is considered a sustainable and transformative model of online teacher professional development using social networking will be described, illustrating the key elements of effective implementation.

In: Advances in Social Networking Research ISBN: 978-1-63485-225-8
Editor: Salvador Reese © 2016 Nova Science Publishers, Inc.

Chapter 1

NETWORK THEORY APPLIED TO INFORMATION AND COMMUNICATION TECHNOLOGIES: ADVANCES IN TYPOLOGY

María Rosalía Vicente* and Ana Salomé García-Muñiz
University of Oviedo, Avd. Cristo s/n, Oviedo, Asturias Spain

ABSTRACT

Traditionally studies on the sector of Information and Communication Technologies (ICT) have focused on the analysis of its economic impact, not taking into account the qualitative importance of the networked industrial structure. ICT are general purpose technologies, that is, they are characterized by a fast pace of technological progress, they are suitable for a wide variety of activities, and they enable the generation of innovations. Consequently, the importance of ICT do not rely itself on the weight of the producing sector, but on the effects of their widespread diffusion across the economy.

Recent research has applied network theory to the study of ICT. Network analysis can bring some novel insights into the potential of new technologies to facilitate knowledge flows and consequently, to generate new sources of income and wealth. This chapter then present an application of network analysis to characterize the role of the ICT sector as an enabler of knowledge and innovation diffusion across the economy.

* Corresponding author: E-mail: mrosalia@uniovi.es.

Keywords: structural holes, reinforced structural holes, betweenness, information and communication technologies (ICT), input-output (IO) analysis.

INTRODUCTION

The history of the last 20 years cannot be understood without taking into account information and communication technlogies (ICT). Such technologies have brought major social and economic changes. Nowadays, sending emails, reading news online, buying online and doing banking transactions on the internet, among others, have become quite common activities in anyone's daily life. Likewise, firms use ICT more and more to improve the efficiency of their processess and to expand their makerts through e-commerce. Moreover, a full range of new services has emerged with the skyrocketing diffusion of the mobile internet and the development of the well-known apps.

All these changes have been possible due to the fact that ICT are general purpose technologies (Bresnahan and Trajtenberg, 1995). This type of technologies is characterized by three main features: they can be used across a wide range of economic activities, they are subjected to a very fast pace of technological change and they enable the generation of complementary innovations (Bresnahan and Trajtenberg, 1995). As a consequence, the economic importance of these technologies relies on the effects driven by its widespread diffusion across the economy (Colecchia and Schreyer, 2002).

Therefore, a proper analysis of the economic importance of the ICT sector requires taking into account its role as a catalyst of knowledge flows and innovation throughout the economy. In this context, it becomes essential to consider the intersectoral relationships established between the industries. Input-ouput (IO) analysis reveals as a very useful tool to achieve this goal, since it details the interdependencies between sectors. Several papers have then applied IO analysis to identify the economic importance of the ICT sector (Schreyer, 2001; Roy, Das and Chakraborty 2002; Xing, Ye and Kui 2011; Rohman, 2013; Rohman and Bohlin 2013, among others). Nonetheless, the standard input-output techniques do not capture the qualitative importance of industrial linkages. Such limitation has recently led to apply concepts and techniques developed in the framework of the network theory to IO models in order to extend and improve structural analysis (Soofi and Ghazinoory, 2011; Semitiel and Noguera, 2012; Lopes, Dias and Amaral, 2012; García-Muñiz, 2013; García-Muñiz and Ramos, 2015).

The starting basis to apply the framework of network analysis over IO tables is to identify the flows of goods between the productive sectors as the links of the economic network. Then, the position that a sector holds in this network will be defined by its connections with other industries and the type and quality of such linkages in terms of information provision. In particular, the two latter elements will allow to approach a sector's capacity for innovation generation and diffusion (García-Muñiz, Morillas and Ramos, 2010; García-Muñiz and Vicente, 2014), and hence it constitutes the focus of the present chapter.

The presented analysis follows Burt's (1992, 2015) approach on structural holes. According to this author, among the network of contacts of an individual (firm), there are clear differences in terms of the information and opportunities each of these contacts provide for him. In fact, Burt (1992) states that there are two main types of connections: redundant and non redundant. Non redundant links are those which make possible to access to varied information, and hence they are essential for knowledge transmission and innovation diffusion, allowing to gain competitive advantages over other elements of the network. These non redundant links are connected by structural holes, as called by Burt (1992). Recently, Burt (2015) has studied and proposed a measure of how these holes can be reinforced by the existing organization around them. In particular, he highlights that the more reinforced the hole, the more difficult the access to it, but in case of managing to access, the greater benefits for those acting as bridges since they will have access to valuable novel information (Burt, 2015).

Within this framework, this paper focuses on analyzing the role of the ICT sector as an enabler of technological diffusion and innovation in the European economy. In particular, attention is paid to identifying to what extent the European ICT sector acts as a bridge that enables the flow of information and knowledge across the economic network. Moreover, the author explore its level of access to reinforced structural holes, and hence the extent to which it allows to reach these hard-to-access holes which can provide with valuable information and knowledge. In addition, the association between the holes and complementary topological network measures is exposed. The connections between all these measures and some basic economic indicators are also considered.

Empirical evidence is shown for the European Union (EU). With that aim, the most recent IO information published by Eurostat is used: in particular, the consolidated IO tables of the EU for the year 2011.

Since the year 2000, the European Union has considered information and communication technologies as key elements in order to achieve its growth and competitiveness goals. Hence, ICT have been at the core of the European actions for economic growth and development for the last two decades. Not only were ICT basic elements in the Lisbon strategy launched in the year 2000, but also for the current Europe 2020 with its flagship initiative, the Digital Agenda, aimed at the full development of a European digital economy. Such initiative highlights the importance of the ICT sector in the European economy and draws attention on "the high levels of dynamism and innovation inherent in the sector, and the enabling role the sector plays in changing how other sectors do business" (European Commission, 2010, p.4).

The paper is organized as follows. Next section presents the methodological approach providing some basic ideas on input-output analysis, followed by the description of the employed network metrics: in particular, structural holes (Burt, 1992); reinforced structural holes which is one of the newest measures developed in the field (Burt, 2015) and betweenness (Freeman, 1977, 1979). The following section clarifies the definition of the ICT sector used for the analysis and presents the results on the topological structure of the European ICT sector. Finally, some concluding remarks are drawn.

METHODS

Input-Output Model

Input–output (IO) tables describe a complete picture of the flows of goods and services in an economy for a given year. The Leontief Input-Output Model (1951) can be described by:

$$\mathbf{x} = \mathbf{A}\mathbf{x} + \mathbf{d} \tag{1}$$

where for an economy with n economic sectors, **x** and **d** denote, respectively, the vectors of output and final demands (nx1) and **A** is the technology matrix (nxn) which comprises the ratios known as technical coefficients which indicate how much input from sector i is needed to obtain a unit of output in sector j.

The output matrix can be solved by:

$$\mathbf{x} = (\mathbf{I} - \mathbf{A})^{-1}\mathbf{d} \tag{2}$$

where **I** is the identity matrix and $(\mathbf{I} - \mathbf{A})^{-1}$ is known as the inverse Leontief matrix.

Following the Qualitative Input-Output Analysis (QIOA) (Lantner,1974; Campbell, 1975) the matrix **A** of technical coefficients can be transformed into a Boolean array **W** = $\{w_{ij}\}$, known as the adjacency matrix, in which the coefficients larger than a filter –usually the average- are made equal to one to show that one sector demands significatively goods from another, zero otherwise. This matrix hence highlights the important relationships between industries. When sector i demands inputs from another sector j, it is said that the former is adjacent to the latter and also that they are directly connected. Those relations can be depicted in a directed graph or, properly, a digraph G: (V, E), where V stands for the set of nodes or vertices which represent the analyzed industries and the demands for inputs are represented as arcs, arrows or directed edges (E), stemming from the consuming branch to the supplier. The supporting assumption is that the IO model is demand (and technologically)-driven and when a sector receives a demand order, it adjusts its output correspondingly. The resulting digraph can be understood as an economic network, as both the nodes and the relationships between them are of economic nature. The sectors (nodes) may play different roles in the structure (economic network) depending on the number of connections they maintain with other industries, the intensity of these connections and their type.

Network Metrics

In order to analyze the role that the ICT sector plays in the economic network, this paper relies on Burt's approach on structural holes (1992) and its recent extension with the introduction of the measurement of the access to reinforced structural holes (Burt, 20015). To complement this analysis, the well-known measure of betweeness (Freeman, 1977, 1979) will be considered.

According to Burt's approach (1992), the organization of the economic network defines where opportunities lie and who can acess and then benefit from them. The number of connections a sector has, to whom the sector is connected, and how tight these links are, constitute a series of factors that determine the benefits a sector may gain in terms of advantages of time, exclusivity and access to certain information and knowledge.

Then, intersector relationships differ by the type of information and opportunities they can provide. In this sense, if a sector is connected to other sectors that are connected between them, then the information that flows through this network is very likely to be the same. Consequently, there are little competitive advantages to gain from it. This type of connections is considered to be redundant since the same sectors are involved and same information is exchanged.

Conversely, a sector can establish non redundant links and act as a bridge between different economic activities. In this case, the bridge sector will be able to access to more varied information and will constitute itself as a key element for the diffusion of ideas, knowledge and innovation within the economic network. Economic competitive advantanges lie in these "relationships of non-redundancy between two nodes", the so-called the structural holes by Burt (1992).

There are two basic elements in the analysis of structural holes: network size and the level of redundancy. Burt (1992) defines the effective size as the difference between network size and level of redundancy:

$$TE_i = \sum_j \left[1 - \sum_q p_{iq} m_{jq} \right] \tag{3}$$

where index q refers to the remaining sectors that are related to sector i, p_{iq} shows the proportion of direct links and m_{jq} represents the marginal intensity of sector j in relation to sector q, and x_{ij} represents the relation between the sector i and j:

$$p_{iq} = \frac{x_{iq} + x_{qi}}{\sum_{j=1}^{n} x_{ij} + x_{ji}} \tag{4}$$

$$m_{jq} = \frac{x_{jq}+x_{qj}}{max_k(x_{jk}+x_{kj})} \tag{5}$$

This analysis can be complemented by taking into account the degree of dependence between sectors. In case of high levels of dependence, the benefits of information transmission can be small even for a high-efficiency sector as long as it is negatively affected by the non-favorable conditions of those industries it depends on. Sectoral dependency can be assessed by the following constraint index C_i:

$$C_i = \sum_j c_{ij} \tag{6}$$

where

$$c_{ij} = \left(p_{ij} + \sum_q p_{iq} p_{qj} \right)^2 \; ; \; q \neq i, j \tag{7}$$

p_{ij} is the relative intensity of flows between i and j, p_{iq} (p_{qj}) is the weight of the sector i(q) with q(j). The measure c_{ij} is based on the directed and undirected efforts made to establish the links. The way c_{ij} is built makes that the constraint index takes values from zero to one.

Recently, Burt (2015) has gone further in the concept of structural holes and has studied how the structural organization may variably reinforce structural holes. "Reinforcement around the structural holes to which ego has access is defined by the network around each of ego's contacts" (Burt, 2015, p.11). If an initial hole is reinforced, it will be much more difficult to bridge, but the information to be gained from it will be novel and valuable.

The measure of access to reinforced structural holes (2RSH) is:

$$2RSH = \sum_{i,j} RSH_{ij} \; ; \; i \neq j \tag{8}$$

where

$$RSH_{ij} = \sum_k \left(1 - m_{ij}\right) p_{ik} \left(1 - m_{kj}\right); \; k \neq i, j \tag{9}$$

where p_{ij} is the proportional strenth for i of his linkage with k, and $(1\text{-}m_{kj})$ represents the marginal strength of k's disconnect from j.

This measure of access to reinforced structural holes can take values from zero to an upper bound delimited by the number of structural holes in ego's network.

The analysis of structural holes can be complemented by exploring the levels of betweennes as a basic indicator that can influence structural holes.

Betweenness is a measure of how often a node is located on the shortest path (geodesic) between other nodes. Freeman's geodesic centrality measure (Freeman, 1977, 1979) is a traditional betweenness indicator. Ego network betweenness can be measured as:

$$\sum_{j<k} b_{jke} \tag{10}$$

where b_{jke} indicates the proportion of shortest connections between j and k that go through ego (Everett and Borgatti, 2005).

Results

The described methodology has been applied to the analysis of the ICT sector in the European Union. The statistical information comes from the last consolidated input-output tables published by Eurostat (2015) which refer to the EU in the year 2011[1].

In order to analyze the capacity of the ICT sector for technological diffusion, for enhancing innovation and creating new market opportunities, it is essential to work with a homogeneous and widely accepted definition. Hence, the OECD's current definition of the ICT sector has been used. This definition was agreed in 2011 (OECD, 2011) and includes both ICT products and those related to content and media. Table 1 shows the classification of ICT products according to OECD's definition.

To identify the ICT sector over IO tables, a very careful matching process is necessary (Rohman, 2013). The OECD definition of the ICT sector relies on the International Standard Industrial Classification of All Economic Activities (ISIC, Rev.4) which was released in its fourth revision by the United Nations in August 2008; meanwhile, the consolidated IO tables for the European

[1] In 2011, the EU included 27 countries, that is, the current member states except for Croatia which joined the Union in 2013. The so-called consolidated EU's input-output tables aggregate all the information corresponding to the member states and, therefore, provides a picture of the European Union as a whole.

Union are based on the Statistical Classification of Economic Activities of the European Community (NACE 2), from the year 2002. Following the correspondence between the two classifications, ISIC and NACE, the European ICT sector comprises 13 products/activities out of the 65 products/activities included in the IO table (Table 2).

Table 3 summarizes the results of the networks metrics described in the previous section. Some descriptive statistics are provided: in particular, the mean, the standard deviation and the correlation coefficients for network metrics and two key economic indicators, i.e., value added and output at basic prices. Results are presented as matrix where the elements above the diagonal refer to the 13 activities identified in the ICT sector; whereas those below the diagonal correspond to the 51 non-ICT sectors[2].

Table 1. ICT products classification

ISIC-4 digits	Definition
Classification of ICT products	
2620	Computer and peripheral equipment
2610, 2630	Communication equipment
2640, 2670	Consumer electronic equipment
2610, 2630, 2651, 2670, 2680, 3290	Miscellaneous ICT components and goods
2610, 2620, 2630, 2640, 2680	Manufacturing services for ICT equipment
5820	Business and productivity software and licensing services
6202, 6201, 6311, 7020	Information technoloy consultancy and services
	Telecommunication services
6110, 6120, 6130, 6190	Leasing or rental services for ICT equipment
7729, 7730	Other ICT services
3320, 6209, 7110, 9511, 9512	
Classification of content and media products	
5811, 5812, 5813, 5819, 5820	Printed and other text-based content on physical media and related services
5911-5914, 6010, 6020, 6110, 6120, 6130	Motion picture, video, television and radio content and related services
5920	Music content and related services
5820	Games software
5811-5813, 5819, 5820, 6311, 6312	On-line content and related services
5811, 5812, 5913, 5920, 6391, 6399, 7310, 7420, 9000	Other content and related services

Source: OECD (2011).

[2] The sector which refers to services provided by extraterritorial organisations and bodies (sector number 65) is not included. Network analysis revealed that it is an isolated sector; consequently it has been excluded from the analysis.

Table 2. Identification of the ICT sector over the European IO tables

Sector number	Sector name
17	Computer, electronic and optical products
23	Repair and installation services of machinery and equipment
37	Publishing services
38	Motion picture, video and television programme production services, sound recording and music publishing; programming and broadcasting services
39	Telecommunications services
40	Computer programming, consultancy and related services; information services
46	Legal and accounting services; services of head offices; management consulting services
47	Architectural and engineering services; technical testing and analysis services
49	Advertising and market research services
50	Other professional, scientific and technical services; veterinary services
51	Rental and leasing services
59	Creative, arts and entertainment services; library, archive, museum and other cultural services; gambling and betting services
62	Repair services of computers and personal and household goods

Source: Own.

Results show that the ICT sector has, on average, less constrained networks than non-ICT sectors (note the averages for constraints: 0.151 in the ICT sector compared to 0.209 in the other sectors). In addition, it has more exclusive access to structural holes through a higher betweennes average (39.106 in the ICT sector and 28.357 in non-ICT sectors). Moreover, the ICT sector is connected to more reinforced structural holes than other economic sectors (the former with an average of 240.827, while the latter shows an average of 187.919). These first results indicate that ICT activities have fewer restrictions and need lower investments in the configuration of their network of relationships than the rest of the productive industries. In fact, several studies have pointed out the key importance of ICT to improve the processes of information transmission, by making it faster and more efficient both within and between firms and sectors, (Kretschmer, 2012; García-Muñiz and Vicente, 2014).

It can also be seen that the intensity of correlations in the ICT sector and the rest of the industries are different. Network measures are higher correlated within them in the ICT sector than in others. Moreover, the correlations of these metrics with valued added and output measures are also large. See, for example, the correlation between value added and constraints: -0.8 in the ICT sector and 0.02 in the rest of the productive sectors. It is worth noticing that the correlation patterns are those that could be expected: thus, betweennes, effective size and reinforced holes are positively correlated with the value added and output and negatively correlated with constraints.

Finally, Tables 4 and 5 present the results of the regressions of valued added and output on networks metrics. These network indicators have significant effects in the ICT sector. Note the high levels of goodness of fit in the case of reinforced holes and effective size in the ICT sector (R^2 shows values in the threshold of 0.8). In contrast, networks measures are little associated with economic measures in the non-ICT sectors. The employed topological indicators then predict fairly well the output and valued added in the case of the ICT sector. Such results suggest that the process of technological diffusion is key in the ICT sector and reflects in their economic results. In order to understand this fact, it is important to bear in mind that the effects of ICT extend not only to other industries but also to consumers (Colecchia and Schreyer, 2002). These effects can be directly generated through technological progress or indirectly through their diffusion all over the economy. The boom of mobile devices, of fixed and mobile broadband infrastructure and the expansion of ICT services (e-commerce, electronic administration, e-learning, and e-health) have contributed to more flexible and efficient enterprise organizations, new strategies, business models and distribution channels (Venturini, 2015).

Table 3. Results of network metrics for the European Union productive network: ICT sector (above the diagonal) and non-ICT sectors (below the diagonal)

			Network Metrics				Economic Indicators	
			Constraint	**Effective Size**	**Reinforced Holes**	**Betweenness**	**Output**	**Value added**
		Mean (S.D)	0.151 (0.041)	17.045 (9.473)	240.827 (247.883)	39.106 (28.974)	253,126.5 (149,551.6)	125,544.9 (87,383.4)
Network Metrics	**Constraint**	*0.209 (0.114)*	1	-0.928**	-0.842**	-0.801**	-0.850**	-0.799**
	Effective Size	*14.055 (10.536)*	*0.705***	1	*0.978***	0.671*	0.899**	0.908**
	Reinforced Holes	*187.919 (260.344)*	*-0.585***	*0.978***	1	0.564*	0.875**	0.903**
	Betweenness	*28.357 (39.979)*	*-0.529***	*0.822***	*0.799***	1	0.677*	0.611*
Economic Indicators	**Output**	*397,781.8 (355,396)*	*-0.174*	*0.505***	*0.510***	*0.577***	1	0.978**
	Value added	*189,724.3 (204,998.4)*	*0.027*	*0.393***	*0.440***	*0.377***	*0.909*	1

Source: Own.

Notes: S.D. stands for standard deviation. Figures in italics refer to non-ICT sectors. * and ** indicate, respectively, that the correlation is significant at the 0.05 and 0.01 levels (2-tailed).

Table 4. Regression analysis of value added on network metrics. Coefficients and p-values

	Non- ICT sectors				ICT sectors			
	(1)	(2)	(3)	(4)	(1)	(2)	(3)	(4)
Constraint	47,826.2 (0.853)				-1,747,726 (0.001)			
Effective size		7,654.8 (0.004)				8,715.5 (0.000)		
Reinforced Holes			346.3 (0.001)				331.5 (0.000)	
Betweenness				1,932.9 (0.006)				1,917.8 (0.027)
R^2	0.001	0.155	0.193	0.142	0.638	0.824	0.816	0.373

Source: Own.

Note: Estimations have been run including an intercept though it is not reported in the results. p-values are reported between brackets.

Table 5. Regression analysis of output on network metrics Coefficients and p-values

	Non- ICT sectors				ICT sectors			
	(1)	(2)	(3)	(4)	(1)	(2)	(3)	(4)
Constraint	540,551.4 (0.223)				-3,183,522 (0.000)			
Effective size		17,031.5 (0.000)				14,766.4 (0.000)		
Reinforced Holes			695.9 (0.000)				549.5 (0.000)	
Betweenness				5,130.9 (0.000)				3,638.7 (0.011)
R^2	0.030	0.255	0.260	0.333	0.723	0.808	0.766	0.459

Note: See notes under Table 4.

CONCLUSION

This chapter has presented a novel approach to the analysis of the economic importance of the ICT sector. By combining the frameworks of input-output analysis and network theory, the flows of goods between the productive sectors of the economy have been identified as the links of the economic network. On that basis, the importance of those links have been studied not only through some well-known concepts and measures of the network theory but also through some very recent metrics. In particular, the structural holes approach developed by Burt (1992) has been used together with his latest extension on the measurement of the access to reinforced holes (Burt, 2015). The combination of these measures have allowed to assess the role the ICT sector plays as an enabler of the diffusion of ideas and knowledge across the different sectors of the economic network.

Results have shown that the ICT sector has a more central position and with less constraints than the rest of economic activities. The higher betweeness centrality of the ICT sector implies that it has a larger influence on the diffusion of knowledge and innovations through the network compared to other industries. Moreover, negative economic shocks might have a limited impact over this sector as it has less constrains. In addition, it has a higher level of access to reinforced structural holes. Such result reveals the key role of the ICT sector as a bridge through which it is possible to access to novel information, ideas, and innovations that, otherwise, would be hard to access.

Finally, results show that the main economic measures (output and value added) can be predicted quite accurately in the ICT sector by using network measures and in particular the access to reinforced structural holes and the effective size.

Overall, the analysis presented in this chapter points out that the combination of traditional input-output techniques with networks metrics is a useful and powerful tool for sectorial economic analyses.

References

Bresnahan, T. and Trajtenberg, M. (1995). General purpose technologies: Engines of growth? *Journal of Econometrics*, *65*, 83-108.

Burt, R. S. (1992). *Structural holes: The social structure of competition.* Cambridge: Cambridge University Press.

Burt, R. S. (2015). *Reinforced Structural Holes*. Retrieved from: http://faculty.chicagobooth.edu/ronald.burt/research/files/RSH.pdf.

Campbell, J. (1975). Application of graph theoretic analysis to interindustry relationships. *Regional Science and Urban Economics*, *5*, 91-106.

Colecchia, A. and Schreyer, P. (2002). The contribution of information and communication technologies to economic growth in nine oecd countries. *OECD Economic Studies*, *34*, 153-172.

European Commission, (2010). *A Digital Agenda for Europe*. Brussels: European Commission.

Eurostat, (2015). *Supply, use and input–output tables database*. Retrieved from:http:// epp.eurostat.ec.europa.eu/ portal/ page/ portal/esa95_supply _use_in put_tables/introduction.

Everett, M. and Borgatti, S. P. (2005). Ego network betweenness. *Social Networks*, *27*, 31-38.

Freeman, L. C. (1977). A set of measures of centrality based on betweenness. *Sociometry*, *40*, 35-40.

Freeman, L. C. (1979). Centrality in social networks: I. conceptual clarification. *Social Networks*, *1*, 141-154.

García- Muñiz, A. S. (2013). Input-output research in structural equivalence: extracting paths and similarities. *Economic Modelling*, *31*, 796-803.

García-Muñiz, A. S. and Ramos, C. (2015). Input-output linkages and network contagion in Greece: demand and supply view. *Applied Econometrics and International* Development, 15, in press.

García-Muñiz, A. S. and Vicente, M. R. (2014). ICT technologies in Europe: A study of technological diffusion and economic growth under network theory. *Telecommunications Policy*, *38*, 360-370.

García-Muñiz, A. S., Morillas, A. and Ramos, C. (2010). Spanish and European innovation diffusion: A structural hole approach in the input-output approach. *The Annals of International Regional Science*, *44*, 147-165.

Heng, T. M. and Thangavelu, S. M. (2013). An input–output study of the Singapore information sector. *Economic Systems Research*, *25*, 2, 233-244.

Hong, P., Byun, J. and Kim, P. (2015). Structural changes and growth factors of the ICT industry in Korea: 1995–2009. *Telecommunications Policy*, in press.

Kretschmer, T. (2012). *Information and communication technologies and productivity growth: A survey of the literature* [OECD Digital Economy Papers].OECD. Retrieved from: http:// ideas.repec.org/ p/ oec/stiaab/195-en.html.

Lantner, R. (1974). *Théorie de la dominance economique*. París: Dunod.

Leontief, W. (1951). Input–output economics. *Scientific American*, 15-21.

Lopes, J., Diaz, J. and Amaral, J., (2012). Assessing economic complexity as interindustry connectedness in nine OECD countries. *International Review of Applied Economics*, *26*, 811-827.

OCDE, (2011). *Guide to Measuring the Information Society*. Retrieved from: http://www.oecd.org/sti/measuring-infoeconomy/guide.

Rohman, I. (2013). The globalization and stagnation of the ICT sectors in European countries: An input-output analysis. *Telecommunications Policy*, *37*, 387-399.

Rohman, I. and Bohlin, E. (2013). How important is the media and content sector to the European Economy? In J. Alleman, A. Ní-Shúilleabháin and P. Rappoport (Eds), *Demand for communications services-insights and perspectives: Series the economics of information, communication and entertainment*, (pp. 113-131). New York: Springer.

Roy, S., Das, T. and Chakraborty, D. (2002). A study on the Indian information sectors: An experiment with input–output techniques. *Economic Systems Research*, *14*, 107-129.

Schreyer, P. (2001) Information and communication technology and the measurement of volume output and final demand: A five-country study. *Economic Innovation and New Technology*, *10*, 339-376.

Semitiel García, M. and Noguera Méndez, P. (2012). The structure of inter-industry systems and the diffusion of innovations: The case of Spain. *Technological Forecasting and Social Change*, *79*, 1548-1567.

Soofi, A. and Ghazinoory, S. (2011). The network of the Iranian techno-economic system. *Technological Forecasting and Social Change*, *78*, 591-609.

Venturini, F. (2015). The modern drivers of productivity. *Research Policy*, 44, 357-369.

Xing, W., Xuan, Y. and Kui, L. (2011). Measuring convergence of China's ICT industry: An input–output analysis. *Telecommunications Policy*, *35*, 301-313.

BIOGRAPHICAL SKETCH

Name: María Rosalía Vicente

Affiliation: University of Oviedo

Date of Birth: August 14, 1977

Education: Ph.D. in Economics. University of Oviedo, Spain.

Address: Applied Economics, University of Oviedo, Campus del Cristo s/n, Oviedo-Asturias 33006 Spain

Research and Professional Experience:

I am specialized in the economics of information and communication technologies (ICT), its diffusion and economic effects. I have been visiting researcher at the Organization for Economic Cooperation and Development (OECD) and at Curtin University (Western Australia).

Professional Appointments: Associate Professor. Department of Applied Economics. School of Economics and Business. University of Oviedo.

Publications Last 3 Years:

1. Cruz-Jesus, F., Vicente, M.R., Bacao, F. and Oliveira (2016). The education-related digital divide: An analysis for the EU-28. *Computers in Human Behaviour* (in press).
2. Vicente, M.R. (2015). Determinants of C2C e-commerce: an empirical analysis of the use of online auction websites among Europeans. *Applied Economic Letters, 22*, 978-981.
3. Vicente, M.R., López, A.J. and Pérez, P. (2015). Forecasting unemployment with internet search data: Does it help to improve predictions when job destruction is skyrocketing?. *Technological Forecasting and Social Change, 92*, 132-139.
4. García-Muñiz, A.S. and Vicente, M.R. (2014). ICT technologies in Europe: A study of technological diffusion and economic growth under network theory. *Telecommunications Policy, 38*, 360-370.
5. García-Muñiz, A.S. and Vicente, M.R. (2013) La utilidad de las actividades de evaluación en cursos on-line. Un análisis objetivo a partir de la teoría de la información. *RIDU. Revista d'Innovació Docent Universitaria, 5,* 33 - 41.
6. Vicente, M.R. and Novo, A. (2014). An empirical analysis of e-Participation. The role of social networks and e-government over citizens' online engagement. *Government Information Quarterly, 31*, 379-387.
7. Vicente, M.R. (2013). And the Queen asked: Why economists haven´t been able to predict the economic crisis? Don´t they read the news? ... The importance of using news when teaching Economics. *Estudios sobre el mensaje periodístico*, 19, 523-530.

Name: Ana Salomé García Muñiz
Affiliation: University of Oviedo
Date of Birth: June 13, 1975
Education: Ph.D. Applied Economics, June 2006. University of Oviedo, Spain.

Address: School of Economics and Business, Avd. Cristo s/n. 3306 Oviedo, Spain

Research and Professional Experience:

My PhD thesis is on 'The Network Theory in input-output analysis". My areas of research interests include economic networks, input-output, technological diffusion and applied economics.

Professional Appointments:

- 2007- Assistant Professor (Tenure Track). School of Economics and Business. University of Oviedo.
- 1999-2007. Assistant Professor. School of Economics and Business. University of Oviedo.

Publications Last 3 Years:

1. López, Y. and García-Muñiz, A.S. (2015). Usos del tiempo en las Comunidades Autónomas. Una aproximación a la conciliación laboral y familiar a través de índices de igualdad. *Revista Galega de Economía, 24,* 5-23.
2. García-Muñiz, A.S. and Ramos, C. (2015). Input-output linkages and network contagion in Greece: Demand and supply view. *Applied Econometrics and International Development, 15,* 35-60.
3. García-Muñiz, A.S. and Solís, V. (2014). Comercio internacional: Cadenas globales de valor. Una aproximación desde la Teoría de redes. *Revista de Economía Mundial, 37,* 151-180.
4. García-Muñiz, A.S. and Vicente, M.R. (2014). ICT Technologies in Europe: A study of technological diffusion and economic growth under network theory, *Telecommunications Policy, 38,* 360-370.
5. García-Muñiz, A.S., García-Álvarez, M. and Moreno, B. (2014). Analysis of assessment opportunities of learning spaces: On-line versus face to face methodologies. *Computers in Human Behavior, 30,* 372 - 377.
6. García-Muñiz, A.S. (2013). Input–output research in structural equivalence: Extracting paths and similarities. *Economic Modelling, 31,* 796- 803.

7. García-Muñiz, A.S. (2013). Modelling linkages versus leakages networks: The case of Spain. *Regional and sectoral economic studies, 13*, 43 - 54.
8. García-Muñiz, A.S. and Vicente, M.R. (2013). La utilidad de las actividades de evaluación en cursos on-line. Un análisis objetivo a partir de la teoría de la información. *RIDU. Revista d'Innovació Docent Universitaria, 5,* 33 - 41.
9. Moreno, B. and García-Muñiz, A.S. (2013). Investigating the determinants of higher education mobility into European Union countries. *The International Journal of Learning in Higher Education, 19,* 13-27.

In: Advances in Social Networking Research
Editor: Salvador Reese
ISBN: 978-1-63485-225-8
© 2016 Nova Science Publishers, Inc.

Chapter 2

A CHARACTERISTIC-BASED SIMILARITY ALGORITHM FOR FINDING SIMILAR USERS IN A SOCIAL NETWORK

***Francisco Javier Moreno Arboleda*[*], *José Miguel Arrieta Ramos*[†] *and Juan Pablo Correa Rendón*[‡]**
Universidad Nacional de Colombia,
Sede Medellín, Medellín, Colombia

ABSTRACT

The search for similar people is one of the most desirable aspects by users in a community, e.g., in a social network. The identification of similar people promotes the exchange of information about not only common topics, but can also lead to their participation in projects with shared interests. In marketing, it may also be useful to identify, e.g., potential customers that are similar to the customers who buy the most. It can also be used to recommend potential friends to a new user (the so-called *cold start problem*).

In this chapter, we propose a novel algorithm for computing the similarity of users in a social network considering their characteristics,

[*] Corresponding Author Email: fjmoreno@unal.edu.co.
[†] Email: jmarrietar@unal.edu.co.
[‡] Email: jupcorreare@unal.edu.co.

e.g., musical and literary tastes, gender, race, among others. However, that our proposal is generic in the sense that the social network analyst is free to choose the set of characteristics that will be used to establish the similarity among the users. In addition, we also propose an extension of our algorithm to the identification of similar couples, i.e., we face the *cold start problem for couples*. This could be useful, e.g., when a marriage is looking for similar couples in order to develop joint activities: trips, financial projects, and social meetings.

Keywords: social network, individual's matching, couple's matching, cold start, characteristics-based matching, couple's similarity

1. Introduction

The search for similar people is one of the most desirable aspects by users in a community, e.g., in a social network. The identification of similar people promotes the exchange of information about not only common topics, but can also lead to their participation in projects with shared interests. The search of similar people may also help people to find their soulmate and substitutes for certain tasks (e.g., alternative peer reviewers and travel companions). Similarity of people can also be applied in other domains. For example, in marketing, it may be useful to identify, e.g., potential customers that are similar to the customers who buy the most. It can also be used to recommend potential friends to a new user (the so-called *cold start problem*).

In this chapter, we propose a novel algorithm for computing the similarity of users in a social network considering their characteristics, e.g., musical and literary tastes, gender, race, among others. However, our proposal is generic in the sense that the social network analyst is free to choose the set of characteristics that will be used to establish the similarity among the users. In our algorithm, the analyst can also assign weights to the characteristics, e.g., he/she may consider that the music is the most important characteristic to establish the similarity among the users. In addition, we also propose an extension of our algorithm to the identification of similar couples, i.e., we face the *cold start problem for couples*. This could be useful, e.g., when a marriage is looking for similar couples in order to develop joint activities: trips, financial projects, and social meetings. To the best of our knowledge, our proposal is the first one to consider these issues.

The chapter is organized as follows. In Section 2, we analyze related works. In Section 3, we present some basic definitions about the characteristics and their types. These definitions will be used to develop our similarity model, which is presented in Section 4. In Section 5, we extend our model for couples, i.e., a cold start algorithm for couples. Finally, in Section 6, we conclude the chapter and propose future works.

2. Related Works

Adam's patent [1] proposes a social network that connects people who have friends in common, simulating personal relationships in which an individual introduces two of his/her friends who he/she considers can establish a relationship, assuming that if people have a friend in common they may share some interests. This idea is extended with the theory of the six degrees of separation [2], according to which everyone is six or fewer steps away, by way of introduction, from any other person in the world. The author presents an algorithm which shows how the matching between users is made, where the geographical distance between people is considered as a fundamental characteristic for the matching to occur; however, this is the only characteristic used to make the matching.

Kaufman [3] analyzed 10000 marriages, their personalities and their level of satisfaction in marriage. It was found that 66% of people are matched with people of different personalities ("the opposites attract"), but couples with more similarities in their personality, were slightly more satisfied with their marriages than those with more differences.

Eagle and Pentland developed Serendipity [4], a mobile application that uses the profiles of people from other applications such as LinkedIn and Match.com. With these data a new profile is formed that is subsequently used to compare and connect users via Bluetooth. Although it is not explained how the matching process is performed, it is possible to give weighs to the characteristics of the generated profile to customize such process.

Kautz and Selman [5] proposed a referral web model (called ReferralWeb) that combines social networks (people who perform the same activities) and collaborative filtering (a technique in which the information that exists in the system is used to predict or infer new information for another user) in order to help reduce ambiguity in matchings. Profiles of users are constructed and characteristics are inferred (which are not specified), from which people are matched. The authors do not present the algorithm with which the people are matched neither the method to infer characteristics.

Only one of the related works proposes an algorithm to perform the matching [1]; however, this work does not consider the variety of characteristics that a user may have and that may be of interest for the matching as proposed in our work. Meanwhile in [3, 4, 5] the characteristics considered for the matchings are neither specified nor is it determined how similar two people are.

Furthermore, no papers addressing the problem of *start cold for couples* neither the algorithms for this purpose were found. On the other hand, few studies considered the characteristics inherent to a couple and among the few that have done it [6, 7], there is still no consensus about it, neither how the similarity between couples can be calculated. Our work is a first step regarding these aspects.

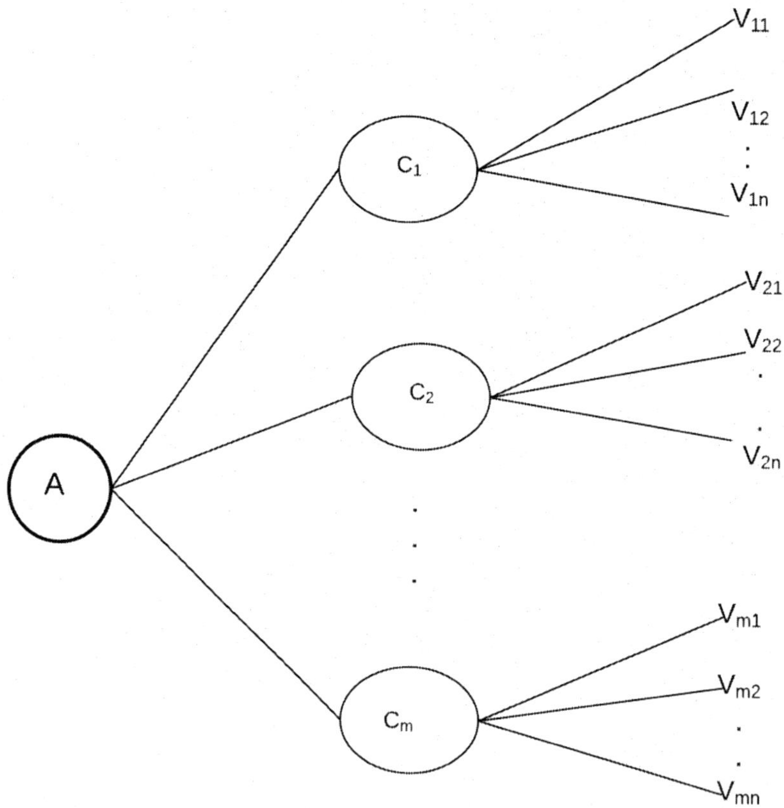

Figure 1. Individual with characteristics and values.

3. Characteristics Associated with an Individual

Consider an individual A who has a set of characteristics $C = \{C_1, C_2, ..., C_m\}$. Each characteristic C_i is associated with a domain (set of values) $V_{Ci} = \{V_{i1}, V_{i2}, \ldots, V_{in}\}$, see Figure 1. The individual can satisfy in a percentage p a value $V_{ik} \in V_{Ci}$ associated with the characteristic C_i. This percentage is denoted PV_{ik}(A).

Figure 2. Example of an individual with characteristics and values.

Example: Let the set of characteristics C = {Sport, Gender, Reading, Music, Nationality, Race}. Each characteristic is associated with a set of values as follows: V_{Sport} = {Cycling, Football, Martial arts, Skating, Swimming, Table tennis, Tennis}, V_{Gender} = {Female, Male}, V_{Music} = {Classical, Electronic, Metal, Pop, Rock, Salsa, Vallenato}, $V_{Reading}$ = {Academic text, Action novel, Adventure Novel, Romance novel, Self-help, Science fiction novel}, $V_{Nationality}$ = {Argentinian, Colombian, Chinese, Paraguayan, Russian, Spanish, Venezuelan}, and V_{Race} = {Black, White, Yellow}.

Consider an individual Danny associated with these characteristics. In Figure 2, we show the values that Danny satisfies in these characteristics with their respective percentage. For instance, P_{Rock}(Danny) = 60%.

From the total number of values $V_{ik} \in V_{ci}$ that an individual can satisfy *simultaneously* of one characteristic C_i, we consider three types of characteristics:

- Characteristics of type 1, in which an individual can satisfy a unique value of the domain of the characteristic and this value is satisfied in 100%, e.g., the characteristic Gender.
- Characteristics of type 2, in which an individual can satisfy several values of the domain of the characteristic and each value is satisfied in 100%, e.g., the characteristic Nationality.
- Characteristics of type 3, in which an individual can satisfy several values of the domain of the characteristic, each value with their respective percentage and where the sum of all percentages is 100%, e.g., the characteristics Music, Reading, and Sport, see Figure 2.

4. Similarity between Two Individuals Based on Their Characteristics

Consider two individuals each one with the same characteristics C and where each individual satisfies in a given percentage one or several values of each characteristic $C_i \in C$ depending on its type.

For determining similarity between two individuals their characteristics and their respective values are compared as explained next.

4.1. Similarity Level between Two Individuals Based on One of Their Characteristics

Let A, B individuals, $C_i \in C$ a characteristic, S_{Vik}(A, B) the similarity level of individuals A and B in a given value $V_{ik} \in V_{Ci}$, and R_{Ci}(A, B) the similarity level of individuals A and B in characteristic C_i. To calculate R_{Ci}(A, B) the type of the characteristic should be considered, see previous section, as follows:

Type 1: In this type of characteristics, where the individual can satisfy just one value of V_{Ci}, if the individuals do not satisfy the same value they are considered *different* in that characteristic then R_{ci}(A, B) = 100, otherwise R_{ci}(A, B) = 0.

Example: Consider two individuals A and B, where A gender is Male and B gender is Female, then R_{Gender} (A, B) = 100.

Type 2: For the characteristics of type 2, we propose two alternatives to compare the two individuals:

a) Individuals are considered equal in the characteristic if they satisfy in common *at least one* value of the characteristic. For instance, consider the characteristic Nationality. Suppose A has four nationalities and B has two nationalities. A and B could be considered as equal in this characteristic, i.e., $R_{Nationality}$(A, B) = 0, if they share at least one nationality, since this gives them, e.g., the same privileges in a given situation (e.g., permission to enter a country).
b) Individuals are considered equal in the characteristic if they satisfy in common *exactly* the same values of the characteristic. In the former example because A has more nationalities than B, then they are considered different, i.e., $R_{Nationality}$(A, B) = 100.

Type 3: For this type of characteristics we proceed as follows.

- For each value $V_{ik} \in V_{Ci}$ common to the two individuals in the characteristic C_i the subtraction (in absolute value) of their respective percentages is done. This subtraction (i.e., $S_{Vik}(A, B) = |PV_{ik}(A) - PV_{ik}(B)|$) represents how different the two individuals are in the value V_{ik} of the characteristic C_i.
- For each value $V_{ik} \in V_{Ci}$ satisfied by A and not satisfied by B then it is considered that the individuals are different in the percentage associated of A with V_{ik}, i.e., $S_{Vik}(A, B) = PV_{ik}(A)$. Likewise, it is

proceeded for each $V_{ip} \in V_{Ci}$ satisfied by B and not satisfied by A, i.e., $S_{Vip}(\text{A, B}) = PV_{ip}(\text{B})$.

- For each value $V_{ik} \in V_{Ci}$ not satisfied neither by A nor by B then $S_{Vik}(\text{A, B}) = 0$.

Then $R_{Ci}(\text{A, B}) = \sum_{i=1}^{n} S_{V_{ik}}(\text{A, B})$ where n = Cardinality(V_{Ci}).

R_{Ci} is normalized (a scale of 0 to 1, where 1 represents no similarity and 0 total similarity) thus:

As 200 is the maximum possible value of $R_{ci}(\text{A,B})$ then:

$R'_{Ci}(\text{A, B}) = R_{Ci}(\text{A, B})/200$.

Example: Suppose the individuals A and B satisfy the values of the characteristic Music as shown in Figure 3.

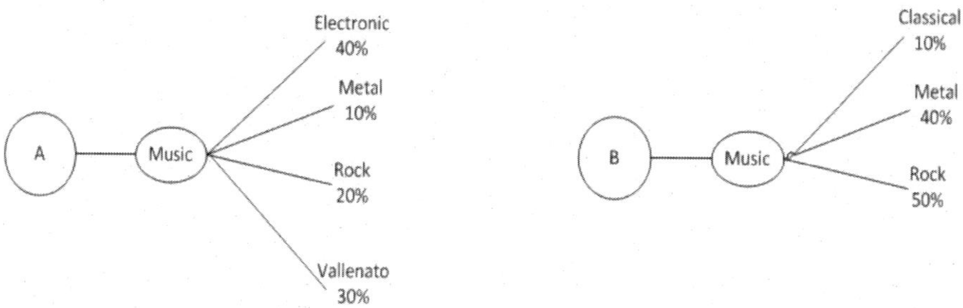

Figure 3. Individuals *A* and *B* with characteristics of type 3.

Let V_{Music} = {Classical, Electronic, Metal, Pop, Rock, Vallenato}. According to Figure 3 we have:

- As A and B share the values Metal and Rock then $S_{Metal}(\text{A, B}) = |10 - 40| = 30$ and $S_{Rock}(\text{A, B}) = |50 - 20| = 30$.
- As A has two values which does not share with B (Electronic and Vallenato) then $S_{Electronic}(\text{A, B}) = 40$ and $S_{Vallenato}(\text{A, B}) = 30$.
- As B has one value which does not share with A (Classical) then $S_{Classical}(\text{A, B}) = 10$.
- As the value Pop is not satisfied neither by A nor by B then $S_{Pop}(\text{A, B}) = 0$.

Therefore, $R_{Music}(\text{A, B}) = 140$ and the normalized value is $R'_{Music}(\text{A, B}) = 0.7$.

4.2. Similarity Level between Two Individuals Based on All of Their Characteristics

Let A, B individuals, C_i a characteristic, R_{Ci}(A, B) the similarity level of individuals A and B in the characteristic C_i. Let T(A, B) be the similarity level of A and B considering the similarity level in each one of the characteristics C_i: $T(A, B) = \sum_{i=1}^{m} R'_{ci}(A, B)$, where m = Cardinality(C).

Example: Suppose that R'_{Gender}(A, B) = 0, $R'_{Nationality}$(A, B) = 1, and R'_{Music}(A, B)= 0.7 then T(A, B) = 1.7.

Note that if we have m characteristics the maximum value of T(A, B) is m, when this value is normalized, we obtain T'(A, B) = T(A, B)/m. For the former example T'(A, B) = 0.56.

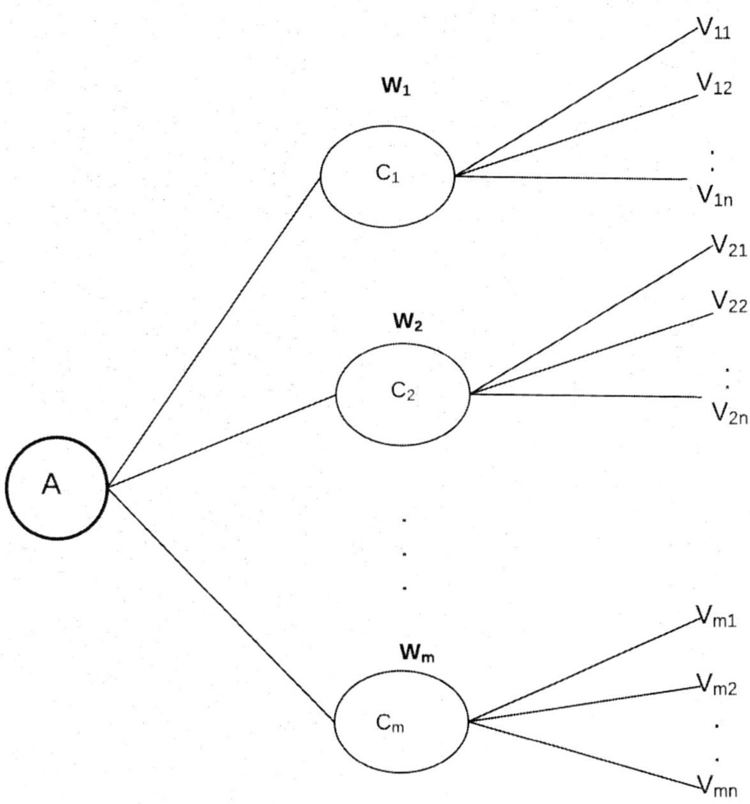

Figure 4. Individual with characteristics with weights.

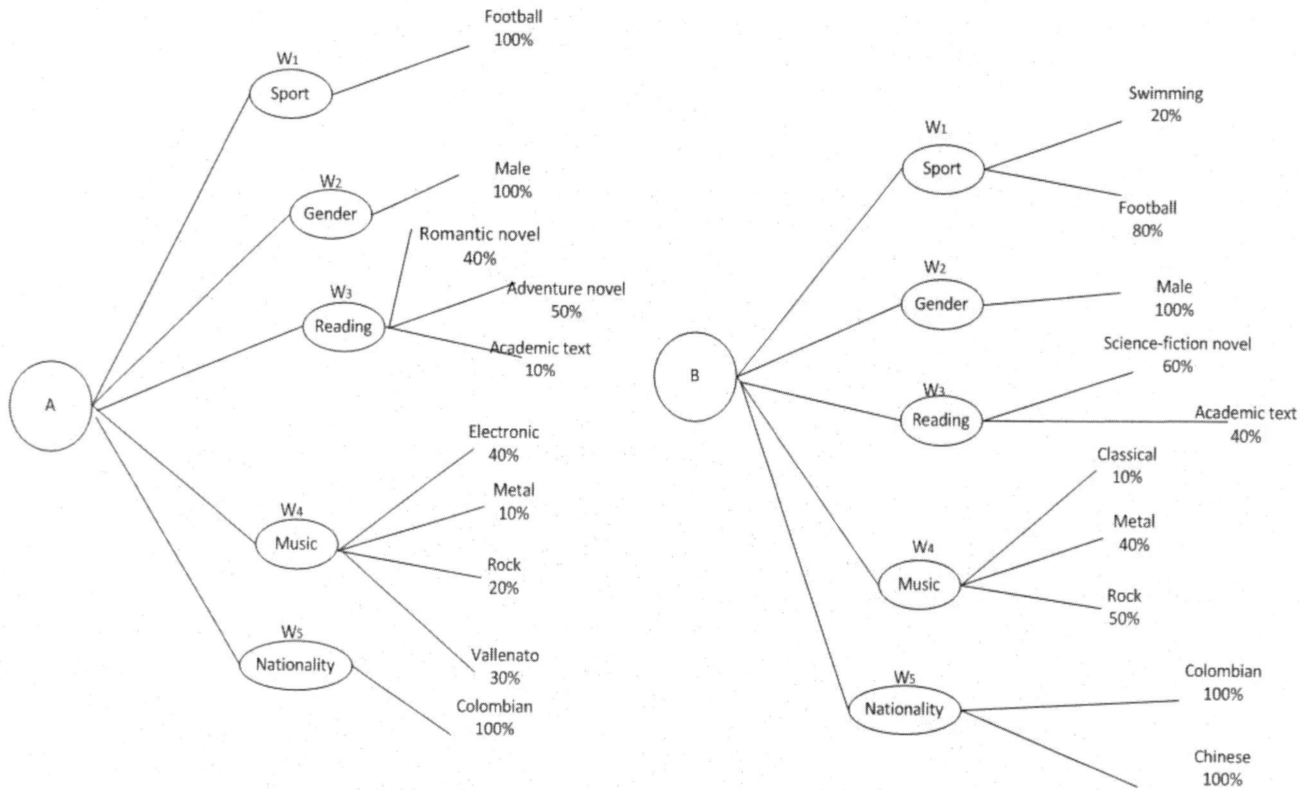

Figure 5. Example of two individuals with characteristics and their respective values and weights.

4.3. Similarity Level between Two Individuals Considering Weighs

An extension to the proposed model is to consider weighs for the characteristics as shown in Figure 4; thereby, the greater weigh a characteristic has the greater the incidence it will have in the similarity level between the two individuals.

Let W_i be the weigh assigned to characteristic C_i, then $T(\text{A, B}) = \sum_{i=1}^{m}(R'c_i * W_i)$. Moreover, $\sum_{i=1}^{m} W_i = 100$.

Example: Suppose two individuals A and B satisfy the values of the characteristics shown in Figure 5.

In Table 1 we show the results for T(A, B) considering that the characteristic Gender is the most important (W_{Gender} = 60). The alternative a) was used for characteristics of type 2, see Section 3.

Table 1. Result for *T(A, B)*

Weighs	W_1 = 10	W_2 = 60	W_3 = 10	W_4 = 10	W_5 = 10
Characteristic	C_1 = Sport	C_2 = Gender	C_3 = Reading	C_4 = Music	C_5 = Nationality
	$S_{Football}$(A, B) = 20		$S_{Adventure\ novel}$(A, B) = 50	$S_{Classical}$(A, B) = 10	
	$S_{Swimming}$(A, B) = 20		$S_{Science\text{-}fiction\ novel}$(A, B) = 60	$S_{Electronic}$(A, B) = 40	
			$S_{Romantic\ novel}$(A, B) = 40	S_{Metal}(A, B) = 30	
			$S_{Academic\ text}$(A, B) = 30	S_{Rock}(A, B)= 30	
				$S_{Vallenato}$(A, B) = 30	
R_{Ci}(A, B)	40	0	180	140	0
R'_{Ci}(A, B)	0.2	0	0.9	0.7	0
T'(A, B)	3.6				

Here, T(A, B) = 3.6. Now considering that the weighs of the characteristics are W_1 = 20, W_2 = 60, W_3 = 5, W_4 = 5, and W_5 = 10 we obtain T'(A, B) = 2.4. Finally, if the weighs are W_1 = 20, W_2 = 20, W_3 = 20, W_4 = 20, and W_5 = 20 we obtain T'(A, B) = 7.2.

Example:

Consider the individual of Figure 6.

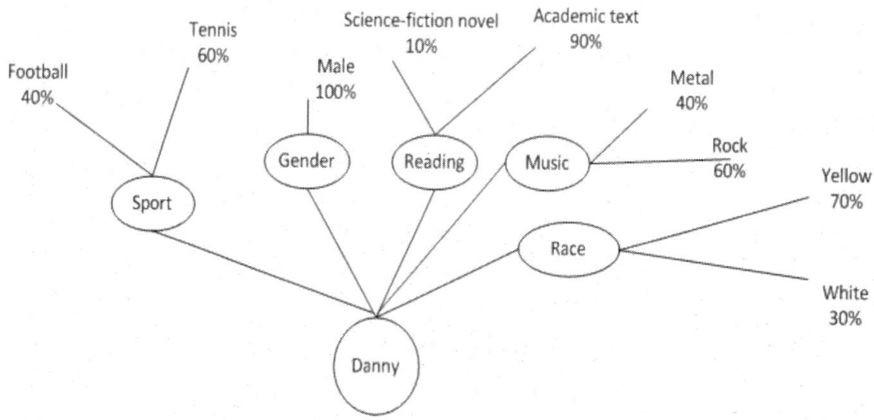

Figure 6. Example of an individual (Danny) and his characteristics and values.

We want to calculate Danny's similarity level against each one of the individuals from the network shown in Figure 7.

If Music is the most important characteristic (W_{Music} = 70), the results are shown in Table 2.

Table 2. Similarity: Danny vs. John with $W_{Músic}$ = 70

Weighs	$W_1 = 5$	$W_2 = 10$	$W_3 = 10$	$W_4 = 70$	$W_5 = 5$
Characteristic	C_1 = Sport	C_2 = Gender	C_3 = Reading	C_4 = Music	C_5 = Race
	S_{Tennis}(Danny, John)= 60		$S_{Academic\ text}$(Danny, John)= 90	S_{Rock}(Danny, John)= 30	S_{Yellow}(Danny, John)= 40
	$S_{Football}$(Danny, John)= 10		$S_{Science\text{-}fiction\ novel}$(Danny, John)= 30	S_{Metal}(Danny, John)= 30	S_{White}(Danny, John)= 40
	$S_{Swimming}$(Danny, John)= 50		$S_{Action\ novel}$(Danny, John)= 60		
R_{Ci}(Danny, John)	120	0	180	60	80
R'_{Ci}(Danny, John)	0.6	0	0.9	0.3	0.4
T'(Danny, John)	7				

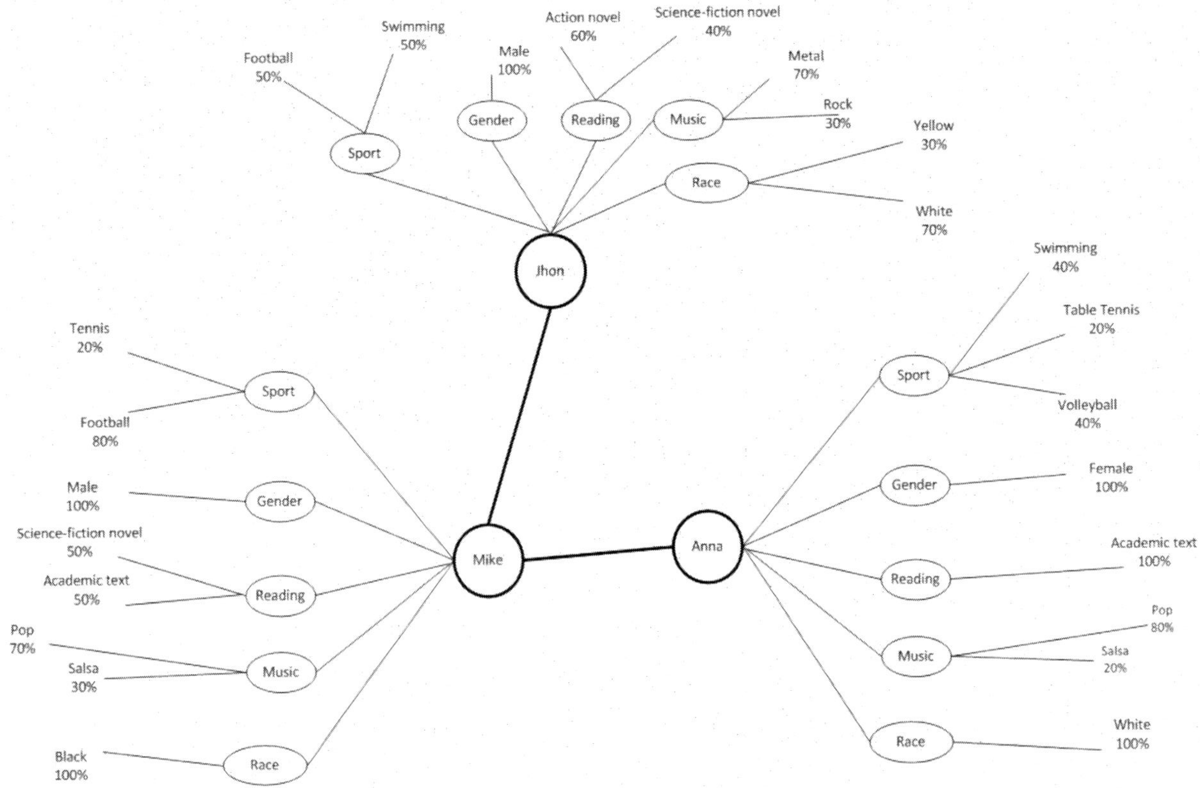

Figure 7. Social network example.

The same procedure is done for Danny vs. Anna and for Danny vs. Mike. The results are *T'*(Danny, John) = 7, *T'*(Danny, Anna) = 17.9, and *T'*(Danny, Mike) = 16.2. Here we see that Danny and John are the individuals who have greater similarity level (7).

If Sport is the most important characteristic (W_{Sport} = 60), the results are shown in Table 3.

Table 3. Similarity: Danny vs. John with $W_{Sport} = 60$

Weighs	W_1 = 60	W_2 = 5	W_3 = 20	W_4 = 10	W_5 = 5
Characteristic	C_1 = Sport	C_2 = Gender	C_3 = Reading	C_4 = Music	C_5 = Race
	S_{Tennis}(Danny, John) = 60		$S_{Academic\ text}$ (Danny, John) = 90	S_{Rock}(Danny, John) = 30	S_{Yellow}(Danny, John) = 40
	$S_{Football}$(Danny, John) = 10		$S_{Science\text{-}fiction\ novel}$(Danny, John) = 30	S_{Metal}(Danny, John) = 30	S_{White}(Danny, John) = 40
	$S_{Swimming}$(Danny, John) = 50		$S_{Action\ novel}$ (Danny, John)= 60		
R_{Ci}(Danny, John)	120	0	180	60	80
R'_{Ci}(Danny, John)	0.6	0	0.9	0.3	0.4
T'(Danny, John)	11.8				

The same procedure is done for Anna and Mike. The results are T'(Danny, John) = 11.8, T'(Danny, Anna) = 16.1, and T'(Danny, Mike) = 9.4. Here we see that Danny and Mike are the individuals who have greater similarity level (9.4).

If Reading is the most important characteristic ($W_{Reading}$ = 80), the results are shown in Table 4.

The same procedure is done for Danny vs. Anna and for Danny vs. Mike. The results are *T'*(Danny, John) = 15.86, *T'*(Danny, Anna) = 5, and *T'*(Danny, Mike) = 9.64. Now Danny and Anna are the individuals who have greater similarity level (5).

If all the characteristics have the same weigh, the results are shown in Table 5.

Table 4. Similarity: Danny vs. John with $W_{Reading}$ = 80

Weighs	$W_1 = 3$	$W_2 = 2$	$W_3 = 80$	$W_4 = 5$	$W_5 = 10$
Characteristic	C_1 = Sport	C_2 = Gender	C_3 = Reading	C_4 = Music	C_5 = Race
	S_{Tennis}(Danny, John) = 60		$S_{Academic\ text}$ (Danny, John) = 90	S_{Rock}(Danny, John) = 30	S_{Yellow}(Danny, John) = 40
	$S_{Football}$(Danny, John) = 10		$S_{Science\text{-}fiction\ novel}$ (Danny, John) = 30	S_{Metal}(Danny, John) = 30	S_{White}(Danny, John) = 40
	$S_{Swimming}$(Danny, John) = 50		$S_{Action\ novel}$(Danny, John)= 60		
R_{Ci}(Danny, John)	120	0	180	60	80
R'_{Ci}(Danny, John)	0.6	0	0.9	0.3	0.4
T'(Danny, John)	15.86				

Table 5. Similarity: Danny vs. John, all the characteristics has the same weigh

Weighs	$W_1 = 20$	$W_2 = 20$	$W_3 = 20$	$W_4 = 20$	$W_5 = 20$
Characteristic	C_1 = Sport	C_2 = Gender	C_3 = Reading	C_4 = Music	C_5 = Race
	S_{Tennis}(Danny, John) = 60		$S_{Academic\ text}$(Danny, John) = 90	S_{Rock}(Danny, John) = 30	S_{Yellow}(Danny, John) = 40
	$S_{Football}$(Danny, John) = 10		$S_{Science\text{-}fiction\ novel}$(Danny, John) = 30	S_{Metal}(Danny, John) = 30	S_{White}(Danny, John) = 40
	$S_{Swimming}$(Danny, John) = 50		$S_{Action\ novel}$(Danny, John)= 60		
R_{Ci}(Danny, John)	120	0	180	60	80
R'_{Ci}(Danny, John)	0.6	0	0.85	0.3	0.4
T'(Danny, John)	8.8				

The same procedure is done for Danny vs. Anna and for Danny vs. Mike. The results are *T'*(Danny, John) = 8.8, *T'*(Danny, Anna) = 15.2, and *T'*(Danny, Mike) = 11.2. Now Danny and John are the individuals who have greater similarity level (8.8).

4.4. System Architecture

Next, in Figure 8, we propose a system architecture to solve the problem of matching of individuals in a community, e.g., in a social network, in which users have some characteristics and some values associated with these. These values can be obtained through a survey or extracted by an inference module of both their characteristics and their values, an issue that is outside the scope of our work (see section of future works). Then this architecture is extended to consider the problem of matching for couples, see Figure 9.

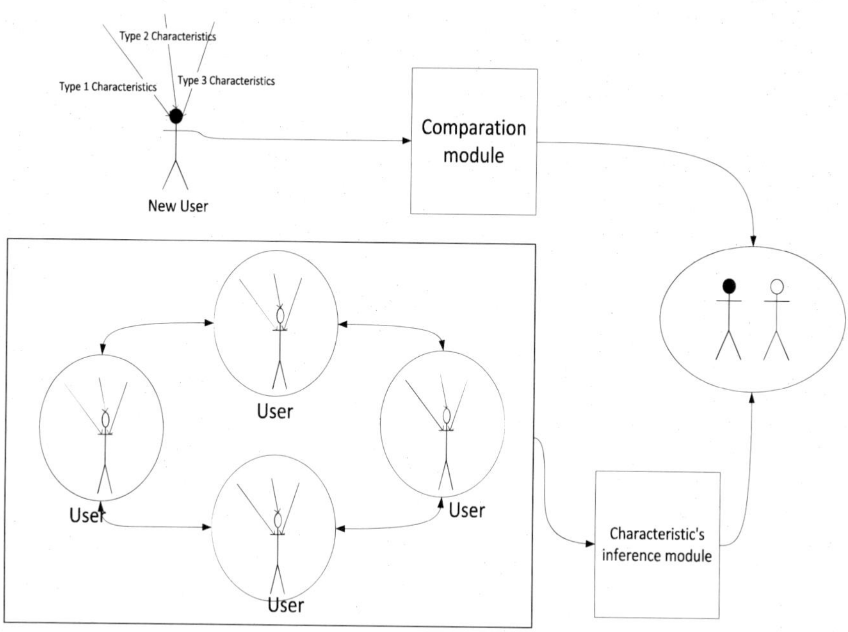

Figure 8. Individual matching system's architecture.

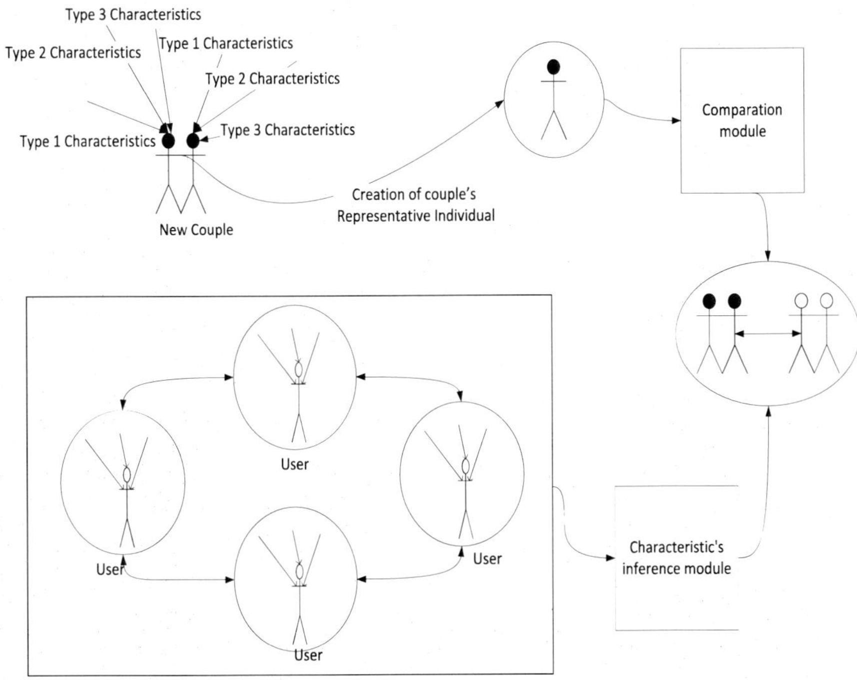

Figure 9. Couple matching system's architecture.

5. Algorithm to Obtain the Most Similar Couple to Another in a Social Network

Given a couple of individuals who will join a social network, our goal is to identify in the network the most similar couple to the new couple, i.e., a *cold start for couples*. Initially, we propose an algorithm to calculate the similarity of two individuals as defined in Section 4.

Next we create a *couple's representative individual* that we will use to calculate the couples similarity, this is consistent with works such as that of Luo et al. [6].

Finally, we propose an algorithm for solving the problem of cold start for couples in a social network.

Algorithm 1: Compute similarity between two individuals in a social network

Data: individual_1, individual_2, they represent the two users of the social network whose similarity will be computed.

Result: grade of similarity of the two individuals

```
compute_Similarity(individual_1, individual_2){
T=0
foreach characteristic in Characteristics do /* Set of
    characteristics considered to compute the similarity
    between the two individuals                          */

    Rci=0
    foreach value in characteristic.values() do /* Set of values of
        the current characteristic                       */

        a=individual_1.get(value)
        b=individual_2.get(value)
        Rci = Rci + | a-b |
    end
    Rci=Rci/200 // Normalization

    T=T+ (Rci * characteristic.weight)
end
T=T/Characteristics.length // Normalization

return T
}
```

Algorithm 2: Construction of a couple's representative individual

Data: individual_1, individual_2, they represent the two users of the social network whose couple's representative individual will be created.

Result: couple's representative individual

```
create_representative_individual(individual_1, individual_2){
representative_ind = new Individual() /* An individual that
   represents the characteristics of the couple                    */

foreach characteristic in Characteristics do /* Set of
   characteristics considered to compute the couple's
   representative individual                                       */

   foreach value in characteristic.values() do /* Set of values of
      the current characteristic                                   */

      representative_ind.set(characteristic, value,
         getValueCRI(individual_1.get(value),
         individual_2.get(value))) /* Set the value of value as
         the result of the function getValueCRI(), designed
         by the analysts. For example, it could be the
         average of the values of the two individuals              */

   end
end
return representative_ind
}
```

Algorithm 3: Cold Start for Couple's

Data: individual_1, individual_2, they represent a couple whose most similar couple of users in the social network will be found.

Result: the most similar couple in the social network with regard to the input couple

```
start_cold(individual_1, individual_2){
representative_ind_new_couple =
create_representative_individual(individual_1, individual_2)
min_T=infinity
most_similar_couple=(none,none)
foreach user in Users do // Set of users in the community
    (social network)

    foreach friend in user.getFriends() do // Set of friends, in the
        social network, of the current user

        representative_ind = create_representative_individual(user,
        friend)
        T = compute_Similarity(representative_ind_new_couple,
        representative_ind)
        if T < min_T then
            min_T = T
            most_similar_couple = (user, friend)
        end
    end
end
return most_similar_couple
}
```

CONCLUSION AND FUTURE WORKS

In this chapter, we proposed a method to make the matching of individuals based on some characteristics, to which the social network analyst can assign weighs. Then, the method was extended to couples. Finally, we present the algorithms which apply the developed theory along the work.

As future work we consider the building of an inference module of values for the characteristics, in order to complement the comparison module proposed in our work and that was specified in the diagram of the system architecture. As starting points can be considered the works of Eagle [4] and Kautz [5]. This information could be obtained from the analysis of the information that users use to post and produce in a social network, e.g., the information usually published in Facebook: artists, movies, books, among others, to which users give "Like" on their websites and other contents they mark as their favorite.

In addition, we also consider improving the algorithm so that it considers the intrinsic characteristics of a couple while advancing research on this topic. Some related ideas are presented in [6]. We also aim to propose more ways (other than the average) to calculate the value of the function *getValueCRI*() presented in the Algorithm 2. For instance, it could be obtained using the absolute value of the difference of the values of each individual or ADS (Absolute Difference Score), presented in [6]. Finally, we expect to generalize both the definitions and the algorithms so that the problem of a *start cold for groups* is solved. Ideas from [8, 9], and [10] may be useful.

REFERENCES

[1] Adams, J. H., 2006. System, method and apparatus for connecting users in an online computer system based on their relationships within social networks. U. S. Patent No. US7069308 B2. Washington, DC: U.S. Patent and Trademark Office. http://www.google.com/patents/US7069308.

[2] Watts, D. J., 2004. *Six degrees: the new science of networks*. London: Random House.

[3] Kaufman, A., 2011. Personality, Partner Similarity and Couple Satisfaction: Do Opposites Attract or Birds of a Feather Flock Together? [Electronic text] https://www.prepare-enrich.com/pe/pdf/research/2011/personality_and_couple_satisfaction_kaufmann_2011.pdf.

[4] Eagle, N., Pentland, A., 2005. Social serendipity: mobilizing social software. *IEEE Pervasive Computing*. 4(2), 28-34.

[5] Henry, A., Kautz, B. S., 1997. Referral web: combining social networks and collaborative filtering. *Communications of the ACM*. 40(3), 63-65.

[6] Luo, S., Chen, H., Yue, G., Zhang, G., Zhaoyang, R., Xu, D., 2008. Predicting marital satisfaction from self, partner, and couple characteristics: is it me, you, or us? *Journal of Personality*. 76(5), 1231-1266.

[7] Ben-Ari, A., Lavee, Y., 2005. Dyadic characteristics of individual attributes: attachment, neuroticism, and their relation to marital quality and closeness. *The American Journal of Orthopsychiatry*. 75(4), 621-631.

[8] Pedroche, F., Moreno, F., González, A., Valencia, A., 2011. Leadership groups on social network sites based on personalized pagerank. Mathematical and Computer Modelling. 57(7-8), 1891-1896.
[9] Carlier, G., Ekeland, I., 2008. Matching for teams. *Economic Theory.* 42(2), 397-418.
[10] Quijano-Sánchez, L., Bridge, D., 2013. A Case-Based Solution to the Cold-Start Problem in Group Recommenders. *Proceedings of the Twenty-Third International Joint Conference on Artificial Intelligence.* Beijing, China, August 2013.

Name: Francisco Javier Moreno Arboleda
Affiliation: Universidad Nacional de Colombia - Campus Medellín
Date of Birth: August 11 – 1972
Education: PhD. Systems Engineering and Informatics
Address: Facultad de Minas, Building M8A, Office 312, Medellín, Colombia

Research and Professional Experience: Databases and Algorithms, Associate teacher since 2003, at Universidad Nacional de Colombia - Campus Medellín.

Professional Appointments: Meritorious Teaching Universidad Nacional de Colombia - Campus Medellín.

Honors: PhD degree *cum laude*.

Publications Last 3 Years

Edison Ospina, Francisco Javier Moreno Arboleda, Iván Amón Uribe: Using Criteria Reconstruction for Low-sampling Trajectories as a Tool for Analytics. ICCS 2015: 366-373.
Francisco Javier Moreno Arboleda, Santiago Hernández, Edison Ospina: My Best Current Friend in a Social Network. ICCS 2015: 2903-2907.
Francisco Javier Moreno Arboleda, Andrés Felipe Pineda, Renato Fileto, Vania Bogorny: SMoT+: Extending the SMoT Algorithm for Discovering Stops in Nested Sites. Computing and Informatics 33(2): 327-342 (2014).
Francisco Javier Moreno Arboleda, Andrés González, Andrés Valencia: NewFriends: an algorithm for computing the minimum number of friends

required by a user to get the highest PageRank in a social network. Int. J. Comput. Math. 91(2): 278-290 (2014).

Francisco Pedroche, Francisco Javier Moreno Arboleda, Andrés González, Andrés Valencia: Leadership groups on Social Network Sites based on Personalized PageRank. Mathematical and Computer Modelling 57(7-8): 1891-1896 (2013)

Francisco Javier Moreno Arboleda, Sebastian Munera, Luis Munoz: A Trajectory Model to Deal with Transmission Failures. TrustCom 2012: 1692-1697.

Name: José Miguel Arrieta Ramos

Affiliation: Universidad Nacional de Colombia - Campus Medellín

Date of Birth: October 22 – 1992

Education: Graduate of Systems Engineering and Informatics at Universidad Nacional de Colombia – Campus Medellín

Address: Facultad de Minas, Building M8A, Office 415, Medellín, Colombia

Research and Professional Experience: Independent Consultant.

Professional Appointments: None.

Honors: None.

Publications Last 3 Years: None.

Name: Juan Pablo Correa Rendón

Affiliation: Universidad Nacional de Colombia - Campus Medellín

Date of Birth: November 29 – 1993

Education: Undergraduate Student of Engineering of Systems and Informatics at National University of Colombia – Campus Medellín

Address: Street 59 A # 63-20 Medellín, Colombia

Research and Professional Experience: Independent Consultant.

Professional Appointments: None.

Honors: None.

Publications Last 3 Years: None.

In: Advances in Social Networking Research
Editor: Salvador Reese
ISBN: 978-1-63485-225-8
© 2016 Nova Science Publishers, Inc.

Chapter 3

MODELING AND CONTROL OF USER INTEREST DICTATED INFORMATION DISSEMINATION IN COMMUNICATIONS AND SOCIAL NETWORKS

***Eleni Stai*[*]*, Vasileios Karyotis*[†] *and Symeon Papavassiliou*[‡]**
National Technical University of Athens, Zografou, Greece

Abstract

Information dissemination is one of the most critical processes in modern societies and one of the most important reasons for the proliferation of communications networks, especially of online social networks that have enabled global information exchange at rapid scales. This chapter will focus on information dissemination models that compared to the current literature, they specifically take into account aspects related to user interest and its temporal variability in the dynamics of information spreading. We focus on a dissemination framework regarding solely useful information, where users of communications and online social networks are willing to accept information and potentially further propagate it to their uninformed peers, depending on the interest each user has on specific topics. This is a novel perspective to consider information dissemination under inhomogeneous mixing, since the time-varying user

[*]E-mail address: estai@netmode.ntua.gr.
[†]E-mail address: vassilis@netmode.ntua.gr.
[‡]E-mail address: papavass@mail.ntua.gr.

interests affect significantly the outcome and the dynamics of information propagation and have an impact on its control process. Such models can be employed for further improving information dissemination analysis and control methodologies, and they can be exploited in various application domains, e.g., from infrastructure design and management, to marketing and advertising improvement. This chapter addresses both the modeling of information dissemination, especially via epidemics and evolutionary game theoretic techniques, as well as their control via optimal control frameworks and dual optimization techniques.

1. Introduction

Computer and communications networks have been fundamentally developed to transfer information, initially for restricted academic and military communities, and nowadays for any individual with access to a smart handheld device or more sophisticated computing machinery. Furthermore, the technological advances of the last decade have enabled the proliferation of online social networks, which have further propelled the more widespread and faster spreading of information. Thus, it is very important to analyze and model in detail the emerging information dissemination mechanisms, and further obtain control means that allow better serving the information volumes anticipated in future infrastructures/applications within the forthcoming 5G era [3, 35, 37].

In this chapter, we will be specifically concerned with the modeling and control of useful information, and not the undesired or malign information that can cause any form of damage in infrastructures and users. For the latter, various relevant works can be found in the literature, e.g., [4, 5, 6, 7] and references therein. Furthermore, we will focus on a very critical aspect affecting the speed and breadth of information propagation, namely user interest. It has been observed that user interest, in the form of user willingness to accept/acquire and communicate information can affect drastically the way specific information propagates over a network and various communities existing within it, and even determine the final outcome of the corresponding process [45, 53, 36]. Thus, this chapter will be specifically involved with information dissemination models developed for complex and especially online social networks that consider explicitly user interest.

Several works have suggested different approaches for modeling information diffusion, including epidemics, stochastic branching processes, queuing networks, etc., and others have exploited them for optimally controlling the speed or breadth of information dissemination, e.g., optimal control frameworks, simple feedback control, etc. These models will be analyzed in the following sections of this chapter in various capacities. However, irrespective of the adopted methodology, some common assumptions and objectives are in order. For instance, it is assumed that random interactions take place between humans, machines or 'actors' in general, involved in information spreading, based on their underlying network connections. However, by also considering the fact that user interest may vary among actors, user interaction is eventually characterized by heterogeneity, leading to "heterogeneous mixing" regimes. Common objectives among the relevant frameworks apply, e.g., the maximization of the speed or breadth of information propagation. Additionally, information dissemination is analyzed and studied from a macroscopic perspective, where the cumulative number/percentage of non-informed/informed users is of interest, and not the explicit system state determined by the state of each node. Furthermore, the ultimate goal of each approach is to reveal the macroscopic parameters that affect information dissemination, and exploit them for dictating the dissemination process. In this chapter, special attention will be paid to the impact of user interest on the above objectives of modeling information dissemination.

The rest of this chapter is organized as follows. In Section 2, we list notable approaches for modeling user behavior in information propagation. In Section 3, we present and explain the most popular tools for modeling information dissemination, i.e., those based on epidemics (Section 3.1) and those based on evolutionary game theory (Section 3.2) along with relevant literature for each one. In Section 4, we present analytical models based on epidemics for modeling information dissemination in social networks that take into account evolving user interests, while in Section 5, we present analytical models based on evolutionary game theory for the same purpose. In Sections 6.1, 6.2, we present a framework for optimally controlling information dissemination under evolving user interests based on epidemic modeling and evolutionary game theory, respectively. Next, Section 7 provides some indicative numerical results of information dissemination and its control under evolving user interest in social networks based on both synthetic and real data sets. Finally, Section 7.2 concludes the chapter and provides some directions for future research emphasizing on bigdata aspects related with information propagation.

2. Mathematical Modeling of User Behavior

User behavior has been shown to play a key role in the emergence, diffusion and final outcome of information spreading [8, 42, 53]. Furthermore, user behavior tends to be rather dependent on user interest [9], which cumulatively describes human character, desires, objectives, etc., that shape one's personality and determine the way one acts everyday. We consider that all these elements shape one's willingness to accept or discard information received from various means. As already mentioned, in this chapter we focus on the impact of such interest on information dissemination, and more specifically on useful information. Thus, within this setting we describe and analyze the positive or negative effect that user interest can have on information diffusion in online social networks.

User interests, their temporal variability and their impact on information diffusion have been considered already up to a limited degree, e.g., [10, 11, 12]. The authors in [11] aim at computing the minimum number of seed users capable of spreading information to all interested users for specific topics over multiple online social networks, while the work in [10] addresses the role of information diffusion in topology evolution considering the link formation process with respect to sources/retransmitters of the information, based on users' preferences. The work in [12] attempts to infer the impact of user interests in the information topics propagated in the network, with the ultimate goal to detect the truly active links in the diffusion of a given message. In general, most of the available relevant works, except from considering contact-related and topological factors affecting information diffusion dynamics [13, 14], they occasionally consider static user interests, e.g., [12, 11]. As an excemption, [16] studies the spatio-temporal dynamics of information diffusion, while incorporating time-varying (decreasing) users' interest, an aspect which will be also addressed in this chapter extensively. In a similar fashion, [15] studies malicious software dissemination in the Internet, where the infection rate decreases with time, modeling more accurately the actual propagation of CodeRed worm virus, since the worm spread can be slowed down by countermeasures employed by users and congestion points arising over the Internet. As in [15], in our approach the introduction of the time-evolving users' interests in the information propagation decisions along with the consideration of a network substrate abolishes the homogeneity assumption. However, contrary to [15] and [16], in this work we are not restricted only to time-decreasing user interest functions, but we apply diverse forms of the latter (e.g., periodic).

Taking the above into account, it is possible to define several types of functions describing the evolution of user interest with respect to time. Typically, user interest does not remain fixed with time for most types of information, e.g., memes, news, gossip, sports, etc. For some of these types of information, time-decreasing functions such as exponential, or other functions exhibiting "heavy-tail" like behavior are suitable. Especially for breaking news and other similar types of information, a more accurate function is the one obtained from the PDF of the Weibull distribution (Table 1), as it initially provides a sharp increase of interest, followed by a peak and then a rapidly decreasing but relatively long tail with respect to time (Fig. 1). A logarithmic user interest function, describes the cases where one is initially eager for a specific type of information, but as the user becomes very informed his/her interest saturates, yet still increasing very slowly. Finally, user interest can vary periodically, e.g., interest for summer vacations, seasonal sports, etc. Several periodic functions, e.g., having sinusoidal forms, can be employed for this purpose (Table 1).

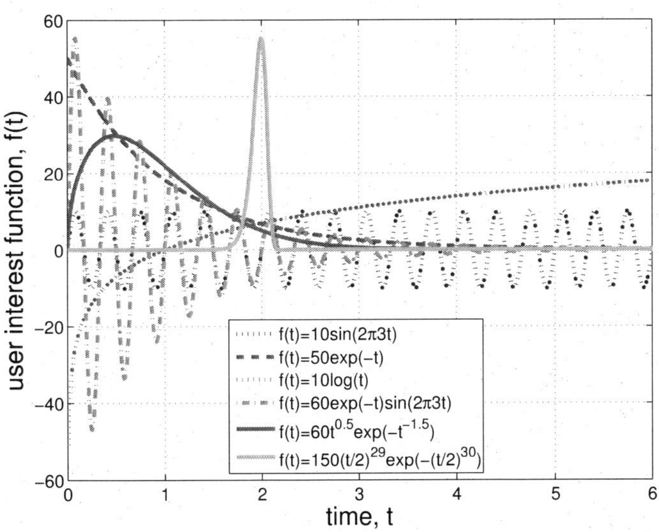

Figure 1. Examples of function forms modeling user interest (Table 1).

Table 1 summarizes some of the aforementioned functions modeling user interest and maps them to the type of information best suited for. Fig. 1 presents pictorially these functions. In the table, parameters A and k are constants. So are

Table 1. Mapping of various functions to different types of user interest.

Function	Form $f(t)$	Type	Interest Mapping
Constant	A	fixed	non-varying
Linear	$At + k$	incr./decr.	persistent/extincting
Exponential	$A\exp(-kt)$	decreasing	persistent decaying
Logarithmic	$A\log(kt)$	increasing	time-saturating
Sinusoidal	$A\sin(2\pi kt)$	periodic	seasonal (periodic)
Damped cosine	$e^{-t}\cos(2\pi kt)$	decreasing	decreasing periodic
Weibull	$F(t;k,\lambda) = \frac{k}{\lambda}(\frac{t}{\lambda})^{k-1}e^{-(t/\lambda)^k}, t \geq 0$	heavy-tailed for $k < 1$	memes, trends, etc.

parameters k, λ for the Weibull distribution function. In the following subsections, we provide some specific example scenarios where user interest is modeled with some of the aforementioned time functions and for different groups of users exhibiting different interest behaviors.

3. Modeling of Information Propagation in Social Networks

As already mentioned, various approaches have been employed for modeling information dissemination in complex networks (e.g., in telecommunications, social, hybrid, generalized, sensor, etc.) in general, and in online social networks in particular. This section describes the most popular tools for modeling information propagation in complex and social networks along with the corresponding literature.

More specifically, there are two major frameworks currently available for modeling information dissemination. One based on epidemic models, e.g., [7, 38, 13], and the other based on game theoretic models, and specifically on Evolutionary Game Theory (EGT), e.g., [33, 34]. Both are temporal frameworks, describing information spreading in the course of time. The main difference between them is that for the epidemic based approaches user decisions on whether to diffuse or not information, namely their dissemination strategy, are not modeled explicitly. Thus, users may not have decision-making capabilities and may acquire knowledge or diffuse information in a random manner. On the contrary, the EGT based models of information propagation are founded on modeling users' decisions via appropriately defined payoff functions and strategy update rules. In simpler terms, the EGT based framework is more appropriate for cases where users have the ability to choose and apply different strategies, e.g., [32, 39], while the epidemics based framework is more appropriate for scenarios that do not allow for such flexibility to users. However, both frameworks allow studying the basic characteristics of information propagation in complex/social networks, which include the dynamics of its evolution along with the stable points that the propagation arrives at.

In terms of mathematical machinery, the epidemics framework adopts the so-called epidemic equations [38, 7], an example of which will be described in the following subsection, and obtains solutions of a system of ordinary differential equations describing the variation of each group in the population, according to state dynamics. On the other hand, the EGT approaches assume equations describing the variation of groups in the population adopting different strategies, aiming to compute the balance point of the strategy evolution and whether this is a stable strategy or not [52, 33].

These two frameworks will be applied in the subsequent sections for developing more elaborate models of the dynamics of the information diffusion process and frameworks of the control of the latter, while considering user interest and its related impact. The notation we employ between epidemics and EGT based approaches varies, following practices compatible within each individual research community. However, in each case, we define explicitly the employed symbols, so that direct associations can be made straightforwardly.

3.1. Information Epidemics

Information dissemination resembles the spread of a virus in humans or animals, thus, the first approaches for modeling information dissemination were inspired by epidemic models for humans [38, 7] and computer worms [17, 15]. Some of the most recently proposed models for information dissemination based on epidemics are [13, 19, 20, 14], while more can be found in the references therein. Under epidemic models, network nodes that have not received information yet are denoted as susceptible or non-informed (similar to non-infected nodes), while nodes that have already received the information are denoted as infected, i.e., informed. All of these models are characterized by the succession of possible states the population can have. Thus, if nodes initially start susceptible (susceptible state is denoted by S), then become infected (infected state is denoted by I) and recover eventually with permanent immunity (recovered state is denoted by R), the corresponding epidemic model is referred to as SIR. Furthermore, if the nodes of the population can ultimately be completely removed, i.e., die (dead state is denoted by D), the epidemic model is referred to as SIRD [17]. The most general epidemic model is referred to as compartmental model (MSEIRS model, where M denotes the state of maternally acquired immunity and E stands for the exposed state before an individual becomes infected but is prone to receive infections). Each state is considered as a compartment, and the model is analytically described in [38].

In this chapter we will be specifically concerned with the Susceptible-Infected-Susceptible (SIS) epidemic model, where users start susceptible, corresponding to non-informed nodes, then they are considered as infected (i.e., informed) when the desired information is obtained, and then return to the susceptible state, possibly expecting other information or new information for their topics of interest. This behavior is described in the general case by the following set of differential equations:

$$\frac{dS}{dt} = -\frac{\beta SI}{N} + \mu(N - S) + \gamma I, \tag{1}$$

$$\frac{dI}{dt} = \frac{\beta SI}{N} - \gamma I - \mu I, \tag{2}$$

where S, I is the number of susceptible/infected nodes respectively, μ is the individual death rate, assumed equal to the individual birth rate, β is the rate of infection (assumed homogeneous for all population in the above set), and γ is the considered recovery rate.

Epidemic models can be segregated in deterministic and stochastic [22, 23]. Stochastic epidemic models treat information propagation as a discrete time process (Discrete Time Markov Chain) [22, 23] being more suitable for small-scale systems whereas deterministic models assume continuous processes relying on the law of large numbers and applying differential equations or inclusions [15, 21], thus being more suitable for large-scale systems. Most of the deterministic models focus on the macroscopic evolution of the diffusion dynamics computing the evolution of the cumulative system state, expressed by the number of infected individuals, while assuming homogeneous infection rates for all population members [38, 24]. These models are denoted as "population dynamics". However, there are deterministic models defined over networks that study the state of each individual separately and segregate infection rates between different pairs of individuals [23]. However, system state transitions depend on the state transition models developed for each individual, e.g., SIS, SIR, etc. [38, 23]. Contrary to deterministic network models, a typical assumption in population dynamics is that of homogeneous mixing, where contact patterns between individuals are considered highly homogeneous [24] and thus the infection rates (β in Eq. (2)) are the same for all pairs of individuals. Both approaches, account for the endogenous (transition that takes place owe to internal individual operation, e.g., recovery transition) and exogenous (transitions dictated by external factors, e.g., infection transition) transition rates expressing the topological and operational, endogenous or exogenous, factors that affect the evolution of the system [23].

Information dissemination epidemic models have been developed for different types of networks, e.g., wireless [27], social [38] multiple social [11], and generalized networks [13]. More specifically, epidemic models, e.g., SIS, SIR and SI [38, 16] have been adopted and adapted over diverse network topologies to describe the spreading of useful or malicious information. In this chapter, and specifically in the corresponding section (Section 4), we will focus on the diffusion of useful information over social networks considering deterministic epidemic modeling (over networks) and time-varying infection rates. Although we will consider heterogeneous infection rates per pairs of individuals depending on their interests on the propagated information, we will analyze the latter on an approximate basis using approximate infection rates, common for all pairs of interacting nodes.

3.2. Evolutionary Game Theory

This section describes the evolutionary game theoretic tool and mentions related literature in the domain of applying EGT for studying information propagation in social networks. As mentioned before, EGT emphasizes on modeling users' decisions related to the information propagation. Specifically, EGT applies concepts of game theory (strategies, payoff values, strategy update rules, etc.) [52] to populations that exhibit evolutionary features, similar to those observed by various forms of life in biology, e.g., mutation, birth, death, etc., [31]. Compared to classical game theory, EGT focuses more on the dynamics of strategy change that depend both on the quality of the strategy, i.e., the payoff values it ensures for the players and the extent of the adoption of the strategy by the members of the population. In EGT, a game is played repetitively, as a repetition game [31, 29], studying the dynamics of the strategies' distribution within the population along with its stable points and its shift by the effect of *mutants*, namely nodes that introduce another strategy influencing the rest of nodes. Since the evolution of most systems is naturally taking place over networked environments, EGT on graphs or equivalently referred to as Graphical EGT [52] becomes the basic tool for its study.

To facilitate the presentation of the EGT, initially we do not assume an underlying network structure. Thus, we assume an infinitely large (in the sense of a deterministic limit), well-mixed population (namely that all individuals are equally likely to interact with each other). To begin with the basics, an evolutionary game is characterized by a set of players (nodes), a set of strategies $\mathcal{X} = \{1, 2, ..., m\}$ and an $m \times m$ payoff matrix U, each entry $u_{i,j}$ of which denotes the payoff of strategy i versus strategy j. The matrix U is called the *fitness matrix*, and the system state can be defined via the vector $p = [p_1, ..., p_i, ...p_m]^T$, where p_i is the relative frequency of strategy i, i.e., the fraction of the population using strategy i. Thus, $\sum_{i=1}^{m} p_i = 1$. The fitness of strategy i can be obtained as $f_i = \sum_{j=1}^{m} u_{ij}p_j = \mathbf{e}_i U p^T$ ($\mathbf{e}_i$ is a unit vector with 1 in position i and 0 elsewhere), while the average fitness of the population as $\phi = \sum_{i=1}^{m} p_i f_i = pUp^T$.

The EGT dynamics are described by the fundamental *replicator equation*:

$$\frac{dp_i}{dt} = p_i(f_i - \phi), \ i = 1, ..., m. \tag{3}$$

The replicator equation shows the dynamics of the evolution of the information propagation over the population and dictates that the population distribution of those types of strategies that perform better than average will grow further, while those that perform less will extinct. With respect to the stability of the above dynamics, the concept of the Evolutionarily Stable State (ESS) is defined [33]. Intuitively and given that an evolutionary game is a repetitive process, an ESS is a stable equilibrium after a period of strategic interactions. ESS is a refinement of the Nash equilibrium for symmetric games, where now even if a small fraction of players do not behave rationally and deviate from equilibrium strategies, ESS will be still a locally stable state. More formally, a state p^* is an Evolutionarily Stable Strategy/State (ESS) if for all strategies $p \neq p^*$, we have:

$$pUp^{*T} \leq p^*Up^{*T}, \tag{4}$$

$$pUp^{*T} = p^*Up^{*T} \Rightarrow pUp^T < p^*Up^T. \tag{5}$$

The first condition is equivalent to the Nash equilibrium condition, while the second further guarantees the stability of the ESS, p^*.

Above, we described a classical evolutionary game, i.e., in the case of population dynamics, as also explained in Section 3.1, which considers a complete graph of connections for the members of the population (there is a connection between each pair of members of the population). However, as it was mentioned before, most systems evolve assuming an underlying network structure. This means that not every pair of members of the population is connected and a member of the population is affected only by its connections (i.e., neighbors) and not by the whole population. In this case, Graphical EGT [34, 52] is developed to study the evolution of strategies in a structured population, where the interactions are described by a non-complete network graph. Most of the notation employed in the classical EGT is adopted by the Graphical EGT and below we present only their differentiations.

According to [52], the study of a graphical evolutionary game, i.e., an evolutionary game over a structured population, needs the following:

- the existence of a network graph over the population, e.g., an online social network is considered in this chapter;
- a set of strategies of the players of the game or the members of the population, where this set is the same for all the players and each player chooses one strategy per iteration of the game;
- a payoff function providing the payoff value of a player given his/her strategy choice and those of his/her neighbors;
- a strategy update rule that determines the next strategy choice of a player given the strategies and the payoff values of his/her neighbors.

The set of strategies of the users of the online social network with respect to the information propagation will be determined in the corresponding section that elaborates more on the Graphical EGT model (Section 5). The fitness of a player following the strategy i (similarly to the fitness matrix defined for classical EGT above), denoted as π_i, is locally determined from interactions with all adjacent players given by the equation:

$$\pi_i = (1 - \alpha) \cdot B_i + a \cdot U_i, \tag{6}$$

where B_i is the baseline fitness that represents inherent player properties (with respect to the strategy i) and U_i is the player's payoff derived via the payoff matrix U and the graph structure (i.e., neighboring relations). Let B stand for the vector expressing collectively the B_i values for all m strategies. The parameter α represents the selection intensity, where the case $\alpha \to 0$ represents the limit of *weak selection* and $\alpha \to 1$ the *strong selection* regime where fitness equals payoff.

In Graphical EGT, the strategy evolution dynamics (i.e., similarly to the replicator equation, Eq. (3)) depend on the rule applied for the strategy update of the players given their fitness values (i.e., Eq. (6)). Some characteristic strategy update rules are the following [33, 52]:

- **Birth-Death (BD) rule**: A player is chosen for reproduction with probability being proportional to fitness (Birth process). Then, the chosen player's strategy replaces one of his/her neighbors' strategies with uniform probability (Death process).
- **Death-Birth (DB) rule**: A random player is chosen to abandon his/her current strategy (Death process). Then, the chosen player adopts one of his/her neighbors' strategies with the probability being proportional to their fitness (Birth process).
- **Imitation (IM) rule**: Each player either adopts the strategy of one of his/her neighbors or remains with his/her current strategy, with probability being proportional to fitness.
- **Unconditional Imitation with Fixed Priority rule**: The strategy of a player is selected as the best strategy from the strategies of his/her neighbors (best strategy is one achieving the highest fitness value). In case that there are more than one best strategies, selection among them is performed assuming a fixed priority.
- **Unconditional Imitation with Equal Probability for Best Strategies rule**: The strategy of a player is selected as the best strategy from the strategies of his/her neighbors. In case that there are more than one best strategies, selection among them is performed randomly with equal probability.
- **Simplified Femi rule**: A player randomly selects one of his/her neighbors. It adopts the strategy of his/her randomly chosen neighbor, only if the latter has achieved a higher fitness value compared with the player's one.

Through analyzing the system dynamics under some specific strategy update rule, the final ESSs can be found at the stable points of the dynamics. The replicator equation on graphs has been studied in [31], where a generally defined replicator equation is derived and appropriately adapted for each one of the above update rules. Throughout this chapter, we assume the BD strategy update rule, without loss of generality, since similar results can be obtained for the other rules by appropriately adapting the process followed for the BD update rule.

Some of the available works, apply game theoretic concepts instead of epidemics for studying the behavior of users or network nodes with respect to the propagation of information, i.e., the decision on whether to forward the information or not (as in [43]). More specifically, these works consider the existence of two strategies in the population or network graph (Section 5), namely forward or not forward the information and either study the dynamics of the evolution of these strategies in the population or network graph, e.g., [34], or extend to the study of the stability of such dynamics such as in [33, 40, 41]. However, none of the previous works addresses the issue of the effect of the evolving, i.e., time-varying, user behavior on his/her strategy choice, which however has significant impact on the diffusion of useful information (Section 2). For example, the interest of users of a social network on advertisements regarding vacations, follows a periodic behavior, peaking during summer months and dropping in winter. Regarding the problem of incorporating the time-evolving behavior/payoffs in EGT, to the best of our knowledge, there is limited work that applies a time-varying fitness matrix U only in the case of population dynamics, [30]. The time-variation of the fitness matrix considered in [30] is of periodic form and the authors study the conditions for the existence of a periodic stable orbit of the strategy dynamics. In this chapter, we will define a framework for Graphical EGT with a time-varying fitness matrix U of general form, targeting at modeling and studying the impact of time-varying user interests on the information propagation. We consider that the elements of the time-varying fitness matrix U depend on the time-varying user interests and they can thus be determined using the user interest modeling of Section 2. Based on this framework, we will design a control framework over EGT aiming to control the dynamics and the ESSs of the evolution of the information propagation.

4. Information Propagation in Social Networks under Evolving Users' Interests Using Epidemic Modeling

In this section, we show how the epidemic based models can be extended to take into account user interest in the process of information dissemination. In the general case, M classes of information, denoted by $m = 1, ..., M$ as in [54], are assumed. Each consists of messages on a specific topic, e.g., summer vacations advertisements, and dissemination is considered separately for each class. Interactions among separate classes are probabilistically considered. Each node i is characterized by its interest in class m at time t, denoted as $R_i^m(t)$, where $\sum_{\forall m} R_i^m(t) \leq 1,\ \forall i$ (i.e., the interest of a user is split among potentially all classes). Information diffusion is modeled via an SIS paradigm [7], assuming the mapping that a node i is considered Infected (i.e., informed) for a specific class m of information if it possesses at least one message belonging in this class, otherwise i is considered Susceptible (i.e., not informed) for class m. The transition from the susceptible state to the infected one for a particular class takes place when a node receives information about this class, while an infected node transits back to the susceptible state when it deletes all messages for this class. Let us denote with $\mathbb{I}^m(t)$ the set of infected/informed nodes at time t for class m.

With respect to information diffusion, a node i is expected to perform/experience one of the following actions at each time t.

1. For the classes for which i is infected/informed at time t, denoted as $i \in \mathbb{I}^m(t)$:

   (a) i diffuses information about class m with probability $f_1(R_i^m(t))$ ($f_1(t)$ for simplicity). Specifically, node i transfers the information to each one of its neighbors j in the social network with probability equal to $f_3(R_j^m(t))$ ($f_3(R_j^m(t))$ for all j neighbors of i do not sum to one, i.e., do not form a probability distribution).

   (b) i deletes all messages about class m with probability $qf_2(R_i^m(t))$(also $f_2(t)$ for simplicity), where the parameter q is introduced to control the deletion process.

We consider that the duration of each time slot permits only the completion of one action, thus only one class m will be selected and either (a)

or (b) will happen. This means that

$$\sum_{m:\, i \in \mathbb{I}^m(t)} (f_1(R_i^m(t)) + qf_2(R_i^m(t))) \leq 1.$$

2. Node i performs another action - which is not of interest for the information diffusion - with probability equal to $1 - \sum_{m:\, i \in \mathbb{I}^m(t)} (f_1(R_i^m(t)) + qf_2(R_i^m(t)))$.

The above diffusion process requires that there is always an informed node for every class to maintain the spreading. However, all informed nodes for a particular class may delete their information for this class, thus disrupting its diffusion. Exogenous impact such as the optimal control which will be introduced in the following sections, may be leveraged to alleviate the case of extinction of a whole information class.

It is fairly straightforward to approximate the dynamics of the evolution of the information diffusion process described above. If the number of infected nodes for each class m is now denoted by $I^m(t)$, the differential equation describing the average (approximate) dynamics of $I^m(t)$ is:

$$\frac{dI^m(t)}{dt} = f_1^{avg}(t) f_3^{avg}(t) \frac{S^m(t)}{N} I^m(t) N_s^{avg} - qI^m(t) f_2^{avg}(t), \tag{7}$$

where $f_1^{avg}(t)$, $f_2^{avg}(t)$, $f_3^{avg}(t)$ are the average (or the expected values) of all f_1, f_2, f_3 functions correspondingly over the network at time t for the corresponding class m. N_s^{avg} stands for the average number of neighbors in the social network. The initial conditions are $I^m(0) = I_0^m, \forall m$, i.e., I_0^m nodes are initially infected for each information class m.

ODE (7) has a unique solution when $f_1^{avg}(t)$, $f_2^{avg}(t)$, $f_3^{avg}(t)$ are continuous functions with respect to time (Cauchy-Lipschitz Theorem [55]). The right hand side is obviously Lipschitz continuous with respect to I^m. This fact has an impact on the design of possible forms for the interests' functions $R_i^m(t)$, $\forall m, i$, which should be continuous in time. It also has impact on the design of possible formats for the functions $f_1(t)$, $f_2(t)$, $f_3(t)$ with respect to user interest.

A suitable selection for the functions f_1, f_2, f_3 in the working example scenarios that follow is:

$$f_1(R_i^m(t)) = \frac{R_i^m(t)}{2M},$$
$$f_2(R_i^m(t)) = \frac{1 - R_i^m(t)}{2M},$$
$$f_3(R_j^m(t)) = R_j^m(t). \tag{8}$$

This configuration is not restrictive in the sense that others may be designed for other scenarios/applications. It is important to note that Eq. (7) is approximate since average (expected) values of the functions f_1, f_2, f_3 are used. However, such an approximate form can be used to demonstrate the important characteristics of information diffusion dynamics in specific cases, as follows.

4.1. Examples of Forms of User Interest Functions

In this subsection, we provide some indicative examples of the forms that user interest functions may employ according to different scenarios. We discuss briefly three scenarios, one with periodic interests, one with groups exhibiting different interests, and one of an increasing-versus-decreasing interest.

4.1.1. Periodic Users' Interests

Consider two classes of information, where the time continuous interests' functions take sinusoidal forms to express time periodicity of user interest. Specifically, $R_i^1(t) = 1 - A_i \sin^2(a(t + b_i)) + B_i,\ \forall i$, for class $m = 1$, where $a > 0$ determines the period of users' interests and $A_i,\ b_i,\ B_i$ are appropriately defined constants. Then, $R_i^2(t) = A_i \sin^2(a(t + b_i)) - B_i,\ \forall i$, so that $R_i^1(t) + R_i^2(t) = 1,\ \forall t, i$. Note that, we consider the same frequency for all sinusoidal interests assuming the propagation of information that intrigues the attention of all users over specific time periods such as vacations, summer sports, Halloween, etc.

Based on this scenario, the average values for the functions f_1, f_2, f_3 for the class 1 become:

$$f_1^{avg}(t) = \frac{1 - A\sin^2(a(t + b)) + B}{2M},$$
$$f_2^{avg}(t) = \frac{A\sin^2(a(t + b)) - B}{2M},$$
$$f_3^{avg}(t) = 1 - A\sin^2(a(t + b)) + B,$$

where $b_i = b, \forall i$, and the constants A, B are computed by averaging the interests over all users at time t. The average values of functions f_1, f_2, f_3 for class 2 are defined similarly.

It can be assumed that $f_1^{avg}(t), f_2^{avg}(t), f_3^{avg}(t)$ represent the expected values of the corresponding expressions of the users' interests at time t. Thus, users' interests will vary randomly according to a distribution with mean value $1 - A\sin^2(a(t+b)) + B$ for class 1, letting the complementary interest (i.e., with mean value $A\sin^2(a(t+b)) - B$) to be assigned to class 2.

In this case, the ODE (7) for class 1, becomes:

$$\frac{dI^1(t)}{dt} = \frac{N_s^{avg}}{N}(N - I^1(t))I^1(t)\frac{(1 - A\sin^2(a(t+b)) + B)^2}{2M} - qI^1(t)\frac{(A\sin^2(a(t+b)) - B)}{2M}, \tag{9}$$

and similarly, for class 2, it can be obtained as:

$$\frac{dI^2(t)}{dt} = \frac{N_s^{avg}}{N}(N - I^2(t))I^2(t)\frac{(A\sin^2(a(t+b)) - B)^2}{2M} - qI^2(t)\frac{(1 - A\sin^2(a(t+b)) + B)}{2M}. \tag{10}$$

The solution of both Eqs. (9), (10) takes a complex form which does not provide any intuition regarding the dynamics of change of the number of infected nodes for each class, $I^1(t), I^2(t)$. For this reason, a finite difference approach to approximate them can be employed. For more details on this approach, the interested reader may have a look at [45].

4.1.2. Information Diffusion Dynamics among Groups with Different Characteristics

In this example, constant interests are assumed exhibiting how information of a specific subject spreads in groups characterized by different features, e.g., news about a football match propagating within the members of a football team compared with their propagation within members of a dance team. This special case is similar to the SIS models developed in literature [38, 7] in the sense that the parameters applied in the ODEs describing the dynamics of information diffusion are constant, contrary to the time varying parameters $(f_1^{avg}(t), f_2^{avg}(t), f_1^{avg}(t))$ considered in this chapter. Thus, several existing schemes in literature, e.g., [38, 7, 37] may be considered as special cases of our proposed diffusion model.

For simplicity, two groups and one information class (e.g., class 1) are considered. For both groups $R_i^1(t) = a, \forall i, 0 < a < 1$, where for the first group a

is close to 1, while in the second group a gets closer to 0. In this particular case of constant interests, the solution of Eq. (7) attains a less complex form.

4.1.3. Increasing vs. Decreasing Users' Interest

In this scenario, there exist two classes of information, while the population has increasing interest for the one class and decreasing for the other. The appropriate interest functions for this case are formulated, $\forall i$, as follows:

$$R_i^1(t) = B\frac{At}{At + C}, \; R_i^2(t) = B\frac{C}{At + C}, \tag{11}$$

where $A,\ B,\ C$ are constants.

As previously, the finite difference approximation described in [45] can be employed for obtaining approximate solutions.

5. Information Propagation in Social Networks under Evolving Users' Interests Using EGT Modeling

In this section, we study information diffusion dynamics over social networks via EGT. Specifically, Graphical EGT is suitable since the players deciding for their strategies correspond to users of a social network, which do not form a well-mixed population but develop specific interconnections among them (i.e., the social network graph). As also mentioned in Section 3.2, by applying Graphical EGT, we can model and analyze the evolution of the strategy dynamics with respect to information diffusion over the users of a social network and we can infer their stable points. Importantly, EGT is more adequate for studying information diffusion dynamics when users have the possibility to decide about which strategy they will follow in terms of information propagation, e.g., forward a specific information message or not. The epidemic based modeling does not pre-assume such possibility for network users.

As the definition of a graphical evolutionary game requires a set of strategies (which should be the same for all the users, Section 3.2), as a first step, we need to explore strategies related to information diffusion in a social network. We have identified three different (general) types of strategies, namely, the strategy S_f which translates to "forward the information/message", the strategy S_n which translates to "do not forward the information/message" and the strategy S_d which translates to "delete the information/message". We characterize them as general strategies because we believe that other more specific ones can be cast under the umbrella of the above three. Indeed, as information propagates within the network, nodes decide to forward it, not forward it or delete it depending on their interest on the latter and their interactions with their neighbors. Although these strategies are quite general to cover a broad range of information diffusion cases, they can be adapted and complemented for specific problems if needed. The adaptation of the problem formulation and solution that will be presented below will be straightforward, although it may lead to seemingly more complex systems. As also argued in Section 2, the dynamics and extent of information diffusion depend on the interest that the users of the social network show for its corresponding topic. This interest depends on the content of the information [53], the target social network's user composition and it is time-varying, e.g., dependent on the epoch of the year.

We assume a population of users (players) each one currently having a given strategy that belongs to the specific set of strategies/behaviors mentioned above. In this chapter, we focus on symmetric games, i.e., the outcome depends only on the strategies adopted by the players and the interactions of the latter, and not on the users themselves. This means that if user A with strategy S_f interacts with user C with strategy S_n, the outcome will be the same with the case where user C with strategy S_f interacts with user A with strategy S_n. The outcome of each encounter of pairs of strategies (i.e., between strategies of neighboring players in the social network) yields payoffs described by the fitness matrix [33] (Section 3.2). Due to our considered setting of time-varying evolution of users' interests/needs, we adopt a time-varying payoff (fitness) matrix, defined as follows:

$$U(t) = \begin{bmatrix} u_{ff}(t) & u_{fn}(t) & u_{fd}(t) \\ u_{nf}(t) & u_{nn}(t) & u_{nd}(t) \\ u_{df}(t) & u_{dn}(t) & u_{dd}(t) \end{bmatrix} \tag{12}$$

where all elements are assumed normalized in $(0, 1)$. This means that depending on users' interests at time t, the payoff of, e.g., strategy S_f versus strategy S_n is given by $u_{fn}(t)$, and the same holds between the other pairs of strategies. Similarly to the elements of the fitness matrix U (Eq. (12)), the elements of the baseline fitness vector B (Section 3.2) attain time-varying forms as imposed by users' evolving interests and needs. Then, according to the Graphical EGT (Section 3.2) the fitness of a player following the strategy i, denoted as π_i, is locally determined from interactions with his/her neighboring players given by the equation:

$$\pi_i(t) = (1-\alpha)\cdot B_i(t) + a \cdot U_i(t), \tag{13}$$

where $B_i(t)$ stands for the also time-varying baseline fitness that represents inherent player properties (with respect to the strategy i) and $U_i(t)$ is the player's payoff derived via the payoff matrix U and the graph structure (i.e., neighboring relations), more explicitly given in the following.

Similarly to Section 4, let $R^m_{avg}(t)$ stand for the expected interest of the users of the online social network for the information class m being under propagation at time t. Note that a separate graphical evolutionary game should be defined for each information class under propagation. In order to model the impact of the user interest in the information diffusion dynamics, we should express the elements of the fitness matrix and the baseline fitness values in terms of R^m_{avg}. As an example, $u_{ff}(t) = f_1(R^m_{avg}(t))$ and $u_{dd}(t) = f_2(R^m_{avg}(t))$, where f_1 is an increasing function of R^m_{avg} and f_2 is a decreasing function of R^m_{avg}, i.e., for all times t that R^m_{avg} is high, the payoff for two interacting nodes both with strategy S_f is high, while the payoff for two interacting nodes both with strategy S_d is low. The other elements of the payoff matrix $U(t)$ and of the baseline fitness $B(t)$ can be defined in a similar fashion according to the specific application. Similar conditions should apply for the elements of $U(t)$, $B(t)$ as the ones defined in Section 4 for the functions $f_1(t), f_2(t), f_3(t)$, with respect to time continuity.

In the remaining of this section, in order to ease the presentation and simplify the analysis, we focus on the two strategies S_f, S_d. Generally, we will follow a problem formulation and analysis similar to the one followed in [33], although incorporating time-varying user interests. Then, the network state is given by the following variables:

- p_f, p_d: the percentage of nodes that adopt strategy S_f, S_d, respectively.
- p_{ff}, p_{dd}: the percentage of edges, both endpoints of which adopt strategy S_f, S_d correspondingly.
- p_{df}, p_{fd}: the percentage of edges, one endpoint of which adopts strategy S_d and the other S_f.

Furthermore, we define as $p_{f|d}$, the percentage of the neighbors of a user that adopt strategy S_f given that the user employs strategy S_d. We define $p_{f|f}$, $p_{d|f}$, $p_{d|d}$ in a similar fashion. We consider one information class, e.g., m

and we omit its indication on the state variables for brevity. The network state variables need to satisfy the following relations for each time t [33] (in general we omit time-dependence of the state variables for brevity):

$$p_f + p_d = 1, \tag{14}$$

$$p_{ff} = p_f p_{f|f},\ p_{dd} = p_d p_{d|d},\ p_{fd} = p_f p_{d|f} + p_d p_{f|d}, \tag{15}$$

$$p_{f|f} + p_{d|f} = 1,\ p_{f|d} + p_{d|d} = 1,\ p_f p_{d|f} = p_d p_{f|d}. \tag{16}$$

Due to the system of Eqs. (14)-(16), we only need two variables to describe the network state, e.g., p_f, p_{ff} suffice.

After defining the strategies and the payoff matrix of the graphical evolutionary game, we will proceed with modeling the dynamics of the strategy distribution evolution in the social network and find its ESS points (Section 3.2). Based on the above, we need first to derive the dynamics of the state variables, p_f, p_{ff}, as differential equations and then define the balance points of their nonlinear dynamic system satisfying the conditions for stability that will be specified in the following.

We define as $\lambda(.)$ the node degree distribution, i.e., $\lambda(k)$ is the probability that a node has degree k at the social network. The mean node degree is given by $\overline{k} = \sum_{k=0}^{\infty} k\lambda(k)$. Let k_f stand for the number of neighbors of a node that use strategy S_f. Note that if the user adopts S_f, then $k_f = kp_{f|f}$, else $k_f = kp_{f|d}$. The probability of the configuration "a user with strategy S_f has k neighbors among which k_f follow the strategy S_f" is equal to

$$\theta^f(k, k_f) = \binom{k}{k_f} p_{f|f}^{k_f} (1 - p_{f|f})^{(k-k_f)}.$$

Similarly, the probability of the configuration "a user with strategy S_d has k neighbors among which k_f follow the strategy S_f" is equal to

$$\theta^d(k, k_f) = \binom{k}{k_f} p_{f|d}^{k_f} (1 - p_{f|d})^{(k-k_f)}.$$

The dynamics of the state p_f of the network depend on the chosen update rule (Section 3.2). Without loss of generality and for easier presentation of our results, we apply the BD update rule (Section 3.2). Thus, based on all the above, the fitness of a player adopting the strategy S_f becomes equal to ([33]):

$$\pi_f(k, k_f, t) = (1-a)B_f(t) + a\left[k_f u_{ff}(t) + (k-k_f)u_{fd}(t)\right]. \tag{17}$$

Similarly, the fitness of a player adopting the strategy S_d becomes:

$$\pi_d(k, k_f, t) = (1-a)B_d(t) + a\left[(k-k_f)u_{dd}(t) + k_f u_{df}(t)\right]. \tag{18}$$

At this point, we define the probability $P_{S_d \to S_f}(k, k_f, t)$ at time t, that a user who uses strategy S_d changes his/her strategy to S_f [33], according to the BD rule described in Section 3.2.

$$P_{S_d \to S_f}(k, k_f, t) = p_f \theta^f(k, k_f) \frac{\pi_f(k, k_f, t)}{\Pi(t)} \frac{k-k_f}{k}, \tag{19}$$

where $\Pi(t)$ stands for the sum of the fitness values of all nodes at time t.

The dynamics of the network state p_f take the form of the following differential equation [33]:

$$\frac{dp_f}{dt} = \frac{1}{N}\mathcal{P}^t(\Delta p_f = \frac{1}{N}) - \frac{1}{N}\mathcal{P}^t(\Delta p_f = -\frac{1}{N}), \tag{20}$$

where the exponent t denotes time dependence and

$$\mathcal{P}^t(\Delta p_f = \frac{1}{N}) = \sum_{k=0}^{\infty} \lambda(k) \sum_{k_f=0}^{k} P_{S_d \to S_f}(k, k_f, t),$$

$$\mathcal{P}^t(\Delta p_f = -\frac{1}{N}) = \sum_{k=0}^{\infty} \lambda(k) \sum_{k_f=0}^{k} P_{S_f \to S_d}(k, k_f, t).$$

In the special case that $u_{df}(t) = u_{fd}(t) = u(t),\ B_f(t) = B_d(t) = 1,\ \forall t$ (also considered in [33]) Eq. (20) takes the simple form:

$$\frac{dp_f}{dt} = \frac{a p_{fd}(\overline{k}-1)}{2N\Pi(t)}((u_{ff}(t) - u(t))p_{f|f} - (u_{dd}(t) - u(t))p_{d|d}). \tag{21}$$

The dynamics of the network state p_{ff} take the form of the following differential equation which is explained in [33]:

$$\frac{dp_{ff}}{dt} = \frac{(\overline{l}-1)p_{f|d}+1}{\overline{k}N/2}\mathcal{P}^t(\Delta p_f = \frac{1}{N}) - \frac{(\overline{m}-1)p_{f|f}}{\overline{k}N/2}\mathcal{P}^t(\Delta p_f = -\frac{1}{N}), \tag{22}$$

where $\bar{l}$, $\overline{m}$ stand for the mean degrees of the replaced users that differ from the mean degree of the whole network, i.e., $\bar{k}$ [33]. Also, according to [33], $\bar{l} = \overline{m} = \frac{\overline{k^2}}{\bar{k}}$. Eq. (22) becomes:

$$\frac{dp_{ff}}{dt} = \frac{p_{fd}}{N\Pi(t)} \left(\frac{(1-a)}{\bar{k}} + au(t) \right) [((\bar{l}-1)p_{f|d}+1) - (\overline{m}-1)p_{f|f}]$$

$$+ \frac{p_{fd}(\bar{k}-1)p_{f|f}a}{\bar{k}N\Pi(t)}[((\bar{l}-1)p_{f|d}+1)(u_{ff}(t)-u(t)) - (\overline{m}-1)p_{d|d}(u_{dd}(t)-u(t))]. \quad (23)$$

Since the average user interest varies with time, the parameters of the ODEs (21), (23) attain also time-varying forms. Therefore, for each selection of parameters' values the ESS points will be different leading to ESS curves with time. Indeed, in order to obtain the ESS loci, we need to solve the system of equations

$$\frac{dp_f}{dt} = 0, \quad \frac{dp_{ff}}{dt} = 0, \quad (24)$$

at different time instances characterized by different parameters' values. Then, a solution (rest point) is an ESS point of the system of the (nonlinear) Eqs. (24), if for the Jacobian matrix J of the system, we have that $det(J) > 0$ and $tr(J) < 0$, where det, tr stand for the determinant and the trace of the Jacobian matrix, respectively.

6. Framework for Optimally Controlling Information Propagation in Social Networks under Evolving Users' Interests

In this section we design and study appropriate frameworks for controlling the diffusion of useful information according to the employed modeling approach, i.e., epidemics or Graphical EGT. The first is studied in Section 6.1 and the second in Section 6.2. Controlling the information diffusion over various types of networks via explicit, e.g., [23, 18, 17, 25, 26] or implicit control, e.g., [21] is highly important, and this subject has been extensively studied in the literature mostly for malware propagation and based on the epidemic information dissemination framework. In this chapter we employ a different approach.

Since we consider the case of propagating useful information, we aim at the maximization of the number of infected (informed) nodes for a topic/class m by applying an exogenous aid/force, i.e., the control, while taking into account associated control costs, e.g., advertising cost. Intuitively, we can identify two roles that the control may play and thus become necessary. Firstly, a control action may be needed in order to boost users' interest and increase information spreading, while not allowing an information class to extinct. Secondly, more resources might be required (by increasing a control signal) when users are more interested in a topic in order to conserve resources by not wasting them when users are not interested in the propagated information. Indeed, in this chapter, we control the propagation of information within the social network, by actually controlling the users' interests on the propagated information. The control might take the form of incentives for increasing user interest, or it may exploit the increased user interest in order to reinforce information spreading. Such behavior is thoroughly explored in [45].

6.1. Control Framework Assuming Epidemic Based Modeling of Information Propagation

In this section, we present a framework for optimally controlling information propagation for a specific topic-class m assuming epidemic modeling. A thorough overview of the current epidemic based control frameworks can be found in [23], including heuristic feedback methods and optimal control policies for both population dynamics and deterministic models for networks along with spectral control policies for the latter. The authors adopt optimal control frameworks for obtaining features allowing the control of the corresponding diffusion processes, which are modeled via differential equations (deterministic models). The work in [17], studies the possible attack strategies of malware over wireless networks and the extent of damage they can sustain. The control parameters consist of the transmission range and the media scanning rate of the worm targeting at accelerating its spread. Malicious software (malware) information dissemination is also studied in [18], where the control signal distribution time is determined, aiming to minimize the number of infected nodes and the cost of control. Similar approaches for malware quarantining and filtering (e.g., configurable firewall) are developed and analyzed in [25, 26, 28]. Considering implicit control, in [21], malware information propagation is studied and analyzed over a homogeneous mixing network, where control takes the form of updates to nodes from an external source to which nodes reply via a best response (game theoretic) scheme. Also, in [21], there is an implicit introduction (i.e., via the time-varying state of the system) of time-varying behavior on the parameters of the information diffusion epidemic model. However, this takes place in a more restricted sense compared to the approach followed in this chapter.

To begin with, we define the control signal as the time function $u(.) = \{u(t)|t \in [0,T]\}$ and based on our discussion on the introductory part of this section, we aim at maximizing the objective function:

$$J(u(.)) = \int_0^T (k_1 I^m(t) + k_2 u(t))\, dt + k_I I^m(T), \tag{25}$$

where $k_1, k_I \geq 0$, $k_2 \leq 0$ are parameters expressing the trade-off between diffusion efficiency and control cost. We aim at finding an optimal control $u^*(.)$ such that:

$$J(u^*(.)) = \max_{u(.)} J(u(.)). \tag{26}$$

The problem of Eq. (26) will be solved subject to the (approximate) controlled evolution dynamics equations of the number of informed nodes, given by:

$$\frac{dI^m(t)}{dt} = \frac{N_s^{avg}}{N} f_1^{avg}(t) f_3^{avg}(t)(N - I^m(t))I^m(t)g_1(u(t)) - I^m(t) q f_2^{avg}(t) g_2(u(t)), \tag{27}$$

with $I^m(0) = I_0^m$ ($S^m(0) = N - I_0^m$). Also the following state conditions should hold:

$$N = I^m(t) + S^m(t),\ 0 \leq I^m(t) \leq N,\ \forall t \in [0,T]. \tag{28}$$

Note that Eq. (27) differs from Eq. (7) due to the introduction of the control $u(t)$ in the summands of its right hand side, where the probabilities $f_1^{avg}(t)$, $f_2^{avg}(t)$ have been replaced with $f_1^{avg}(t)g_1(u(t))$, $f_2^{avg}(t)g_2(u(t))$. The control $u(.)$ depends on the controller's budget for topic m, while the control region is defined as $\Omega = \{u(.) : [0,T] \rightarrow \Re | u_{\min} \leq u(t) \leq u_{\max},\ \forall\ t\}$ where also each $u(.)$ is a piece-wise continuous function such that its left and right limits exist. Functions g_1, g_2 are non-negative, differentiable and either convex or concave with respect to u. While g_1 is increasing with u, g_2 is decreasing, and $g_1, g_2 : [u_{\min}, u_{\max}] \rightarrow [0,1]$. We should note that the controller applies one kind of control with aim to increase $I^m(t)$ trading-off cost, but this impacts in a different way each part of the information propagation differential equation (i.e., Eq. (27)) via the functions $g_1(u), g_2(u)$.

The solution of such an optimal control problem is analytically given in our previous work [45] and is based on both the Pontryangin's Maximum Principle [2, 1, 17] (for proving the existence of the optimal control) and on the

Hamilton-Jacobi-Bellman equation [1], [2] (for numerically solving for the optimal control). Initially, we provide the definitions of the admissible and the optimal control.

Definition 1. *The pair $(I^m(.), u(.))$ is an admissible pair if the following hold: i) $u(.) \in \Omega$, ii) the state $(I^m(.))$ constraint of Eq. (27) holds. Then $u(.)$ is called an admissible control [17].*

Definition 2. *An admissible control $u(.)$ is an optimal control, if $J(u(.)) \geq J(\underline{u}(.))$ for all admissible controls $\underline{u}(.)$ [17].*

Then, based on the above definitions, Pontryagin's Maximum Principle is applied for deriving the functional form of the optimal control and studying its properties. Let us denote as $\lambda(t)$ the adjoint/costate variable of the Pontryagin's Maximum Principle [1] at time $t \in [0, T]$. First, we define the Hamiltonian function, $\mathcal{H}$, at time t as:

$$\begin{aligned} \mathcal{H}(I^m(t), u(t), \lambda(t)) &= k_1 I^m(t) + k_2 u(t) + \\ +\lambda(t) &\left[\frac{N_s^{avg}}{N} f_1^{avg}(t) f_3^{avg}(t)(N - I^m(t)) I^m(t) g_1(u(t)) \right. \\ &\left. -q I^m(t) f_2^{avg}(t) g_2(u(t)) \right]. \end{aligned} \tag{29}$$

Assuming that $u^*(.)$ is the optimal control and $I^{m^*}(.)$ is the corresponding state trajectory, i.e., the one solving Eq. (27) for $u^*(.)$, according to the Pontryagin's Maximum Principle [1], there exists a function (optimal costate) $\lambda^*(.) : [0.T] \rightarrow \Re$ such that

$$\frac{d\lambda^*(t)}{dt} = -\frac{\partial \mathcal{H}}{\partial I^m} = -k_1 - \lambda^*(t) \left[\frac{N_s^{avg}}{N} f_1^{avg}(t) f_3^{avg}(t)(N - 2I^{m*}(t)) g_1(u^*(t)) \right. \\ \left. -q f_2^{avg}(t) g_2(u^*(t)) \right], \tag{30}$$

$$\lambda^*(T) = k_I (\text{transversality condition}), \tag{31}$$

where $\lambda^*(.)$ is the optimal costate (adjoint) function and also the optimal control, $u^*(.)$, is computed as:

$$u^*(t) = u(t) \in \arg\max_{\underline{u} \in \Omega} \mathcal{H}(I^{m^*}(t), \underline{u}, \lambda^*(t)),\ 0 \leq t \leq T. \tag{32}$$

Then, depending on the forms of the functions g_1, g_2 with respect to the control u (convex or concave), the optimal control can be computed. Here, we will provide an example of determining the optimal control $u(.)$ by choosing a non-trivial form for the functions $g_1(u),\ g_2(u)$, as follows:

$$g_1(u) = 1 + \frac{\ln(1+u)}{\ln(1+u_{\max})},$$
$$g_2(u) = \frac{\ln(1+u_{\max}) - \ln(1+u))}{\ln(1+u_{\max})}. \tag{33}$$

This choice serves the purpose of boosting the number of infected (informed) nodes for the examined class by increasing probabilities of communicating/transferring knowledge via $g_1(u) > 1$ in the first summand of the right hand side of Eq. (27), and by decreasing probabilities of knowledge "deletion" via $g_2(u) < 1$ in the last summand of the right hand side of Eq. (27). Then, after some analysis inlcuded in detail in [45], the optimal control takes the following formula (neglecting the time indices):

$$u^* = \left\{-1 - \frac{\lambda\Gamma}{k_2}\right\}_{u_{\min}}^{u_{\max}}, \tag{34}$$

where $\{\ \}_{u_{\min}}^{u_{\max}}$ expresses projection to $[u_{\min}, u_{\max}]$ and

$$\Gamma = \frac{1}{\ln(1+u_{\max})}\left[\frac{N_s^{avg}}{N} f_1^{avg} f_3^{avg}(N - I^m)I^m + qI^m f_2^{avg}\right]. \tag{35}$$

To shed more light on the expression of Γ, if the types of $f_1^{avg},\ f_2^{avg},\ f_3^{avg}$ are given by Eqs. (8), then Γ is increasing with R_{avg}^m, i.e., $\frac{\partial\Gamma}{\partial R_{avg}^m} > 0$ if

$$I^m < N - \frac{qN}{N_s^{avg} 2R_{avg}^m} = I_{TH}. \tag{36}$$

Therefore, Γ will become an increasing function of interest for class m only if the number of infected nodes for class m becomes less than the threshold I_{TH}. This behavior is also expected for the optimal control itself, u^* (Eq. (34)), since it holds $-\frac{\lambda}{k_2} > 0$ as shown in [45] (if one ignores the dependence of λ on R_{avg}^m). Indeed, in [45], it is shown via numerical evaluations that if the number of infected nodes for class m is high enough, higher that I_{TH}, the optimal control saves resources when the corresponding user interest for class m increases. When the number of infected nodes falls below I_{TH}, the control increases with user interest, aiming at leveraging on higher values of interest to drastically boost the number of infected nodes for class m. This behavior emerges also in the case of power control in a wireless channel, where high power values are optimal under good channel conditions, to exploit the maximum possible data transfer rates [46]. Since I_{TH} (Eq. (36)) is time-varying, as R^m_{avg} evolves with time, the monotonicity of Γ may also change with time.

Although via the Potryangin's Maximum Principle approach we obtain the form of the optimal control, computing the optimal control value is more complex, demanding the knowledge of the value of the adjoint variable, λ, for each t. As a result, the computation of the optimal control is performed using the Hamilton-Jacobi-Bellman (HJB) equation [45] and solving it via a numerical approach (e.g., a finite difference scheme) within the control time interval ($[0, T]$).

6.2. Control Framework Assuming EGT Based Modeling of Information Propagation

To the best of our knowledge, there exists a limited number of works in the literature addressing the problem of optimally controlling information propagation modeled as a graphical evolutionary game. Indeed the optimal control of evolutionary games on networks remains a challenging open problem [47]. The majority of the existing approaches [47, 48] focus on controlling the evolutionary game over the network in order to achieve a desired outcome of strategies by solving the so called Minimum Agent Consensus Control Problem (MACC problem) [47]. More specifically, these works consider that there exist some users in the network, also denoted as control agents, that can be exogenously fixed to a specific strategy choice, and they seek the smallest set of control agents that will guarantee convergence of the network to a specific strategy state. In [47, 48], the MACC problem is solved over diverse network topologies (e.g., tree or regular networks) and strategy update rules (Section 3.2). Note that for arbitrary topologies the MACCP is solved approximately based on graph partitioning to recursively decompose a larger problem into several smaller problems, the solutions of which can be used to construct an approximate solution on the original network, while greatly reducing computation complexity. Indeed, it also remains an open question whether the MACC problem belongs to an NP-hard class, however its computational complexity is high limiting its efficiency only over small topologies and demanding approximations for larger ones [47].

In this chapter, we follow a differentiated approach for controlling the graphical evolutionary game modeling the information diffusion than the MACC problem of [47, 48]. In this section, we assume the same notation and assumptions as in Section 5. Specifically, instead of seeking for the minimum set of control agents that will spread a specific strategy ($S_f,\ S_n,\ S_d$) to the whole network, we aim at implicitly controlling the network state variables e.g., $p_f,\ p_n,\ p_d$, etc. via appropriately configuring the entries of the payoff matrix $U(t),\ \forall t$. Since we focus on the propagation of useful information within the network (without loss of generality), we aim at providing incentives to the users to decide in favor of the S_f strategy thus implicitly aiming to maximize the number of infected/informed users as also stated in the introductory part of this section. Suppose that we affect the entries of the payoff matrix via a control signal function $u_c(.) = \{u_c(t)|t \in [0, T]\}$ (defined similarly and satisfying the same properties with the one in Section 6.1). Then, the payoff matrix could be reconfigured as follows:

$$U(t, u_c) = \begin{bmatrix} u_{ff}(t, u_c) & u_{fn}(t, u_c) & u_{fd}(t, u_c) \\ u_{nf}(t, u_c) & u_{nn}(t, u_c) & u_{nd}(t, u_c) \\ u_{df}(t, u_c) & u_{dn}(t, u_c) & u_{dd}(t, u_c) \end{bmatrix} \tag{37}$$

As an example, u_{ff} will be an increasing function of users' interest, R^m_{avg}, for the information class m and of the control value u_c. Thus, higher values of users' interest and of the control at time t should assign higher payoff for the interaction of users both adopting the strategy S_f at this time. Similarly to Section 5, for the ease of presentation, in the following we focus uniquely on the strategies S_f, S_d. Also, we employ the special case that $u_{df}(t) = u_{fd}(t) = u(t),\ B_f(t) = B_d(t) = 1,\ \forall t$ (also considered in [33]), thus we develop the control framework based on the information diffusion dynamics expressed by the Eqs. (21), (23).

In the following, we describe the framework for controlling information propagation modeled via Graphical EGT that consists of two possible schemes. Both schemes aim at maximizing the percentage of the users of the social network that decide in favor of the strategy S_f and support the propagation of the useful information. The first scheme is based on directly controlling the dynamics of change of $p_f,\ p_{ff}$ during a specific control horizon, while the second scheme aims at controlling the ESS points of the state dynamics for each selection of parameters (e.g., user interests). These two schemes are directly related, however, the optimization tools applied in each one of them differ.

6.2.1. Scheme 1: Optimal Control of Useful Information Propagation Based on EGT over a Finite Horizon

For the first scheme, the objective function can be defined in a similar spirit with Section 6.1 (Eq. (25)), i.e., as:

$$J(u_c(.)) = \int_0^T (k_1(p_f(t) + p_{ff}(t)) + k_2 u_c(t))\, dt + k_I(p_f(T) + p_{ff}(T)), \tag{38}$$

where $k_1, k_I \geq 0$, $k_2 \leq 0$ are parameters expressing the trade-off between diffusion efficiency, by adopting the strategy S_f, and control cost. Then, the optimal control $u_c^*(.)$ of the first scheme is obtained by solving:

$$J(u_c^*(.)) = \max_{u_c(.)} J(u_c(.)). \tag{39}$$

The control problem of Eq. (39) is subject to the controlled evolution dynamics of the percentage of users adopting strategy S_f. Similarly to Section 5, the controlled evolution dynamics of p_f and p_{ff} derive according to the BD update rule, as follows:

$$\begin{aligned}\frac{dp_f(t)}{dt} = \frac{ap_{fd}(t)(\overline{k}-1)}{2N\Pi(t)}&((u_{ff}(t,u_c(t)) - u(t,u_c(t)))p_{f|f}(t)\\ &-(u_{dd}(t,u_c(t)) - u(t,u_c(t)))p_{d|d}(t)),\end{aligned} \tag{40}$$

$$\begin{aligned}\frac{dp_{ff}(t)}{dt} &= \frac{p_{fd}(t)}{N\Pi(t)}\left(\frac{(1-a)}{\overline{k}} + au(t,u_c)\right)[((\overline{l}-1)p_{f|d}(t)+1) - (\overline{m}-1)p_{f|f}(t)]\\ &+\frac{p_{fd}(t)(\overline{k}-1)p_{f|f}(t)a}{\overline{k}N\Pi(t)}[((\overline{l}-1)p_{f|d}(t)+1)(u_{ff}(t,u_c(t)) - u(t,u_c(t))) -\\ &(\overline{m}-1)p_{d|d}(t)(u_{dd}(t,u_c(t)) - u(t,u_c(t)))].\end{aligned} \tag{41}$$

The difference of Eqs. (40), (41) with Eqs. (21), (23) lies in the dependence of the parameters of the former ones on the control signal $u_c(.)$. Also, the following state conditions should hold for each $t \in [0,T]$:

$$p_{f|d}(t) = 1 - p_{d|d}(t), \tag{42}$$

$$\frac{p_f(t)(1-p_{f|f}(t))}{1-p_f(t)} - p_{f|f}(t) = 0. \tag{43}$$

Therefore, in order to optimally control the propagation of useful information modeled based on EGT, we should solve the optimal control problem of Eq. (39) subject to the dynamics of Eqs. (40), (41) and the state constraints of Eqs. (42), (43). We do not delve into the solution of this optimal control problem in this chapter, however, we indicate that it follows the lines of the solution of the optimal control of information diffusion based on epidemic modeling (Section 6.1), i.e., it is based on the Potryangin's Maximum Principle and the Hamilton-Jacobi Bellman equation, although exhibiting a more complicated form.

6.2.2. Scheme 2: Optimal Control of Useful Information Propagation Based on EGT on per Time Instance Basis

Before formulating this scheme, we note that as was also indicated in Section 5, the ESS points should be determined for each selection of the user interests' parameters (since these are time-varying). For the second scheme, we target at biasing the ESS points (at each particular value of the average user interest) of the state dynamics expressed via Eqs. (21), (23) (and the related state contraints, Section 5) towards high values of p_f, $p_{f|f}$ (i.e., towards high percentage of adoption of the S_f strategy) via introducing appropriate control signals in the equations that determine these ESS points. Therefore, we aim at controlling the ESS curves of the graphical evolutionary game modeling the information diffusion dynamics. According to the above, we focus at particular values of average user interest (i.e., time), and the objective function becomes:

$$J(u_c) = k_1(p_f + p_{f|f}) + k_2 u_c, \tag{44}$$

where $k_1 \geq 0$, $k_2 \leq 0$ retain their meaning as in Scheme 1. Then, for a particular time instance, t, (i.e., for a fixed value of average user interest), the optimal control $u_c^*(t)$ of the second scheme is obtained by solving:

$$J(u_c^*(t)) = \max_{u_c} J(u_c), \tag{45}$$

subject to the following constraints which are necessary for determining the ESS points (Section 5):

$$(u_{ff}(t,u_c) - u(t,u_c))p_{f|f} - (u_{dd}(t,u_c) - u(t,u_c))p_{d|d} = 0, \tag{46}$$

$$\begin{aligned} &\big((1-a) + a\bar{k}u(t,u_c)\big)\left[((\bar{l}-1)p_{f|d}+1) - (\overline{m}-1)p_{f|f}\right] \\ &+(\bar{k}-1)p_{f|f}a[((\bar{l}-1)p_{f|d}+1)(u_{ff}(t,u_c) - u(t,u_c)) \\ &-(\overline{m}-1)p_{d|d}(u_{dd}(t,u_c) - u(t,uc))] = 0, \end{aligned} \tag{47}$$

$$p_{f|d} = 1 - p_{d|d}, \tag{48}$$

$$\frac{p_f(1-p_{f|f})}{1-p_f} - p_{f|f} = 0. \tag{49}$$

The optimization problem defined via Eqs. (45)-(49) can be solved via dual decomposition techniques for equality constraints [49, 50]. However, we accept only those values of control (u_c) leading to corresponding values of p_f that satisfy the conditions $det(J) > 0$ and $tr(J) < 0$ (J is the Jacobian matrix of the system of Eqs. (46)-(49)).

The collection of the controlled ESS points for all times, t, provides us with the controlled ESS curves.

7. Indicative Evaluation Results of User Interest Dictated Information Diffusion Modeling Approaches in Social Networks

In this section we will provide indicative results on the dynamics of information propagation in social networks and its control when considering user interests. We will also show the importance of considering user interests when studying and predicting the information propagation in social networks via utilizing real data sets. The former is studied in Section 7.1 when considering epidemic modeling. Similar evaluations (numerical and simulation based) subject to EGT based modeling are part of our future work. The latter is presented in Section 7.2.

7.1. Evaluation of the Information Diffusion and Control in Social Networks Based on Epidemic Modeling

The objective of this section lies in observing the dynamics of information diffusion and clarifying the impact of control on the latter by comparing controlled versus non-controlled information propagation for diverse thematic classes. In our previous work [45], there exist extensive numerical and simulation results also with respect to the behavior of the control over time compared with the evolution of the user interest and the number of infected/informed nodes. More specifically, we present simulation and numerical results for the case that the user interest attains a periodic form (Section 2). The simulation results refer to the realization of the diffusion model described in Section 4 in MATLAB, while the numerical results correspond to the expected values theoretically, i.e., they refer to the approximate solution (e.g., via finite difference scheme) of the ODEs (7), (27) (with and without control correspondingly) with the same parameters as in the corresponding simulation.

The simulation setting was as follows. We considered a social network with $N = 500$ nodes having a scale-free structure [56]. For obtaining a scale-free network topology, the social degree for each node was drawn from the power-law degree distribution with exponent 3, as observed for many social networks [44] (specifically the probability density function is $f(x) = \left(\frac{2}{x}\right)^3$, $x \geq 2$), and the corresponding social neighbors of each node are chosen randomly. The expected node degree is equal to $N_S^{avg} \cong 4$. All simulation results were obtained as averages over multiple repetitions ($\#10$) for the diffusion. Finally, 10 nodes out of the 500 nodes were initially infected for each class in all simulation and numerical results that follow.

We considered two thematic classes of information over the social network while the users' interests varied uniformly and randomly with periodic mean value of the form: $1 - \frac{1}{4}\sin^2(\frac{\pi}{0.5}(t + 0.2)) - \frac{1}{8}$ for the first class and of the form: $\frac{1}{4}\sin^2(\frac{\pi}{0.5}(t + 0.2)) + \frac{1}{8}$ for the second class, with the constraint that the interests of one node for the two classes are complementary. Therefore, the period of the user interest functions was equal to one time unit (e.g., one year as in realistic situations such as summer vacation advertisements of the Halloween). Note that the users of the social network were more interested in information messages, posts, etc. that correspond to the first class for all the times, although their interest values varied in periodic form for both classes and when their interest for the first class reduced, their interest for the second class increased.

Fig. 2 presents comparative numerical and simulation results with and without control for both information classes. We should note that the control was applied to only one class at each time, while the other class remained uncontrolled. However, we were mostly interested in the second class in order to evaluate how information diffusion behaves under low values of interest when introducing control, and compare this behavior with the case when no control was applied. In order to perform simulations when considering control, we adapted the diffusion model of Section 4 in order to introduce control by replacing the probabilities $f_1^{avg}(t)$, $f_2^{avg}(t)$ with $f_1^{avg}(t)g_1(u(t))$, $f_2^{avg}(t)g_2(u(t))$, as implied by comparing the Eq. (27) with the Eq. (7). Every simulation runs for 400 time iterations i.e., for a control time $T = 4$ which was divided in smaller time intervals each having a duration of 0.01.

Fig. 2(a) presents numerical and simulation results with and without control for the second class of information while Fig. 2(c) includes the same information for the first one. Firstly, we observe that for both classes of information, the periodicity of users' interests is reflected to the dynamics of information diffusion as these are expressed via the evolution of the number of infected/informed nodes over time. Note that Eq. (27) is solved numerically in a similar way to Eq. (7) and the results in Fig. 2(a) are after the convergence of the numerical solution. Also, for both classes, it can be stated that the numerical results mostly overestimate the number of infected nodes. From Fig. 2(a) we observe that for the second class, the introduction of control leads to a better approximation of the simulation results from the numerical ones, compared to the absence of control. For the first class (Fig. 2(c)) we do not observe such improvement, however, for this class, the numerical results approximate well the ones obtained from simulations. Therefore, the deletion process which happens more frequently in the second information class affects the quality of the approximation of the simulation results from the numerical ones (see also [45]).

Importantly, the introduction of control significantly improves the expected number of infected/informed nodes (there is an increase of approximately seventy nodes) in the case of the second class which corresponds to lower user interest values (Fig. 2(a)). Such a control may correspond to providing incentives to the users in variable degrees over time in order to increase their responsiveness in information propagation. On the contrary, for the first class (Fig. 2(c)), the introduction of control does not improve the number of infected/informed nodes (for the numerical results the number of infected nodes was the maximum possible even without control), thus it does not bring any benefit. This is due to the increased user interest in the information that renders the exogenous control superfluous and thus only costly. Finally, Fig. 2(b) presents only the numerical results for the second class with and without control, in order to indicate in a clearer way the periodicity in the information diffusion dynamics as the latter were obtained theoretically.

7.2. Information Diffusion in Twitter Considering User Interest

In the sequel, in order to further validate our conviction that time-varying user interests should be considered when studying information propagation in complex communications networks, we show an indicative example using a real data set. Specifically, we have collected data from Twitter for the hashtag "tesco" that refers to the announcement of the UK retailer Tesco of an annual loss about 6.4 billion pounds in April 2015 [51]. The propagation of the hashtag "tesco" corresponded to a propagation of useful or informative news to Twitter users. We considered as infected/informed each user of the Twitter that has posted a tweet with this hashtag or that was a follower of another user that has posted a tweet with this hashtag. We counted the number of infected users of Twitter at different times in a sequence and we maintained a set of infected users over time. Then we fitted the number of infected nodes over time to an appropriate epidemic model that is an adapted version of the epidemic model of Eq. (7) for information propagation in the Twitter network. We examined both constant and time-decreasing user interests.

The results are shown in Fig. 3. The training data set used for the fitting of the epidemic model to the real data collected from Twitter derives from sampling every three hours, while the rest of the data are used for testing. From Fig. 3(a) it is observed that the epidemic model with constant user interests in the propagated information (i.e., the hashtag "Tesco") does not capture satisfactorily the dynamics of information propagation. However, when considering time decreasing user interests in Eq. (7), our model presents a very satisfactory performance in both training and testing data sets, as shown in Fig. 3(b). The latter is expected intuitively, as at the moment that the UK retailer Tesco announced its annual loss, many Twitter users were interested in corresponding discussions and posted related tweets, but as the time passed, similarly to many other real-time events, the interest of the users decreased. The behavior of Fig. 3(b) verifies our intuition that taking the time-varying form of user interests into

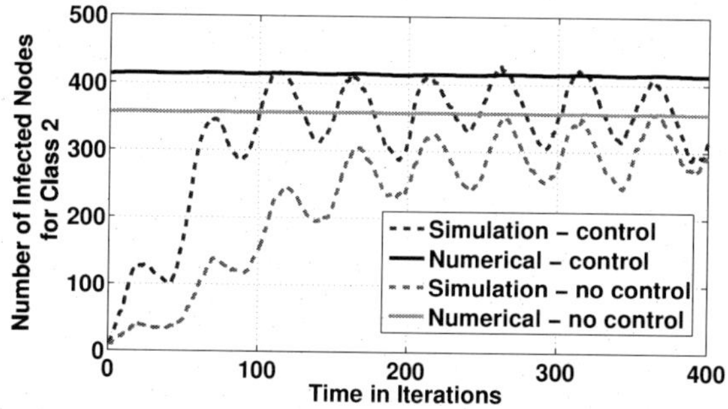

(a) Case of class 2, i.e., of reduced values of users' interests.

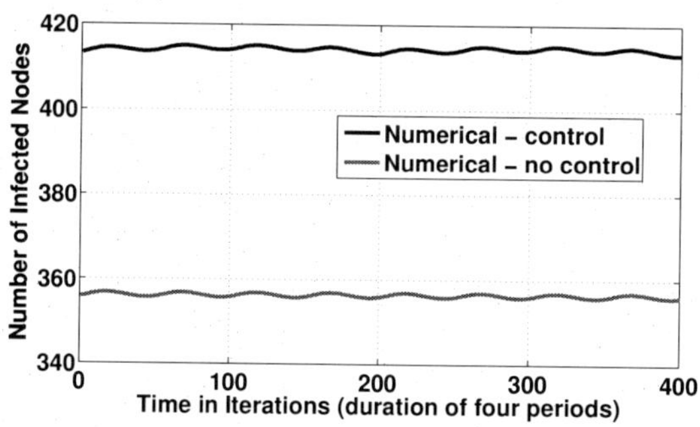

(b) Numerical results with and without control for the case of class 2.

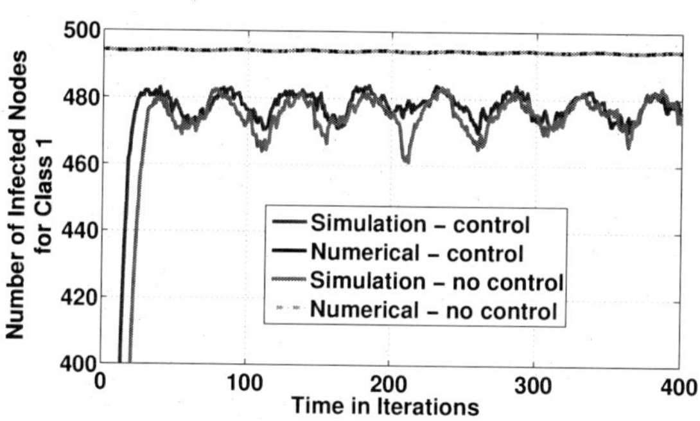

(c) Case of class 1, i.e., of increased values of users' interests.

Figure 2. Comparisons of numerical and simulation results with and without control for both information classes.

consideration when studying information diffusion is necessary for modeling and predicting the dynamics of the information propagation more accurately.

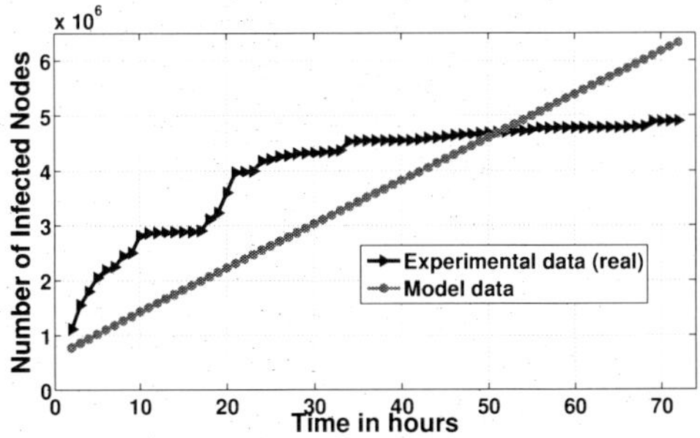

(a) Case of constant with time user interests.

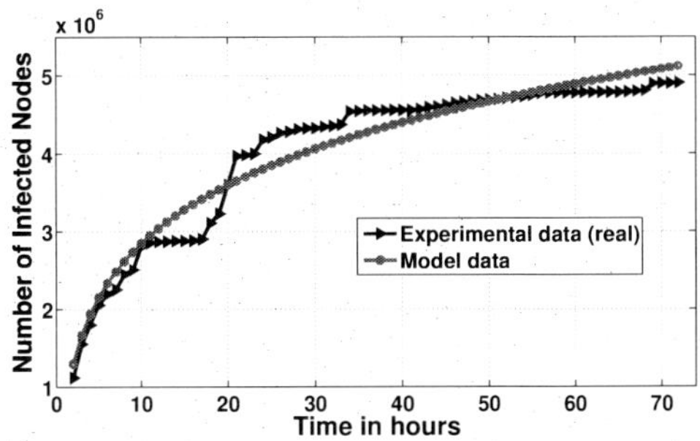

(b) Case of time decreasing user interests in the form of $R_{avg}^{m} \sim \frac{1}{t}$, where m corresponds to the hashtag "tesco".

Figure 3. Hashtag "tesco": Comparison of the numerical results obtained via epidemic modeling and the experimental (real) values of the collected data set. Data for training are sampled every three hours and the rest are used for testing. As information class we consider the one defined by the hashtag "tesco", while other hashtags define other information classes.

Conclusion

In this chapter, we studied models of information diffusion over communication and social networks along with the possibilities of controlling the latter based on each corresponding modeling approach. We briefly reviewed epidemics and EGT, which are both popular tools for modeling information diffusion and allow for the development of efficient frameworks for controlling the extent of the information propagation. We thoroughly evaluated the epidemic based modeling and control of information propagation and we presented an overall framework for the EGT based approach. The design of appropriate algorithms for the EGT based control of the information diffusion extent and dynamics along with their evaluation are prioritized in our future plans. We believe that EGT is a very suitable tool for modeling, studying and controlling information diffusion on social networks where users' decisions is a determinant factor of the outcome of such diffusion processes, since EGT allows for modeling users' decisions more efficiently than epidemics.

Furtheremore, two major issues that emerge through this chapter relate to the identification of the suitable user interest modeling (Section 2) for each application along with the bigdata issues bind with information diffusion in online social networks [57]. Bigdata issues refer to the huge amounts of data produced at incredibly rapid rates by online social networks introducing complexities in their storage and analysis and causing information to become outdated fast [57]. Both issues are strongly interconnected since user interests may be inferred via appropriate analytics over large-scale data collected from (online) social networks [12, 59]. Bigdata issues will also affect user behavior, e.g., user interest may decrease exponentially for an information content due to arrivals/emergence of new information topics. In addition, bigdata issues may impact the fitting of the parameters of developed models for information diffusion and the study of their validity. As the amount of available data from online social networks has already exploded and continues to grow, new software and hardware techniques [58, 60] suitable for bigdata analytics will benefit the study of information diffusion aspects especially when taking users' interests into consideration.

Acknowledgments

E. Stai gratefully acknowledges the Foundation for Education and European Culture (IPEP) for financial support.

References

[1] W. H. Fleming, H. M. Sooner, "Controlled Markov Processes and Viscosity Solutions", *2nd Edition, Springer-Verlag, New York, USA*, 2006.

[2] J. Yong, X. Y. Zhou, "Stochastic Controls, Hamiltonian Systems and HJB Equations", *Springer-Verlag, New York, USA*, 1999.

[3] J. G. Andrews, S. Buzzi, W. Choi, S. Hanly, A. Lozano, A.C.K. Soong, J. Zhang, "What will 5G be?", *IEEE Journal on Selected Areas in Communications (JSAC)*, Vol. 32, No. 6, pp. 1065-1082, June 2014.

[4] V. Karyotis, S. Papavassiliou, "Macroscopic Malware Propagation Dynamics for Complex Networks with Churn", *IEEE Communications Letters*, Vol. 19, No.4, pp. 577-580, April 2015.

[5] V. Karyotis, A. Kakalis, S. Papavassiliou, "Malware-Propagative Mobile Ad Hoc Networks: Asymptotic Behavior Analysis", *Journal of Computer Science and Technology (JCST), Springer*, Vol. 23, No. 3, pp. 389-399, May 2008.

[6] J. Aycock, "Computer Viruses and Malware", *Springer*, Arlington, VA., USA, 2006.

[7] D.J. Daley, J. Gani, "Epidemic Modelling: An Introduction", *Cambridge University Press*, Cambridge, U.K., 2001.

[8] S. Pei, L. Muchnik, S. Tang, Z. Zheng, H.A. Makse, "Exploring the Complex Pattern of Information Spreading in Online Blog Communities", *PLoS One.*, Vol. 10, No. 5, May 2015.

[9] J. Goecks, J. Shavlik, "Learning Users' Interests by Unobtrusively Observing their Normal Behavior", *Proc. of the 5th International Conference on Intelligent User Interfaces*, pp. 129-132, 2000.

[10] L. Weng, J. Ratkiewicz, N. Perra, B. Gonçalves, C. Castillo, F. Bonchi, R. Schifanella, F. Menczer, A. Flammini, "The Role of Information Diffusion in the Evolution of Social Networks", *Proc. of 19th ACM SIGKDD International Conference on Knowledge Discovery and Data Mining (KDD)*, pp. 356-364, 2013.

[11] Y. Shen, T. N. Dinh, H. Zhang, M. T. Thai, "Interest-matching Information Propagation in Multiple Online Social Networks", *Proc. of 21st ACM International Conference on Information and Knowledge Management (CIKM)*, pp. 1824-1828, 2012.

[12] D. Varshney, S. Kumar, V. Gupta, "Modeling Information Diffusion in Social Networks Using Latent Topic Information", *Intelligent Computing Theory (Springer Lecture Notes in Computer Science)*, Vol. 8588, pp. 137-148, 2014.

[13] S.-M. Cheng, W. C. Ao, P.-Y. Chen, K.-C. Chen, "On Modeling Malware Propagation in Generalized Social Networks", *IEEE Communications Letters*, Vol. 15, No. 1, pp. 25-27, January 2011.

[14] Y.-F. Chou, H.-H. Huang, R.-G. Cheng, "Modeling Information Dissemination in Generalized Social Networks", *IEEE Communications Letters*, Vol. 17, No. 7, pp. 1356-1359, July 2013.

[15] C. C. Zou, W. Gong, D. Towsley, "Code Red Worm Propagation Modeling and Analysis", *Proc. of the 9th ACM Conference on Computer and Communications Security (CCS)*, pp. 138-147, 2002.

[16] F. Wang, H. Wang, K. Xu, J. Wu, X. Jia, "Characterizing Information Diffusion in Online Social Networks with Linear Diffusive Model", *Proc. 33rd IEEE International Conference on Distributed Computing Systems (ICDCS)*, pp. 307-316, July 2013.

[17] M.H.R. Khouzani, S. Sarkar, E. Altman, "Maximum Damage Malware Attack in Mobile Wireless Networks", *IEEE/ACM Transactions on Networking*, Vol. 20, No. 5, pp. 1347-1360, October 2012.

[18] P.-Y. Chen, S.-M. Cheng, K.-C. Chen, "Optimal Control of Epidemic Information Dissemination Over Networks", *IEEE Transactions on Cybernetics*, Vol. 44, No. 12, pp. 2316-2328, December 2014.

[19] J. Yang, J. Leskovec, "Modeling Information Diffusion in Implicit Networks", *Proc. of the 2010 IEEE International Conference on Data Mining (ICDM)*, pp. 599-608, 2010.

[20] A. Guille, H. Hacid, C. Favre, D.A. Zighed, "Information Diffusion in Online Social Networks: A Survey", *ACM SIGMOD Rec.*, Vol. 42, No. 2, pp. 17-28, May 2013.

[21] G. Theodorakopoulos, J.-Y. Le Boudec, J. S. Baras, "Selfish Response to Epidemic Propagation", *IEEE Transactions on Automatic Control*, Vol. 58, No. 2, pp. 363-376, Febreuary 2013.

[22] A. Linda, "An Introduction to Stochastic Epidemic Models, Mathematical Epidemiology", *Lecture Notes in Mathematics (Editors: F. Brauer, P. van den Driessche, and J. Wu)*, Springer Berlin Heidelberg, vol. 1945, pp. 81-130, 2008.

[23] C. Nowzari, V. M. Preciado, G. J. Pappas, "Analysis and Control of Epidemics", *asXiv*, 53 pages, May 2015.

[24] S. Bansal, B.T. Grenfell, L.A. Meyers, "When Individual Behaviour Matters: Homogeneous and Network Models in Epidemiology", *Journal of the Royal Society Interface*, Vol. 4, No. 16, pp. 879-891, October 2007.

[25] M.H.R. Khouzani, E. Altman, S. Sarkar, "Optimal Quarantining of Wireless Malware Through Reception Gain Control", *IEEE Transactions on Automatic Control*, Vol. 57, No. 1, pp. 49-61, January 2012.

[26] M. Bloem, T. Alpcan, T. Basar, "An Optimal Control Approach to Malware Filtering", *46th IEEE Conference on Decision and Control (CDC)*, pp. 6059-6064, December 2007.

[27] S. Scellato, C. Mascolo, M. Musolesi, V. Latora, "Epcast: Controlled Dissemination in Human-Based Wireless Networks Using Epidemic Spreading Models", *Bio-Inspired Computing and Communication (Lecture Notes in Computer Science)*, Vol. 5151, pp. 295-306, October 2008.

[28] G.A. Forster, C.A. Gilliga, "Optimizing the Control of Disease Infestations at the Landscape Level", *Proc. of the National Academy of Sciences of the United States of America*, Vol. 104, No. 12, pp. 4984-4989, 2007.

[29] K. Sigmund, "Introduction to Evolutionary Game Theory", *In Proc. of Symposia in Applied Mathematics*, pp. 1-25, 2011.

[30] P. Uyttendaele, F. Thuijsman, P. Collins, R. Peeters, G. Schoenmakers, R. Westra, "Evolutionary Games and Periodic Fitness", *Dyn. Games Appl.*, Vol. 2, pp. 335-345, 2012.

[31] H. Ohtsuki, M.A. Novak, "The Replicator Equation on Graphs", *Journal of Theoretical Biology*, Vol. 243, pp. 86-97, 2006.

[32] C. Jiang, Y. Chen, K.J. Ray Liu, "Distributed Adaptive Networks: A Graphical Evolutionary Game-Theoretic View", *IEEE Trans. on Signal Processing*, Vol. 61, No. 22, pp. 5675-5688, Nov. 2013.

[33] C. Jiang, Y. Chen, K.J. Ray Liu, "Graphical Evolutionary Game for Information Diffusion Over Social Networks", *IEEE Journal of Selected Topics in Signal Processing*, Vol. 8, No. 4, pp. 524-536, Aug. 2014.

[34] C. Jiang, Y. Chen, K.J. Ray Liu, "Modeling Evolutionary Information Diffusion Dynamics over Social Networks", *In Proc. of IEEE Int'l Conference on Acoustic, Speech and Signal Processing (ICASSP)*, pp. 1095-1099, May 2014.

[35] Z. Lu, Y. Wen, G. Cao, "Information Diffusion in Mobile Social Networks: The Speed Perspective", *In Proc. of INFOCOM*, pp. 1932-1940, April-May 2014.

[36] Y. Wang, B. Zheng, "On Macro and Micro Exploration of Hashtag Diffusion in Twitter", *In Proc. of IEEE/ACM International Conference on Advances in Social Networks Analysis and Mining (ASONAM)*, pp. 285-288, Aug. 2014.

[37] Y. Zhang, X. Ruan, H. Wang, "What Scale of Audience a Campaign Can Reach in What Price on Twitter?", *In Proc. of INFOCOM*, pp. 1168-1176, April-May 2014.

[38] H.W. Hethcote, "The Mathematics of Infectious Diseases", *Society for Industrial and Applied Mathematics (SIAM) Review*, Vol. 42, No. 4, pp. 599-653, 2000.

[39] M.F. Amjad, M. Chatterjee, O. Nakhila, C.C. Zou, "An Evolutionary Game Theoretic Framework for Coexistence in Cognitive Radio Networks," *In Proc. of IEEE Global Conference on Signal and Information Processing (GlobalSIP)*, pp.278-282, Dec. 2014.

[40] H. Ohtsuki, M.A. Nowak, "Evolutionary Stability on Graphs", *Journal of Theoretical Biology*, Vol. 251, pp. 698-707, 2008.

[41] P. Shakarian, P. Roos, A. Johnson, "A Review of Evolutionary Graph Theory with Applications to Game Theory", *Biosystems*, Vol. 107, No. 2, pp. 66-80, Feb. 2012.

[42] E. Stai, V. Karyotis, S. Papavassiliou, "User Interest Dictated Information Diffusion over Generalized Networks", *In Proc. of the IEEE International Conference on Communications (ICC), Workshop on Dynamic SOcial Networks (DySON)*, June 2015.

[43] F.C. Santos, J.M. Pacheco, T. Lanaerts, "Evolutionary Dynamics of Social Dilemmas in Structured Heterogeneous Populations", *PNAS*, Vol. 103, No. 9, pp. 3490-3494, Feb. 2008.

[44] R. Albert, A.-L. Barabasi, "Statistical Mechanics of Complex Networks", *Reviews of Modern Physics*, Vol. 74, No. 1, pp. 47-97, Jan. 2002.

[45] E. Stai, V. Karyotis, S. Papavassiliou, "Analysis and Control of Information Diffusion Dictated by User Interest in Generalized Networks", *Journal of Computational Social Networks, Springer*, Vol. 2, No. 18, December 2015.

[46] E. Stai, M. Loulakis and S. Papavassiliou, "Cross-Layer Design of Wireless Multihop Networks over Stochastic Channels with Time-Varying Statistics", *IEEE Transactions on Wireless Communications*, Vol. 12, No. 14, pp. 6967-6980, Dec. 2015.

[47] J.R. Riehl, M. Cao, "Control of Stochastic Evolutionary Games on Networks", *IFAC-PapersOnLine*, Vol. 48, No. 22, pp. 76-81, 2015.

[48] J.R. Riehl, M. Cao, "Towards Control of Evolutionary Games on Networks", in Proc. of 2014 IEEE 53rd Annual Conference on Decision and Control (CDC), pp.2877-2882, Dec. 2014

[49] A. Ribeiro, G. B. Giannakis, "Separation Principles in Wireless Networking", *IEEE Transactions on Information Theory*, Vol. 56, No. 9, pp. 4488-4505, Sept. 2010.

[50] D. P. Bertsekas, "Nonlinear Programming: 2nd Edition", *Athena Scientific*, 2009.

[51] http://www.bbc.com/news/business-32408661, *last access on 10/12/2015*.

[52] D. Cheng, F. He, H. Qi, T. Xu, "Modeling, Analysis and Control of Networked Evolutionary Games", *IEEE Transactions on Automatic Control*, Vol. 60, No. 9, pp. 2402-2415, Sept. 2015.

[53] N. Lee, J.J. Jung, "Content-Based Analytics of Diffusion on Social Big Data: A Case Study on Korean Telecommunication Companies", *Lecture Notes of the Institute for Computer Sciences, Social Informatics and Telecommunications Engineering, Scalable Information Systems, Springer International Publishing*, Vol. 139, pp. 13-27, 2015.

[54] L. Valerio, M. Conti, E. Pagani, A. Passarella, "Autonomic Cognitive-based Data Dissemination in Opportunistic Networks", *IEEE 14th International Symposium and Workshops on a World of Wireless, Mobile and Multimedia Networks (WoWMoM)*, pp 1-9, June 2013.

[55] V.I. Arnold, "Ordinary Differential Equations", *The MIT Press, Cambridge MA, USA*, 1978.

[56] V. Karyotis, E. Stai and S. Papavassiliou, "Evolutionary Dynamics of Complex Communications Networks", *CRC Press - Taylor & Francis Group*, Boca Raton, FL, USA, October 2013.

[57] I. Taxidou, "Realtime Analysis of Information Diffusion in Social Media", *VLDB Endowment* 21508097/13/10, 2013.

[58] C.L.P. Chen, C.-Y. Zhang, "Data-intensive Applications, Challenges, Techniques and Technologies: A Survey on Big Data", *Elsevier Information Sciences*, Vol. 275, pp. 314-347, August 2014.

[59] T.T. Zin, T. Pyke, T. Toriu, H. Hama, "A Big Data Application Framework for Consumer Behavior Analysis", *in 2013 IEEE 2nd Global Conference on Consumer Electronics (GCCE)*, pp. 245-246, Oct. 2013.

[60] E. Stai, V. Karyotis, S. Papavassiliou, "A Hyperbolic Analytics Framework for Big Network Data and their Applications", *IEEE Network Magazine*, Vol. 30, No. 1, pp. 11-17, January-February 2016.

In: Advances in Social Networking Research
Editor: Salvador Reese
ISBN: 978-1-63485-225-8
© 2016 Nova Science Publishers, Inc.

Chapter 4

24/7 EMPOWERED LEARNING IN SOCIALLY NETWORKED SPACES FOR TEACHER PROFESSIONAL DEVELOPMENT

Sarah Prestridge
Griffith University, Queensland, Australia

ABSTRACT

This chapter is designed to explore socially networked spaces as an important process within teacher professional development. Social networking enables teachers to access new ideas, to collaborate and to contribute to a shared knowledge, regardless of time and place. These factors are significant and necessary in a world where a knowledge building economy is a noteworthy indicator of economic prosperity. To live and prosper in the digital age, to understand and function successfully in online spaces and to be able to be self-directed in our learning is foundational for our current and future worlds. The online world has become an integral part of the physical world and with that has come the need for teachers to be fore-runners in shaping our students to live and learn as a basic necessity. The rise of social networking with its inherent disposition for sharing and knowledge-producing exchanges logically suggests a merger with education to improve teaching and learning outcomes (Veletsianos, Kimmons and French 2013).

Teacher professional development has seen a renaissance, and a shift from training or workshops held on school sites to online environments affirming redefinitions of teacher practices to work in new ways, to work in partnership and better focus on high task complexity and continuous learning (Loveless 2008). To support this re-direction towards an online networked professional learning model, an understanding of the advantages social networking can offer teacher professional development is required.

The chapter provides an extensive literature review with illustrations of practice of both the use of social networking in pre-service and in-service teacher professional development contexts that identify relationships and patterns of understanding in each place. What is presented in the chapter are new understandings of the components of effective online professional development in these spaces including critical points for consideration and the dilemmas that can occur around implementation. A final elaboration of what is considered a sustainable and transformative model of online teacher professional development using social networking will be described, illustrating the key elements of effective implementation.

GUIDING PREMISE

In virtual professional development teachers beliefs and practices become the focus and influence of the design of professional development through self-generating content and self-directed pathways for learning. This type of professional development utilises inquiry-based approaches and positions the teacher as the driver rather than the recipient of modular based coursework. Many of the ideas presented here can be applied across a wide variety of fields of employment. They are not limited to Education.

INTRODUCTION

The Link between Social Networking and Professional Development

Social networking platforms such as Facebook, LinkedIn, Snapchat, Instagram, MySpace, Flickr, Friendster and Twitter are pervasive in daily life (Boyd and Ellison 2007). Facebook, for example, is the fastest growing SNS in the world with 1.04 billion daily active users on average for December 2015 with over 350 million photos uploaded daily (http://newsroom.fb.com/Feb-2016). These social platforms are considered popular not just with today's students (Taylor and Keeter 2010), but with people of all ages, who use technologies as part of their seamless social interactions to view, browse and consume life events several times a day. This is a significant part of our socialisation into a connected consumer 21st century culture (Featherstone, 2007).

The rise of the social networking with its disposition for a sharing and knowledge-producing exchange logically suggests a merge with education. At the core face, teachers can use social platforms as pedagogical tools for student engagement, connectedness, online collaboration within class groups and with invited experts; and for teacher professional development, social platforms can be used to build collaborative online communities to improve teaching and learning outcomes. Teachers are the medium through which any curriculum material is enacted. They need support to effectively implement any new educational reform. Teachers need opportunities to discuss pedagogical approaches with like-minded colleagues. They need time to reflect, time to investigate the needs of their students and explore the digital repositories for suitable resources and they need opportunities to investigate what other teachers are doing in their classrooms.

By engaging in social networking teachers could gain an insight into the learning opportunities provided by these online environments, which would inform teachers' use of social networking in the classroom (Prestridge and Tondeur, 2015). Currently, teachers are interested in and want to know how students are reading and writing in online environments so they can harness this power for educational outcomes (Turcsanyi-Szabo 2012). Teachers want to use social networks and powerful mobile tools for real-world applications of knowledge and engagement in learning (Prestridge 2012; Schibeci et al. 2008). Students know how to engage socially online and teachers know how students learn. Bringing this knowledge together would give students the power to learn through these tools as well as the capacity to transfer these new learning approaches to new technologies. A first step towards this would be to leverage social networking as a basis for teacher professional development. In this way teachers are living and learning online and would develop a deeper understanding of the social networking tool itself and the advantages for use in curriculum based student learning activities.

There needs to be a sustainable flow of change continuously shaping teaching in every classrooms in order to educate a generation that can respond to the ever-changing technological demands within the future workplace. Success with one of the major educational reforms- digital technologies- has been based on the quantity of the use of computers, such as the number of laptops rather than the quality of the use of technologies to enhance learning outcomes (Moyle 2010). Many teachers use digital technologies in the same ways they used traditional resources (Prestridge 2012). This causes students to become frustrated and lose interest in lessons. Students need to use digital technologies to help them think deeply about a concept, to examine, investigate, collaborate, critique and create rather than simply present content, research information on websites or email assignments. These higher order thinking skills are difficult to teach and require 'hard thinking.' However, with the use of digital technologies as 'Mindtools' (Jonassen, Carr and Yueh 1998) can both support and help scaffold this kind of thinking for students. Students need to be smart users of technology, to take advantage of the opportunities associated with digital tools. Teachers also need to be smart users of technology so they can facilitate the educational process and know how to use different technologies authentically.

It has long been established that teacher change in pedagogy when using digital technologies does not come about through a training approach (Watson 2001). Rather effective professional development is driven by the teacher through self-directed pathways supported by an online networked community that includes teachers from all educational levels. Such a professional development approach provides teachers with the ability to utilise current technologies such as social networking to research and direct their engagement through generating content at any time during the school day.

Elaborations of Social Networking

Definitions and Educational Potential of Social Networking

The advent of Web 2.0 tools has generated, among other things, social networking sites (SNS). Boyd and Ellison (2007 211) provide a clear definition: 'SNS are web-based services that allow individuals to (1) construct a public or semi-public profile within a bounded system, (2) articulate a list of other users with whom they share a connection, and (3) view and traverse their list of connections and those made by others within the system.'

The term 'network' carries with it an important disposition to the way communication tools are used within sites. Networking does not necessarily mean that people are looking to meet new people; rather, they are primarily communicating with people who are a part of their extended social network or professional circle. What is important with a SNS is that people are able to make visible their social connections and therefore, provide potential connections between individuals that would not otherwise have been made (Haythornewaite 2005).

Characteristics of SNS

Social networking sites such as Facebook and LinkedIn create a personalised approach to networking through the use of personal profiles. The user provides typical information 'about me' to develop a social presence or online identity, by including interests, profession and demographics (see Figure 1 as an example randomly selected from a google search on SNS profile images). Additionally the user is prompted to identify others with whom they have a connection and/or resources they might be interested in through the use of para-data (NSDL Network 2012). By using in situ information about online users' actions that are related to a resource, prompts are provided that direct and suggest further engagement. This creates an intuitive, personalised approach that supports further user interaction.

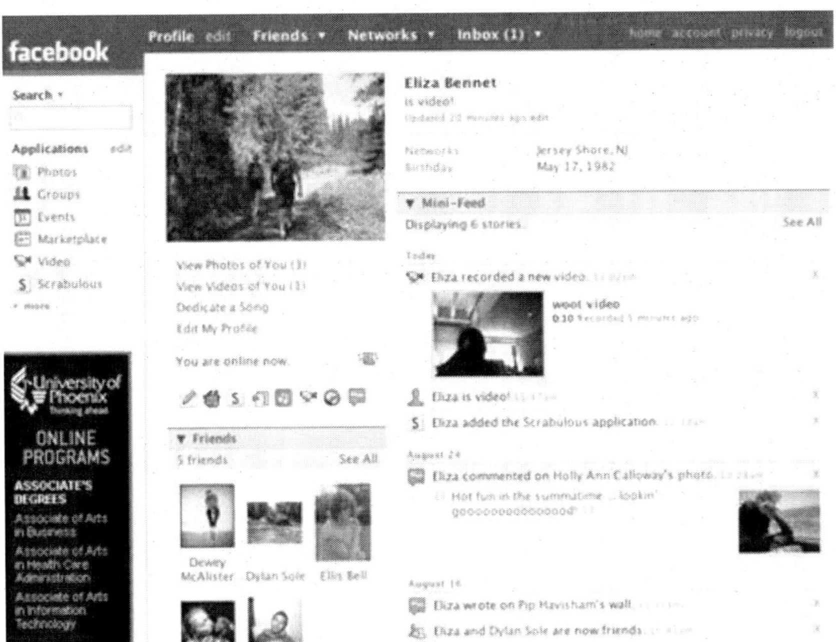

http://www.reuters.com/article/us-britain-facebook-idUSTRE49S3KU20081029.

Figure 1. Example of a profile page.

A SNS employs other tools to support interactivity such as forums, blogs, media sharing, file repositories, messaging, RSS, chats, calendars and tagging. These tools create the 'personal touch' and networking capabilities but more importantly, as suggested by Brady, Holcomb and Smith (2010) these tools put the user at the centre, and have the potential to increase user engagement.

Differences between a SNS and a LMS

One of the first moves to learning online has been to employ a learning management system (LMS) because of its use in higher education systems. LMS like the Blackboard@ platform direct users to engage in ways that are different to SNS.

LMSs serve as management systems that support administrative concerns and use communication management tools more frequently than interactive tools (Dalsgaard 2006). LMSs also engender teacher-centred pedagogies for distributing course content. This has impact on how content and student interaction occurs. In a LMS the instructor provides the content, which is central to activity, whereas in a SNS the content is generated by the user and interaction is the central activity (Mott 2010).

Engagement between student and the content is also different. For example, an instructor in a LMS may pose a question in an online discussion board and each student posts a response, replicating traditional question-and-answer mode. In contrast, discussion in a SNS is self-directed or student-centred (Brady, Holcob and Smith 2010). Veletsianos, Kimmons and French (2013) suggest that a SNS fosters the use of participatory pedagogies and are able to support interactive discussions. Interaction and content are more free-flowing and therefore are more difficult to control. This is why tensions arise when SNS have been used in higher education as personal and professional boundaries for instructors collapse (Marwick and Boyd 2010) and the sites are not conducive to teacher-centred pedagogies.

Developing a sense of community is critically important to student engagement in any online learning environment – LMS or SNS – especially if students do not meet face to face. The tools used in a SNS facilitate the sharing of information. This, plus personal profiling and a student's sense of social presence are key factors that promote a community of practice (Cobb 2009, DeSchryver, Mishra, Koelhler, Francis 2009). LMS have been described as tools that fail to provide users with the social presence necessary for more robust and valuable networking experiences that are essential for learning

(Minocha 2009; Velesianos, Kimmons and French 2013). Therefore, social presence and its critical relationship to building a community of practice indicate the potential of SNS in education.

Personal Learning Networks

Institutions, professionals including teachers and community groups are increasingly turning to Personal Learning Networks (PLN) for the open architecture and customisability of web tools (Mott 2010) making everyday communication, productivity and collaboration easier. A PLN is an informal learning network that consists of the people with whom the student interacts and derives and builds knowledge in a SNS and/or through independent web tools (see Figure 2). The PLN in Figure 2 described by AJ Cann's refers to it as a PLE- Personal Learning Environment. He uses Bloglines as the base and generates interaction with people through various web tools displayed. This suggests that PLN can be infinitely configurable to meet personal needs and interest.

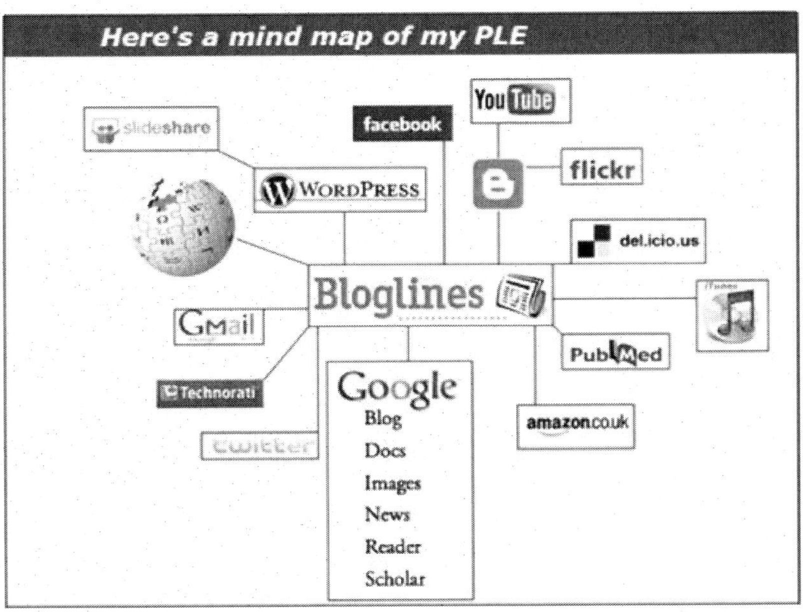

[http://www.microbiologybytes.com/tutorials/ple/ple5.html].

Figure 2. AJ Cann, PLE presentation.

Learning through PLN is illustrated in Figure 3. The diagram emphasises learning processes and action rather than web tools. The PLN is conceptualised in two ways: through the structure (interests, tools, people and content), and through what it enables (competencies, actions and connections).

As previously described, learning in this way has its foundations in social constructivist theories (Smith and Ragan 2005). Brown and Alder (2008, 30) suggest that learning with Web 2.0 tools is so different that it should be called 'Learning 2.0' to emphasise a new learner-centric paradigm that facilitates innovative explorations, experimentations and purposeful tinkering, which often forms the basis of a situated understanding emerging from action, not passivity.

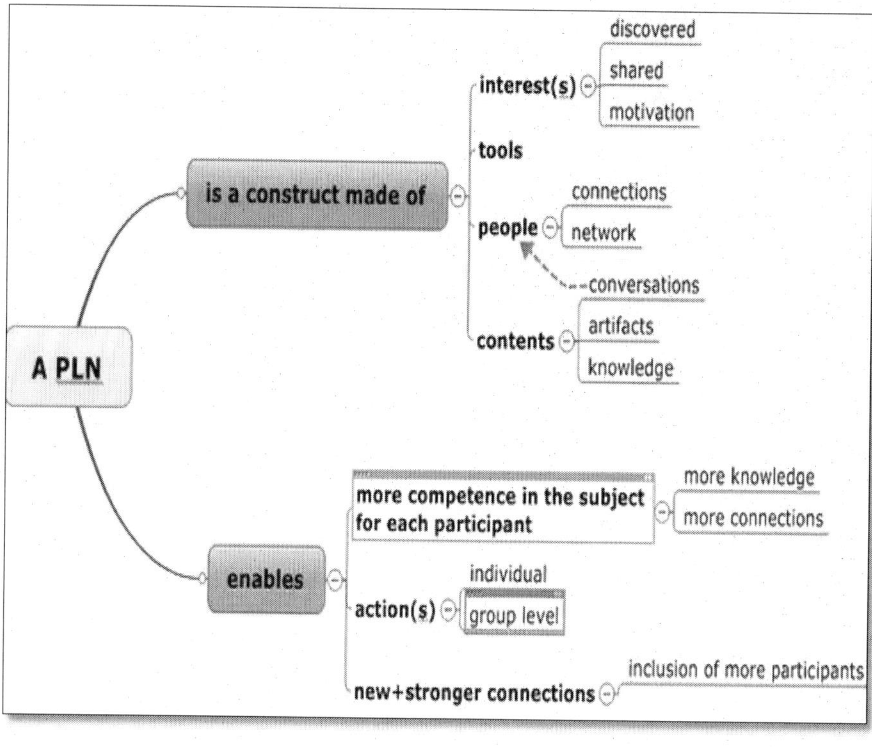

[http://www.edtechpost.ca/ple_diagrams/index.php/A_PLN_is_and_enables].

Figure 3. Vahid Masrour's synthetic view of a PLN.

Use of Social Networking in Higher Education

There is a need to look at what is happening in higher educational institutions to inform our understanding of SNS for teacher professional development, as these sites are still in the emerging stages of experimentation with Web 2.0 tools. Currently, the application of these tools is at a course level rather than a university-wide level and the research is focused to small-scale independent projects employing Facebook, Twitter or Social Networking such as Elgg or NING. As mentioned previously, higher education and distance education institutions have traditionally employed LMS to implement coursework. With the rapid advancement of technologies coupled with changes in work and social life patterns, universities have been hastening to move more course delivery into the online mode.

Online education requires students to engage in self-regulated learning, which is a more difficult learning process (Oliver 2001). It has been plagued by issues of students feeling isolated and a lack of engagement between students and with the instructor, all of which can lead to disengagement and higher drop-out rates (Veletsianos and Navarrete, 2012). Herrington, Reeves and Oliver (2005) identify online courses as having a product orientation for information delivery and they call for a move to more innovative, authentic pedagogies refocusing on course delivery for learning outcomes. There is a very clear requirement also, that instructors need to develop students' self-regulatory and active learning skills through online course delivery.

The employment of social networking tools in higher education has been viewed as one way to address these problems through the tool's potential to create a sense of social presence and commitment to engagement, its role in development of a learning community and enabling student driven participation in interactive discussions through participatory practices. From a sociological perspective, Beer and Burrows (2007) acknowledge social networking as reworking hierarchies, changing social divisions, creating possibilities and opportunities, informing us and reconfiguring our relations with objects, spaces and each other. The following examples of social networking in higher education present a range of benefits with an insight into their role in teacher professional development.

Elgg Platform

Veletsiano and Navarrette (2012) conducted an exploratory study to identify, describe and understand students' experiences in an online course on the Elgg platform. The course ran for six weeks. Students were asked to create a personal profile, including photos of themselves and to view others to help establish a sense of social presence and connectedness. Each day, student activity included reading, watching or listening to resources online, responding to self-reflective questions on personal blogs, reading and commenting on their peers' blogs, and responding to frequent comments and alerts left by the instructor. Figure 4 (copied from Veletsiano and Navartte 2012, 8) displays a typical configuration of a student dashboard showing tools- files, wire posts, blog, pages, bookmarking. The goal of this process was to initiate investigation of content while creating space for learner-centred exploration and discussion.

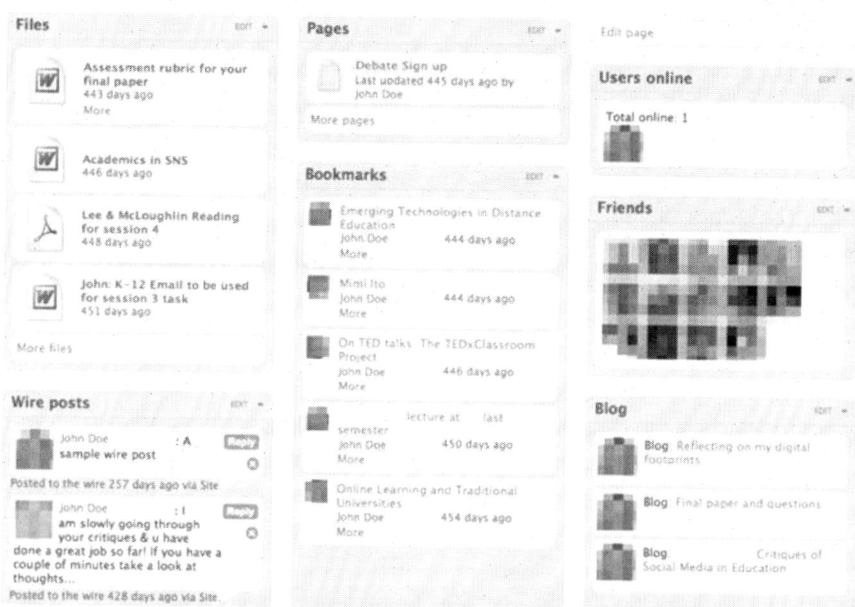

[http://www.irrodl.org/index.php/irrodl/article/view/1078/2077].

Figure 4. Student dashboard from a course site using the Elgg platform.

Findings indicated that students acknowledged that supporting one another enhanced their learning experience. However, students lacked the ability to manage their learning strategies through finding and categorising content for future access and the ability to traverse networks of interest. This study suggested that strategic online activities involving reflection and feedback engendered meaningful knowledge building and social support and alleviated the feeling of isolation.

Dron and Anderson (2009) implemented an Elgg platform for an undergraduate course where the students primarily had only used a LMS. The task of reading analysis with guiding questions was posted each week. Students completed the questions on individual blogs. Much of the interaction was achieved through blog comments. The instructor played a moderately active role through dialogue within the main community page, email responses, real-time sessions and comments on blogs.

As found by other researchers (Anderson, 2006; Brandtzaeg and Heim 2011) around 20% of the students were active in discussions, while the rest tapered off rapidly. However, all students posted regularly to their blogs and participated in specific discussion activities because it was a course requirement. Furthermore, students needed additional support and scaffolding to participate in and access resources in the Elgg environment as they found it confusing and disorientating even though they were active users of other SNS such as Facebook and MySpace.

Facebook

Wang, Woo, Quek, Yang and Liu (2011) explored using Facebook for coursework as a replacement for a LMS by putting up announcements, sharing resources, organising weekly tutorials and conducting discussions at a teacher education institute in Singapore. The researchers were interested in the pedagogical, social and technological affordances.

The findings confirmed that the Facebook group was considered by the students to be just as good as the LMS. The students were able to easily communicate and interact with their peers and the instructor. However, issues associated with Facebook's inability to support certain file formats or the availability of a threaded discussion forum imposed limitations on the implementation of the course. Also students expressed concern with issues of privacy with regard to assessment items.

The authors suggest that were substituting an SNS for a LMS by applying pedagogical approaches associated with a LMS rather than changing to a learner-centred participatory approach, which is required for support effective interaction within a SNS.

NING

Brady, Holcomb and Smith (2010) used a NING platform for an education leadership course to forge and maintain a professional educational network. In the course the NING was employed mainly as a discussion tool for students to share ideas and discuss course content. The NING was compared to face-to-face coursework. The following percentages of students agreed that the NING was more beneficial for collaboration (70%), communication outside of classroom (82%) more time to reflect and comment on peers work (74%) and more convenient for sharing and discussing ideas (50%). However, over half of the students expressed a preference for face-to-face communication and had issues with time to connect and delay with receiving feedback.

The instructors expressed that the greatest benefits for students was the opportunity to expand and enhance their postings with a variety of media and creating their own forums. Overall, the results suggested that the SNS did not fully support a learning community or the development of a strong sense of social presence. The reason suggested was this was a new experience and the instructors were not aware of all the tools available in a NING platform, thus suggesting the need for staff training and more time for further implementation.

Acknowledging that these illustrations are coursework oriented and the movement to sustainable professional development through social networking would require an orientation towards teacher generated content, the pedagogical approach adopted in these studies still provides direction and insight for professional development facilitators or professional development leaders. Velestsiano and Navarrette's (2012) use of social networking employed learner-centred approaches whereby the instructor frequently commented on students' blogs and employed the use of alerts to direct learning. Dron and Anderson (2009) highlight the idea that engagement in activities demands some form of requirement or only the innovators or early adopters will participate (Rogers 1962 2003). Wong, Woo, Quek, Yang and Lie (2011) highlighted the fact that there needs to be a change in the mindset of teachers using an SNS, in that it can not be compared to a LMS and its functionality. Interacting through social networking is self-directed which requires the employment of learner-centred pedagogies. Lastly, Brady,

Holcomb and Smith (2010) identify the need for staff and student support and time for a new technology to be implemented before benefits can be measured.

In concluding this section, the educational potential for teachers to professionally learn through social networking that harnesses PLN is evident in the opportunities for self-generated and shared creation of knowledge, experimentation and participatory learning. There are challenges associated with social networking implementation such that the use requires greater support for teachers, unlike the more familiar LMS, as there is a more dynamic system of interconnected tools. Most importantly, their needs to be a mind-shift for some teachers to conceptualise social networking as opportunities for substantive professional development and for instructors in these environments to use learner-centred pedagogies to facilitate interaction among teachers.

> Teachers have the opportunity to be the drivers of professional development through social networking.

History of Professional Development

Training and Workshop Models – Re-Tooling to Pedagogical Transformation

What constitutes effective models of teacher professional development is highly contested (Becher 1999, Knight 2002, Schulman 1987). Long-standing perceptions of professional development as skill workshops or training approaches indicate a 're-tooling' of teachers that tends to augment the existing curriculum by developing teachers' competencies focused on specific types of digital technologies. These 're-tooling' models serve to reinforce teachers' approach to integrate digital technologies without changing their pedagogy. Lankshear and Bigum (1998) have described this as a 'technologised' approach, and later Bigum (2002) refers more poignantly to such practices as 'domesticating' the computer in classrooms. O'Rourke (2001 13) redirects digital technology professional development towards helping teachers 'to focus on pedagogy than on the technology itself' which is affirmed by Loveless (2003 324) through her premise to build teachers' 'confidence in change … rather than evidence of technological competence.'

As this movement has progressed, Fisher, Higgins and Loveless (2006) call for a cultural change, a 'renaissance,' affirming a redefinition of teacher practice to work in new ways, to collaborate and focus on high task complexity and continuous learning (Loveless 2008, Prestridge 2007). If there is any hope of encouraging teachers to change their pedagogies in ways that will capture a 21st Century curriculum through new learning styles and learning pathways of students living in a digital culture, professional development intentions need to move from 're-tooling' with infrequent curriculum integration to models where teachers will see the 'transforming' pedagogical possibilities of digital technologies and approaches to learning that enable students to create, analyse and transform information.

From Face-to-Face Approaches to Blended Approaches to Fully Online

A shift in teacher professional development from training or workshops held on school sites or in school cluster groups to online environments first utilised the traditional models of professional development. These approaches shifted the content to create online courses that included discussion forums or boards to support teacher engagement. For practicing teachers, the first moves into the online environment mirrored the higher education approach to online courses. In this transition phase, there were still components of face-to-face meetings with facilitators and teachers both individually and in cluster meetings that supported online engagement. Face-to-face (F2F) meetings were perceived as necessary by teachers to provide the social presence for online communication.

Blended Approaches to PD

A good example of this blended approach in Australia was the teacher professional development project run by Henderson (2007). This project involved teachers in Australia and the United Kingdom in an online course through the Blackboard supported by an initial face-to-face training day in each location and the use of forums, chats and emails though the coursework period. In another example, more common by design, is where teachers are given the opportunity to be involved in a year long professional development program facilitated by academic institutions where by the teachers are involved in a project based learning model. Teachers individually or in small cluster groups are mentored face to face to design and implementation a classroom based project. This school-based inquiry is supported by a course based Moodle site that teachers upload and share their projects.

Fully Online- Virtual PD

Another project in Queensland, Australia, involved teachers from four schools engaging in constructive dialogue in a NING environment supported by face-to-face planning and cluster meeting with the facilitator. In this pilot project, teachers were visited by a facilitator who collaborated on teacher inquiry project plans and, at times, organised meeting for groups of teachers involved in similar projects to share what they were doing with other teachers face-to-face.

The NING environment was not populated with content such as in coursework; rather, the content was self-generated by the teacher participants. As the project advanced and moved into a third phase, with the use of a range of online tools and environments, all face-to-face opportunities were removed, as new teachers became involved and geographical distances increased. All professional development activities were conducted online and all content was generated by the teachers (Prestridge, in press). This move to an approach supported solely by online tools is indicative of the capabilities of communication tools to replicate and support the social context teachers require.

By moving professional development into a context that is not limited by place or space, or the need for face-to-face communication, it is anticipated that professional development can become an embedded part of teachers' everyday practice. The issue of time becomes altered within online professional development, as time is considered part of daily practice (Darling-Hammond 1998). Professional development becomes part of the teaching day rather than being tacked on to the end of it as they can access social networking 24/7.

Using online learning pathways for professional development is an innovative approach in this field. The approach enables teachers to direct their learning using social networking tools supported by a networked community with mentor/s. Teachers can build and share their knowledge pathways online, during a period when they are examining their practice in the classroom. The role of both the community or network/s of teachers and the mentor is that of support, critique, collaboration, direction, investigation and celebration.

In concluding this section, using online learning pathways for professional development is a relatively new field in the context of continuing teacher education. The approach to online professional development is significant as it examines how teachers direct and build their own knowledge pathways and thus enable themselves to come in and out of professional knowledge contexts when required. The initial phases of learning in this way are supported by online networks or communities of practice as well as a mentor and knowledgeable others. As the teacher builds competence and confidence through the professional connections and communications, they become the 'knowledgeable others' building inquiry, reformation of practice and professional development into their daily practice. In this way, there are sustainable opportunities for professional renewal and development.

Principles of Professional Development

As identified there has been a movement from training or skilling approaches to professional development that focuses on teachers' attention to examining their own pedagogy. It can be simply stated that teachers' pedagogical beliefs affect their teaching behaviours in the classroom (Bandura 1986, Clark and Peterson 1986). As such, teachers need to be made conscious of their beliefs that are informing their practices. Through professional development, beliefs require interrogation and reformation. Regardless of the medium through which professional development occurs, that is, face-to-face, online or virtually, principles of professional development need to exist for transformative and sustainable outcomes.

There are three principles of professional development that are required for enabling teachers to effect change in their practice. These are investigation, reflection and constructive dialogue. Drawing on action research as a method and guiding ethos, a theoretical professional development model represents the deconstruction and reconstruction of critical professional learning activities or principles for teachers to engage with to change their existing pedagogical beliefs and practices.

Teachers start at the left-hand side of the PD model and move from left to right in a circular motion as indicated by the arrows (see Figure 5). They enter with existing pedagogical beliefs and practices. These existing pedagogical beliefs and practices are shaped through engagement within the core reflective process and are continually evolving. An evolving state implies meaning associated with teachers' understanding of professional development. First, it implies that a teacher considers professional development as continual and an intrinsic part of their professionalism. Secondly, it implies that different pathways are required within professional development.

The capacity for professional development is indicated in the formation of and relationship between the three sections in the centre of the model. This section is named the core reflective process and is made up of three principles:

investigation, reflection and constructive dialogue. As the teacher moves from left to right, he or she engages simultaneously with the three professional learning principles. These three principles must be viewed as dynamically interdependent. Each is required in professional development to initiate teacher engagement that pre-empts reflection to enable further informed strategic action. The innermost shaded intersection of these three activities is where teachers transform their beliefs and practices.

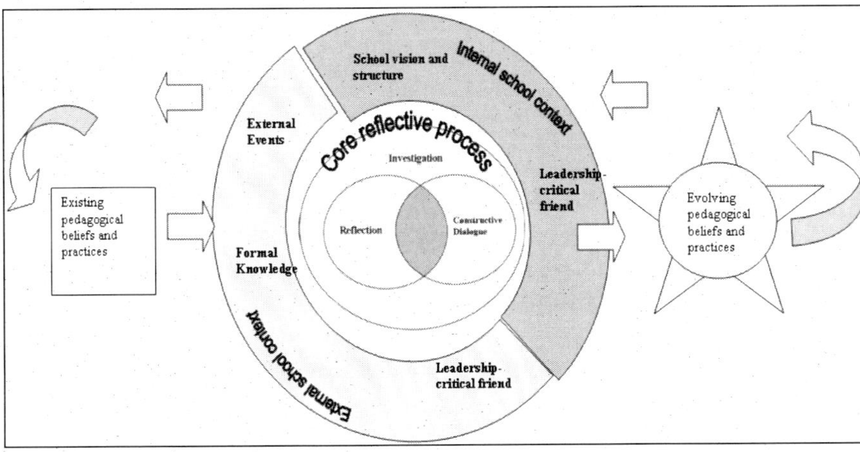

Figure 5. Theoretical professional development model (Prestridge, 2007).

Teacher change (*in belief and practice*) occurs during professional development when teachers' verbal reflection, supported by written reflection, is actioned with critical discourse that is based in collegial formations. Teacher action is best embedded within an investigative context such as a classroom-based inquiry. Teachers engaged in this dynamic interplay of the three professional learning principles make links with elements in the internal and external school contexts when they are required, such that internal and external leaders are drawn on to direct or challenge teachers' pedagogical beliefs; formal knowledge and external events are used to inform teachers' pedagogical practices; and school vision and structures provide opportunities to collaborate with other teachers within and across schools. The core reflective principles of investigation, reflection and constructive dialogue are the three principles that are critical in professional development.

Investigation centralises professional development in the classroom context. Teachers' classrooms become sites for inquiry for making conscious knowledge-of-practice. Essentially, opportunities for professional discourse that are structured and derived from personal investigation acknowledge the value of teacher-constructed knowledge. The generation of knowledge through professional inquiry has the ability to influence change in teachers' beliefs and practices and is imperative to effective professional development. Reflection supports this inquiry through the process of 'sense-making,' providing a lens through which re-conceptualisation of practice can occur. Finally, the interdependent process of constructive dialogue infers that teachers require both collegial and critical discourse to engage in within professional development activity. Collegial discourse is required to build a community of learners or community of practice CoP, which supports the development of social presence or a social context whereas critique or critical discourse supports the learning, the interrogation of established beliefs for the reformation of new beliefs. Engagement in all principles enables change in teacher beliefs and practices.

Principles for Professional Development – Actuality

The guiding assumption of professional development should aim to make teachers conscious of their beliefs, and any activity associated with the professional development should be contextualised to teachers' classrooms. Pedagogical analysis is enabled through the three principles while the building of technological skills is secondary, to support growth in teacher confidence. Professional development is underpinned by action research, where the teacher is considered a researcher.

The guiding three principles of investigation, reflection and constructive dialogue are not constrained to a face-to-face context; the model can be applied in blended and virtual environments. With this in mind, the following is provided below as an actualised example of a professional development model which adopts a strategic approach to enact the three principles.

Investigation

1) The teacher identifies current beliefs and practices through a questionnaire and discussions with peers and the PD leader.
2) A collaborative design of an inquiry project with the PD leader and peers is created. The inquiry project involves: identifying a problem, developing learning materials, implementing and monitoring with data collection, identifying learning outcomes and results, and re-designing learning materials.

3) The teacher examines their own beliefs and makes conscious the links to their practices.
4) A review and redesign points 1, 2 and 3 depending on individual needs.

Reflection

1. Written reflection: undertaken weekly in a journal or blog.
2. Verbal reflection: dialogue and sharing with the PD leader and peers.

Constructive dialogue

1. Teacher planning sessions for inquiry project with the PD leader and group sharing sessions are discussed.
2. Threaded discussion forums led by teachers take place.

Teachers engaging with the in this professional development model are better positioned if they are working with colleagues at their school-based location. This collegial connection supports constructive dialogue with teachers from other schools. Teachers support each other and the PD leader is available if they need help to engage online. It is important that teachers' classrooms are considered the site for investigation. Reflection facilitates sense-making, and collegial dialogue supports the building of a network of colleagues, in which critical dialogue enables learning. On a final note, reflections both verbal and written can occur online as can constructive dialogue using Web 2.0 tools, facilitated by a PD mentor.

Teacher-Led Design-Based Research (TDR)

Bannan-Ritland (2008) offers a similar model based on teacher-led research involving the design and cyclic testing of instructional materials (that include the use of technologies). The model is called 'Teacher-led Design-based Research' (TDR). Its roots are the same as the IRC PD model in that the teacher is considered a researcher, implementing action research methodology. In summary, the TDR process consists of:

- teacher immersion in experiences that involve deep learning
- constructing meaning from current experiences
- focusing on how students learn

- developing sustainable innovative practices
- developing collaborative research competence.

Markauskaite and Reimann Model

Markauskaite and Reimann (2008) also developed a design-based inquiry model to support teachers' engagement with digital technologies. They describe a similar process for teacher-led research: problem-design-implement-monitor-evaluate-reflect-disseminate. Their model is encapsulated in three spaces: design space, collaboration space and decision-making space. Each of these spaces includes a range of interconnected digital tools that can help with the inquiry process.

There are many similarities in the research identifying the essential principles of professional development. First and foremost, when professional development is concerned with transformative outcomes, teachers' beliefs and current practices need to be made conscious so that through professional activity based in investigation and supported by reflection and constructive dialogue, these beliefs can cause tension to enable reformation and inform new practices. Conceptualising professional development in this way provides opportunity for these processes to exist in different contexts such that professional development can occur online and through teachers' self-directed pathways.

LEARNING COMMUNITIES

Professional development has strong links with the role of community in supporting teacher education. The term 'community' is found in the literature under various titles: learning community, communities of practice, online networks, special interest groups, collaboratives, listservs, personal learning networks, research groups, teacher networks and professional communities. These communities signify a group approach to learning that draws on the social nature of meaning (Imel 2001). Literature in this area acknowledges that learning communities require group commitment to long-term needs but must also focus on the daily problems and issues to sustain involvement (Lieberman 2000).

Learning Communities

Learning communities have been found to facilitate teachers' knowledge construction if they are able to evaluate collusions and collisions as part of the learning experiences of a group (Fletcher and Hill 2004). Learning communities have administrative requirements at points in time and may need direction from an administrator (Nickerson and Sowder 2002). Also considerable time is required for teachers to form relationships that enable engaged and enthusiastic discussion (Wineburg and Grossman 1998). Learning communities offer a classroom teacher a forum for discussion and reflection, a place to flag ideas and thoughts, a social support network and an acknowledgement of their commitment.

Characteristics of Communities of Practice (CoPs)

Lave and Wenger's (1991) seminal work exploration of situated learning spawned the concept of a CoP as more than an interest-based grouping, rather a shared practice. Wilson and Ryder (1996) state that groups become communities when they interact with each other and stay together long enough to form a set of habits or when they come to depend upon each other to accomplish a task. Brown et al. (1989) describe a CoP as bounded by intricate socially constructed webs of belief, essential to understanding informed action. In Wegner's (1998a) view, CoPs have three characteristics that define practice and identity that sustains engagement and therefore learning: mutual engagement, a joint enterprise and a share repertoire. The shared repertoire is the shared knowledge, beliefs and practices of the community that support interaction and direction of action.

Lock (2006) highlights the advantages of CoP as they foster a learning culture of transformation rather than a culture that reinforces old or established practice. The learning in a CoP comes from the critique, the collisions and personal and social interrogation of beliefs. In contrast, social and collegial discourse builds the atmosphere of trust and respect, a safe environment to explore teacher beliefs and practices. Prestridge (2009) found that tension arises in a CoP as collegiality is opposed to critique but without critique there is no need for collegiality. In other words, a learning community is built on camaraderie but without the opportunity for learning to occur through critique, there is no point in membership.

Learning Communities and CoPs

Building a learning community is an essential design element of professional development. It is oriented to designing a structure and a process that is purposeful and fluid in nature and meets personal ongoing needs of teachers (Lock 2006). As established in the previous section on the conceptualisation of professional development, it is the necessary ingredient in supporting the social ecology, the climate of the grouping.

A learning community is pivotal for online professional development as it is intrinsically related to the establishment of social presence for teachers. Social presence helps to provide the face-to-face ingredient with which teachers are familiar in professional development. A learning community also provides the underlying social structures and dispositions for critical discourse, required for learning to occur. As established, constructive dialogue is required to build a learning community, where collegial discourse supports the development of social presence and a social context, and critique or critical discourse supports the learning, the interrogation of established beliefs for the reformation of new beliefs.

Much can be learnt from the literature on CoP for its relationship with professional development. Wenger (1998a) provides a learning architecture for the design and evolution of a CoP. There are four dualities that provide the tension to enable learning and change:

- reification/participation – movement between interaction with others and theory building
- design/emergent – movement from conceptualisation of design and actualisation of practice
- local/global – learning within and across communities
- identification/negotiation – movement between individual and distributed ownership of meaning.

Considering these dualities, Wenger (1998a) points out that a CoP is not synonymous with a group or team; rather it is an entity created through mutual engagement and reflection. As explained, this happens through dialogue, a common focus and sustained interaction. Underwriting this is the peer mentoring process where participants share ideas, support each other in dialogue and offer feedback. Lave and Wenger's (1991) term 'legitimate peripheral participation' refers to the process by which newcomers become part of a CoP through an apprenticeship model, or learning with a knowledgeable other. McLoughlin et al. (2008) identify seven dimensions for the design of an online learning community based on Wenger's (1998a) Learning Architecture Framework. These dimensions could be considered as actions in a professional development approach:

Mutuality Competence Continuity Reflection
Exploration Coordination Jurisdiction

The literature on CoP aligns with a culture of learning. Learning can be described as active engagement in discourse and shared knowledge building within the community. Garber (2004) suggests that CoP members need to be contributors, not just observers and/or consumers of group knowledge. However, Lock (2006) suggests that not all teachers are ready to work collaboratively in an online community, as they need to be self-motivated, independent learners with self-confidence.

Social Networking and CoP

Brantzaeg and Heim's (2011) studied users of Social Networking. They found five distinctly different types of users: Socialisers, Debaters and Actives are considered early adopters while Sporadics and Lurkers are late adopters. Sporadics and Lurkers have low levels of participation, with Lurkers making up the largest user category. However, low participation for contributing may not indicate what Garber suggests as a requirement of group membership as Prestridge (2009) found that there is still learning value associated with viewing and listening to group dialogue. It is vital for teachers to have the self-confidence to actively move from viewing or lurking to participating.

Community building takes time, commitment and an understanding that the ebb and flow of knowledge and level of participant action will continually change at any one time in response to the issues being addressed by the group. It cannot be assumed that an online group with a common interest will evolve into a CoP. Murphy and Laferriere (2005) inform us that for a group to develop to a point where there is interdependence or inter-influence, a conscious systematic effort must be deployed. This suggests a role for professional development and the roles and actions of PD leaders.

Online Networks

The English Companion NING is an example of a learning network that utilises social networking tools to collaborate to meet their specific needs. Burke (2009) describes this space as a place where teachers share, discuss and argue over topics central to their teaching, beyond their local districts. Social networking sites such as a NING, enable members to have a personal space as well as a community space. The ability to connect at both levels has the potential for greater impact as it encourages disparate individuals to connect, communicate and take action (Ellison et al. 2009).

Based on a coursework approach, Vrasidas and Zembylas (2004) used an online environment (www.star-online.org) that developed a learning network through asynchronous and synchronous communication tools, enabling participant collaboration through program design and project tasks. They provide lessons learned through the implementation process:

- Promote ownership, commitment and a shared vision among participants.
- Promote interaction be structuring collaborative tasks.
- Choose the right technology for the task.
- Design for cognitive apprenticeship.
- Choose authentic tasks and activities.
- Provide regular feedback regarding participants' work.
- Promote self-reflection.
- Constantly evaluate and revise.
- Use a variety of assessment methods.

Waltonen-Moore et al. (2006) used a threaded discussion tool as a central focus to support student engagement in an online professional development course. They focused on enabling co-construction of knowledge and negotiated meaning as a process that underlined interaction. They identified a model for the stages of online group development that provides insight into the implementation process and time frames for the development of a learning network (see Figure 6).

The introductory stage initiates the sharing and building of personal and professional backgrounds. The identification stage involves participants in affirming interests with one another and identifying similarities and differences. The interaction stage sees an engagement with knowledge by first making conscious links with participant's own professional knowledge. The involvement stage identifies participants working collaboratively, co-constructing knowledge with a sense of group cohesion. In the final stage there is movement to application of knowledge involving reflective, synthesis and evaluation processes - putting it into practice.

These stages have clear implications for leadership in online professional development as different strategies are required for different stages. A coursework-based professional development approach is not considered the most effective approach. However, these stages can provide insights into how leaders can support participants at various constructions of an online learning network.

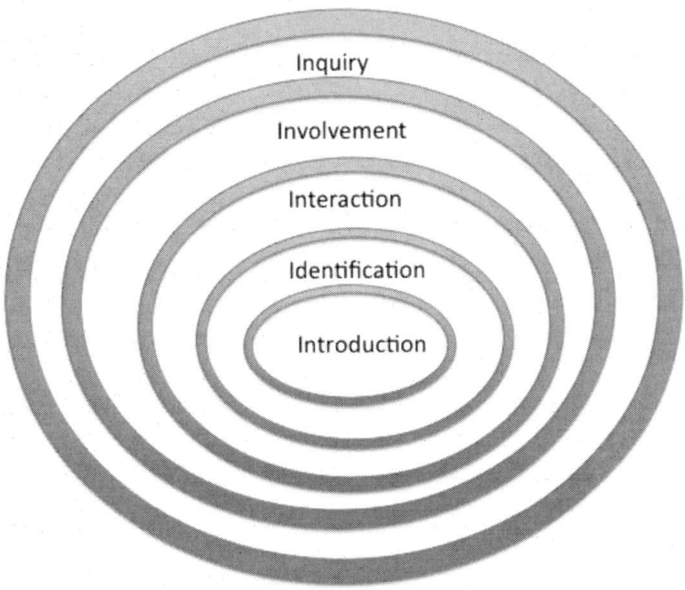

Figure 6. Evolution of online group development (Walton-en-Moore et al. 2006, 297).

Approaches to Leadership in Online Networks

In social networking environments to build an online network or community the use of participatory pedagogies by leaders enable a greater sense of social presence, improved community building and active participation through shared discussion tools (Veletsianos et al. 2013). Participatory pedagogies support collaborative processes that enable learners to connect and exchange information among each other rather than directed by an instructor or network administrator. Communication tools, such as wikis, discussion forums, instant messaging and blogs etcetera allow for freer discussions of topics and issues and can alleviate difficulties associated with user isolation and alienation. One of the advantages suggested by Brady et al. (2010) is that learners can be supported to take ownership of their own learning and personalise their engagement to suit their own needs and time frames.

In an adult learning setting, Veletsianos, Kimmons and French (2013) investigated instructors' approaches to the use of a LMS that integrates a range of social technologies such as personal profiles, friends list, file sharing and discussion boards. They found that all instructors replicated old practices and did not take advantage of the social networking functions for learning. Mentors need to be aware of past experiences in a LMS so their conceptualisation of a social networking environments are based on interactivity and the development of a social presence to ensure robust and valuable networking occur, which is essential for learning. Veletsianos and Kimmons (2013) also found tension arising between instructors and participants as personal and professional contexts can collapse in social networking environments. Naveh et al. (2010) places a high degree of importance on online environments being 'friendly,' easy to use and up to date, in keeping with the advances in technology and new functionality of Web 2.0 tools. This supports novice users as the tools are more intuitive. Therefore engagement can focus on knowledge construction.

Leadership in online networks and professional development is essential. Leaders are the vehicle through which direction, action and engagement occur. The literature provides insight into the various identities they have, the roles that are required and the strategies they need to employ to implement a professional learning environment that enables teachers to change their pedagogical beliefs and practices.

A Case Study: Socially Networked Teacher PD

Background

In 2012, a research project was implemented to investigate the possibility and effectiveness of instituting a personalised and virtually networked mode of professional development to promote teacher confidence and competence with digital technologies and its use as a key component of their pedagogy. The aim of the project was to examine the advantages of online modes of professional development where communities of practice were built without any face-to-face contact and where the direction for professional development was personalised and self-directed within a network.

This project aligned with the implementation of the Australian Curriculum, which was used as a premise for examining teachers' technological pedagogical content knowledge. Griffith Institute of Educational Research and six independent Queensland schools funded the project collaboratively.

Schools

The schools were chosen to represent all educational levels, from primary to secondary and included independent and Catholic colleges, single sex and multi-campus sites and were located across Queensland. Twenty-four teachers participated over the school year.

PD Program

The professional development program implemented the three principles of professional development described above, where the theories of professional development were actualised in a year-long program. The PD program was designed to support the flow of the school year. Term 1 required teachers to make conscious their beliefs and practices though online surveys and interviews; Term 2 involved collaboratively developing classroom Inquiry projects; Term 3 involved implementation and monitoring and Term 4 involved redesign and reflection (see Figure 7).

A mentor (PD leader) was enlisted to facilitate the professional development. His role was to establish a learning network within a social networking environment (project site and repository), to encourage engagement with and among the teachers online, to guide and direct pathways for learning associated with a teacher inquiry and to challenge and make teachers think deeply about how their students learn, their beliefs and practices.

A range of communication and Web 2.0 tools were used to implement the online PD. These included email, a discussion list through Google Groups,

Skype for one-to-one teacher and mentor discussions and wall.fm as the project site. Wall.fm provided an environment where both public and private online communities could be created. This became the central social networking space where teachers had control over and could create their personal profiles, published and shared curriculum materials as well as blog their inquiry project progress and comment on each other's reflections, giving advice and ideas.

Inquiry project outline given to teacher participants

Term 1: Administration elements to get access. Teachers create personal profile pages and begin to communicate in discussion forums and explore social networking tools.

Term 2: Teachers begins to develop an Action Learning Project based on their ICT interests, curriculum requirements and student needs. The Action Learning Project focuses on investigating one aspect of the use of ICT in learning. Examples of projects could be:

Does an established wiki space enable greater engagement and collaboration with community and targeted people so that learning is more authentic?

How can blogging be used as an effective learning tool?

Term 2 is spent investigation these questions through

- formulating a guiding question
- researching online- looking at Twitter, wikis, blogs, professional sites
- discussing options with mentor and other teachers
- posting ideas, thoughts, frustrations etc on a personal blog
- commenting on other teachers' blogs,
- talking virtually in 'real time' with mentor and project colleagues
- reviewing curriculum documents and other teachers' planning
- collaboratively developing a unit/learning sequence for implementation in Term 3 with the mentor.

The mentor will be monitoring your professional blogs, helping you set these up, directing your searches, having conversations through an online environment.

Materials to help guide the development of Action Learning Projects will be available on the Project site. The project site will be both a repository for teacher's planning materials to share, resources and website links, communication forums, lists of important dates and 'talk times' etc. Each teacher will have a profile page on this site that will showcase their Action Learning Project and link to their professional blog.

Term 3: Teachers will be implementing their projects and documenting what happens to their teaching and their students' learning- an action research approach. Weekly posts to blogs are required. The mentor continues to respond to blog posts, have online conversations and group discussions to extend thinking and encourage experimentation in classrooms.

Term 4: Conclusions to class based projects and new opportunities are identified. Teachers are required to present their Action Learning Projects to staff within their school and write a written report.

Figure 7. Example of an Inquiry project outline.

The planning of teachers' inquiry projects became the focal point to develop an online community and sense of an online presence. After initial managerial tasks, the development of personal profiles and the 'about me' postings to the discussion list, teachers were directed to post initial ideas and planning towards their inquiry projects. The emphasis for the PD leaders was to build a community through purposeful engagement among the teachers through the sharing of ideas, feedback and building relationships with those who had the same interests in subject matter and digital technologies. In the formation of teachers' inquiries, the PD leader had a pivotal role in helping teachers identify teaching and learning outcomes and the appropriate and purposeful use of digital technologies within the project (see Figure 8).

Prep/year 1	Use of iPads with specific apps to support literacy and numeracy development in the early years
Year 5	Use of Twitter as a collaborative tool to build students' knowledge about Olympic athletes
Year 7	How can student blogs be used as a reflective tool during the planning of Kids Connect Project?
Year 10	Does the use of a online class environment to support student engagement at any point support their learning of subject matter
Years 11 and 12	Create a connected Learning Community so students can receive peer and community feedback on their films in development stage to inform production.

Figure 8. Example of inquiry projects.

The intended outcome of this approach to professional development was in the process of teacher self-renewal and self-efficacy and not digital technology end products. It was intended to shape teachers' thinking about meaningful and authentic uses of digital technologies, in empowering them to become reflective practitioners who are informed about their beliefs and practices. An inquiry project did not have to have teaching and/or student learning outcomes rather it was important that outcomes were identifies and used to inform future practice. As a sustainable model, it was intended and identified through final teacher survey and interviews that these teachers would continue to act as the knowledgeable others within the online community on a needs basis for the next cycle of teacher participants in the program. (Further details see Prestridge in press).

Key Findings of the Project

1) The driver of this type of professional development is the teacher rather than the PD leader. It can be conceptualised as a demand-driven model in the sense that the participant controls the nature and timing of support activities and services. Activities and services can be offered but not mandated by the PD leader and teachers' responses are critical to informing decisions about further activities and services to provide.
2) Teachers engaged at different levels and in different ways. Even though all teachers constructed inquiry projects, it was found that one-third were active engagers, one-third were sporadic engagers and the other third did not engage significantly, lurked, in online communication and reflections. It is suggested that more explicit and direct guidance and expectations from the PD leader is required at the beginning of professional development as well as greater investment in building as sense of community to support the sporadic and lurkers. Targeting teachers based on their beliefs and practices in the first phase of the model could lead to the creation of smaller interest groups and the level of support required by the PD leader. Knowledgeable others and the functionality of social networking to engender links to resources of interest should also support these lower level engagers.
3) Scheduling personal developmental milestones for each teacher as part of the planning phase of the inquiry project would help shape the

support activities, directions and services offered by the PD leader. This orientates the PD leader strategically and helps to maintain the integrity of teachers' personal agency within a self-generating professional development model.

FINAL WORDS

In professional development teachers beliefs and practices can become the focus and influence of the design of professional development through self-generating content and self-directed pathways for learning. This type of professional development utilises inquiry-based approaches and positions the teacher as the driver rather than the recipient of modular based coursework. The following list of guidelines has been drawn from the review of the literature presented in this chapter. These guidelines provide some direction for both the construction and implementation of professional development within socially networked spaces.

Guidelines for Professional Development in Socially Networked Spaces

- Social networking environments are to be used as sites for a learner-centric paradigm that facilitates innovative explorations, experimentation and purposeful tinkering;
- a mind-shift for some teachers need to consider in the design of online professional development so that opportunities for substantive professional development are considered 'real';
- instructors or mentors in these environments should use participatory pedagogies to facilitate interaction and networking among teachers;
- a generation of social presence and a learning community is required to replicate face-to-face engagement and facilitate deep thinking among teachers
- time to play, establish networks, levels of intensity and moving in and out of groups and or networked spaces is considered common practice and responsive to professional needs at given points of teachers' learning pathways;

- the fact that ongoing technical support to help teachers engage in online environments is an embedded part of teacher professional development but is considered a functional requirement, acknowledging that functionality of social networking helps to make the environment intuitive and user-friendly;
- the fact that teachers' experience of how learning occurs through social networking will encourage repurposing of classroom use of these applications.

Critical Factors

On the basis of these guidelines, the following critical factors associated with teacher professional development needs to be considered when designing online support in socially networked spaces:

- The purpose needs to focus on pedagogical change through analysis of teacher beliefs about how children learn;
- Three principles are required: investigation, reflection and constructive dialogue. Teachers' classrooms are considered sites for investigation. Reflection facilitates sense-making, collegial dialogue supports the building of a community of practice, while critical dialogue enables learning;
- Teacher efficacy needs significant focus to build relationship and a sense of presence online with unknown colleagues;
- Teachers in a PD inquiry direct their learning by drawing on knowledge and interactions from other networks online and within their local school context;
- A sense of a learning community needs to evolve within the PD inquiry network to support the social ecology and the climate of the grouping. A critical indicator of the development of an online community is in the strength of the collegiality to support critical discourse that is required for learning to occur;
- PD leaders direct, shape and encourage teachers to share and leverage online knowledge pathways. Greater direction and instruction are required by the PD leader at the beginning of the professional development to ensure 'introductory' and 'identification' stages which are focused on foundational community building;

- Teachers build competence and confidence through professional connections and communications while implementing classroom-based inquiry. These teachers will become the knowledgeable others, taking on leadership roles in broadening networks.

Dilemmas:

- Teachers move in and out with different levels of engagement in online networks and activities based on their needs and interests at different points in time;
- Teachers generate the content which is dependent upon engagement and is more difficult to manage and propagate;
- It is difficult to shift teachers' conceptualisation of professional development from workshops and online coursework to self-generating and networking as a daily practice;
- Not all teachers are ready to work collaboratively in an online community; development of self-confidence and self-efficacy is the key to increasing teacher engagement;
- PD leaders need to develop the self-confidence necessary for teachers to actively move from viewing or lurking to participating in online networks;
- PD leaders need to employ participatory pedagogies to support and direct collaborative processes that enable teachers to connect and exchange information with each other;
- It takes time to change teacher beliefs and practices and build a learning network, as it requires substantive engagement in investigation, reflection and constructive dialogue over a long period of time.

This chapter has explored the move from the traditional face-to-face model of teacher professional development and even from the online traditional model of course work professional development. It has challenged these ideas and asked for a greater exploration of the use of 21st century thinking to move professional development into the online socially networked space. Fundamental principles of professional development such as classroom based inquiry, reflection and constructive dialogue are relevant to the online mode and could be considered more critical to its success. Teacher learning is considered through teacher agency and efficacy for engagement within both their local context and through socially negotiated spaces. The reciprocal nature of engagement enables one space to inform the other in feedback cycles. A key understanding of effective professional development is in the role it plays in constructing the teacher as a life long leaner valuing the process of learning itself.

REFERENCES

Anderson, T. (2006). Social software applications in formal online education. Paper presented at the 6th IEEE International Conference on Advanced Learning Technologies, Kerkrade, Netherland.

Bandura, A. (1986). Social foundations of thought and action: A social cognitive theory. Englewood Cliffs: Prentice-Hall.

Bannan-Ritland, B. (2008). Teacher design research: An emerging paradigm for teachers' professional development. In A. E. Kelly, R. A. Lesh and J. Y. Bak (Eds.), *Handbook of design research methods in education* (pp. 246-262). New York: Routledge.

Beer, D. and Burrows, R. (2007). Sociology and, of and in Web 2.0: Some initial considerations. *Sociological Research Online, 12*(5), article 17. Retrieved May 21 2013, from http://www.socresonline.org.uk/12/5/17.html.

Becher, T. (1999). Professional practices: Commitment and capability in a changing environment. New Brunswick, NJ: Transaction Publishers.

Bigum, C. (2002). Design sensibilities, schools and the new computing communication technologies. In Silicon literacies. Communication, innovation and education in the electronic age, ed. I. Snyder, 130-140. New Fetter Lane, London: Routledge.

Boyd, D. M.. and Ellison, N. B. (2007). Social network sites: Definition, history, and scholarship. *Journal of Computer-Mediated Communication, 13*(1), article 11. http://jcmc.indiana.edu/vol13/issue1/boyd.ellison.html.

Brady, K., Holcomb, L. and Smith, B. (2010). The use of alternative social networking sites in higher educational settings: A case study of the e-learning benefits of Ning in education. *Journal of Interactive Online Learning, 9*(2), 151-170.

Brandtzaeg, P. and Heim, J. (2011). Typology of social networking sites users. *International Journal of Web Based Communities, 7*(1), 28-51.

Brown, J. and Adler, R. (2008). Minds on fire: Open education, the long tail, and learning 2.0. *EDUCAUSE Review, 43*(1) (January/February), 16–32.

Brown, S., Collins, A. and Duguid, P. (1989). Situated cognition and the culture of learning. *Educational Researcher, 18*(1), 32-42.

Burke, J. (2009). English companion: Where English teachers meet to help each other. *Journal of Adolescent and Adult Literacy, 53*(1), 87-89.

Clark, C. and Peterson, P. (1986). Teachers' thought processes. In M. Wittrick (Ed.), Handbook of research on teaching (3rd ed.: 255 - 296). New York: Macmillan.

Cobb, S. C. (2009). Social presence and online learning: A current view from a research perspective. *Journal of Interactive Online Learning, 8*(3), 241-254.

Dalsgaard, C. (2006). Social software: E-learning beyond learning management systems. *European Journal of Open, Distance and E-Learning, 9*(2). Retrieved July 15, 2012, from http://www.eurodl.org/materials/contrib/2006/Christian_Dalsgaard.htm.

Darling-Hammond, L. (1998). Teacher learning that supports student learning. *Educational Leadership*,55(5), 6-12.

DeSchryver, M., Mishra, P., Koehler, M. and Francis, A. P. (2009). Moodle vs. Facebook: Does using Facebook for discussions in an online course enhance perceived social presence and student interaction? In C. Crawford, D. A. Willis, R. Carlsen, I. Gibson, K. McFerrin, J. Price and R. I. Weber (Eds.), *Proceedings from The Society for Information Technology and Teacher Education International Conference 2009* (pp. 329-336). Chesapeake, VA: AACE.

Dron, J. and Anderson, T. (2009). Lost in social space: Information retrieval issues in Web 1.5. *Journal Of Digital Information*, 10, 2, Retrieved from http://journals.tdl.org/jodi/index.php/jodi/article/view/443/280.

Ellison, N, Lampe, C and Steinfield, C. (2009) Social Networking sites and society: Current trends and future possibilities. Interactions, 16 (1), 6-9.

Facebook. (2012). *Statistics*. Retrieved May 23, 2013, from http://www.searchenginejournal.com/stats-on-facebook-2012-infographic/40301/.

Featherstone, M. (2007) Consumer Culture and Postmodernism. SAGE Publication Inc. (US).

Fletcher, M. and Hill, V. (2004). *Partnerships in Action: Self-Directed Community Learning*. Paper presented at the 2nd Annual International Conference on Cognition, Language and Special Education, Gold Coast, Australia.

Fisher, T., C. Higgins, and A. Loveless. 2006. Teachers learning with digital technologies: A review of research and projects. Bristol: Futurelab.

Haythornthwaite, C. (2005). Social networks and internet connectivity effects. *Information, Communication and Society, 8*(2), 125-147.

Henderson, M. (2007). Sustaining online teacher professional development through community design. *Campus-Wide Information Systems, 24*(3), 162-173.

Herrington, J., Reeves, T. C. and Oliver, R. (2005). Online learning as information delivery: Digital myopia. *Journal of Interactive Learning Research, 16*(4), 353-367.

Imel, S. (2001). Learning communities/communities of practice. *ERIC Clearinghouse on Adult, Career and Vocational Education, Issue Alert No.2*, 2-4.

Jonassen, D., Carr, C. and Yueh, H. (1998). Computers as Mindtools for engaging learners in critical thinking. *Techtrends, 43(2), 24-33.*

Knight, P. 2002. A systematic approach to professional development: Learning as practice. Teaching and Teacher Education 18, no. 2: 229-241.

Lave, J. and Wenger, E. (1991). Situated learning: Legitimate peripheral participation. Cambridge: Cambridge University Press.

Lieberman, A. (2000). Networks as Learning Communities. *Journal of Teacher Education, 51*(3), 221-227.

Lock, J. (2006). A new image: Online communities to facilitate teacher professional development. *Journal of Technology and Teacher Education, 14*(4), 663-678.

Loveless, A. 2003. The interaction between primary teachers' perceptions of ICT and their pedagogy. Education and Information Technologies 8, no. 4: 313-326.

Loveless, A. 2008. 'Retooling or renaissance?': Teacher education, professional knowledge and a changing landscape. http://www.pef.uni-lj.si/tepe2008/papers/Loveless.pdf.

Markauskaite, L. and Reimann, P. (2008). Enabling teacher-led innovation and research: A conceptual design of an inquiry framework for ICT-enhanced teacher innovation. In J. Luca and E. Weippl (Eds.), *Proceedings of World Conference on Educational Multimedia, Hypermedia and Telecommunications* (pp. 3484-3493). Chesapeake, VA: AACE.

Marwick, A. and Boyd, D. (2010). I tweet honestly, I tweet passionately: Twitter users, context collapse, and the imagined audience. New Media and Society, 13, 114–133.

Mott. J. (2010). Envisioning the post LMS Era: The open learning network. *Educause Quarterly, 33*(1), 1-9.

Moyle, K. (2010). *Building innovation: Learning with technologies.* Australian Education Review. Victoria: Australia. Accessible at www.acer.edu.au.

Minocha, S. (2009). Role of social software tools in education: A literature review. *Education and Training, 51*(5/6), 353–369.

McLoughlin, C., Lee, M. and Brady, J. (2008, June). A learning architecture framework (LAF) for developing community, engagement and professional development identity for pre-service teachers. Proceedings of the Emerging Technologies Conference, University of Wollongong.

Naveh, G., Tubin, D. and Pliskin, N. (2010). Student LMS use and satisfaction in academic institutions: The organizational perspective. *The Internet and Higher Education, 13*(3), 127-133.

Nickerson, S. and Sowder, J. (2002). *What factors influence the formation of teachers' professional communities and why should we care?* Paper presented at the annual meeting of the International Group for the Psychology of Mathematics Education, Norwich, England, July. NSDL Network (2012) Paradata Retrieved 5th June 2013 from http://nsdlnetwork.org/stemexchange/paradata.

Oliver, R. (2001). Assuring the quality of online learning in Australian higher education. In M. Wallace, A. Ellis and D. Newton (Eds.), *Proceedings of Moving Online II Conference* (pp. 222-231). Lismore: Southern Cross University.

O'Rourke, M. 2001. Engaging students through ICT: A multiliteracies approach. Teacher Learning Network Journal: Change, Growth, Innovation 8, no. 3: 12-13.

Prestridge, S. (in press). Conceptualising self-generating online teacher professional development. Technology, Pedagogy and Education.

Prestridge, S. (2012). The beliefs behind the teacher that influence their practices. *Computers and Education, 58*, 449–458.

Prestridge, S. (2010, April). *The alignment of digital pedagogy to current teacher beliefs*. Paper presented at the Australian Computers in Education Conference, Melbourne, Australia.

Prestridge, S. (2009). Teachers' talk in professional development activity that supports change in their ICT pedagogical beliefs and practices. *Teacher Development, 13*(1), 43-55.

Prestridge. S. (2007) *Models of teacher information and communication technologies professional development that empower multiliterate classroom practices.* Unpublished doctoral dissertation, Griffith University, Australia.

Prestridge, S. (2007) Engaging with the Transforming possibilities of ICT. *Australian Educational Computing, 22*(2) 3-9.

Prestridge, S. and Tondeur, J. (2015). Exploring Elements That Support Teachers Engagement in Online Professional Development. Education Sciences, 5 (3), 199. doi: 10.3390/educsci5030199.

Rogers, E. (1962, 2003). *Diffusion of innovations*. New York: Free Press.

Schibeci, R., MacCallum, J., Cumming-Potvin, W., Durrant, C., Kissane, B. and Miller, E. (2008). Teachers' journeys towards critical use of ICT *Learning, Media and Technology, 33*(4), 313-327.

Smith, P. and Ragan, T. (2005). *Instructional design*. Hoboken, NJ: Wiley and Sons.

Taylor, P. and Keeters, S. (2010). *Millenials: A portrait of a generation*. Washington, DC: Pew Research Centre.

Turcsányi-Szaba, M. (2012). Aiming at sustainable innovation in teacher education - from theory to practice. *Informatics in Education, 11*(1) 115-130.

Watson, G. (2001). Models of information technology teacher professional development that engage with teachers' hearts and minds. *Journal of Information Technology for Teacher Education, 10*(1-2) 179-190.

Waltonen-Moore, S., Stuart, D., Newton, E., Oswald, R. and Varonis, E. (2006). From virtual strangers to a cohesive online learning community: The evolution of online group development in a professional development course. *Journal of Technology and Teacher Education, 14*(2); 287-311.

Wenger, E. (1998a). Communities of practice: Learning, meaning and identify. Cambridge, MA: Cambridge University Press.

Wegner, E. (1998b). Communities of practice: Learning as a social system. *The Systems Thinker, 9*(5), 1-10.

Wilson, B. and Ryder, M. (1996). Dynamic learning communities: An alternative to designed instruction. Proceedings of Selected Research and Development National Convention of Association for Educational Research and Technology, Indianapolis, IN.

Wineburg, S. and Grossman, P. (1998). Creating a community of learners among high school teachers. *Phi Delta Kappan, 79*(5), 305-356.Wenger, E (1998a) Communities of Practice: Learning, Meaning and Identify, Cambridge, University Press, Cambridge, MA.

Wong, Q., Woo, H., Quek, C., Yang, Q and Liu, M. (2011). Using the Facebook group as a learning management system. An exploratory study. *British Journal of Education Technology*. 43 (3), 428-438.

Veletsianos, G., Kimmons, R., French, K. (2013). Instructor experiences with a social networking site in a higher education setting: Expectations, frustrations, appropriations, and compartmentalization. *Education Technology Research and Development, 61*, 255-278.

Veletsianos, G. and Kimmons, R. (2013). Scholars and faculty memberslived experiences in onlinesocial networks. *The Internet and Higher Education.* 16(1) 43-50.

Veletsianos, G. and Navarrete, C. (2012). Online social networks as formal learning environments: Learner experiences and activities. *The International Review of Research in Open and Distance Learning, 13*(1), 144-166.

Vrasidas, C. and Zembylas, M. (2004). Online professional development: Lessons from the field. *Education and Training, 46*(6/7), 326-334.

In: Advances in Social Networking Research ISBN: 978-1-63485-225-8
Editor: Salvador Reese © 2016 Nova Science Publishers, Inc.

Chapter 5

BIBLIOGRAPHY

21 days to success with LinkedIn: business social networking the Gnik Rowten way LCCN: 2015031747 Personal name: Sukenick, Ron, author. Main title: 21 days to success with LinkedIn: business social networking the Gnik Rowten way / by Ron Sukenick and Ken Williams. Published/Produced: Medford, New Jersey: CyberAge Books, [2016] Description: pages cm ISBN: 9781937290054

A colorful history of popular delusions LCCN: 2015018990 Personal name: Bartholomew, Robert E. Main title: A colorful history of popular delusions / by Robert E. Bartholomew and Peter Hassall. Published/Produced: Amherst, New York: Prometheus Books, 2015. Description: 363 pages; 23 cm Links: Cover image 9781633881228.jpg ISBN: 9781633881228 (paperback) LC classification: HM866 .B36 2015 Related names: Hassall, Peter. Scope and content: "This eclectic history of unusual crowd behavior describes a rich assortment of mass phenomena ranging from the amusing and quirky to the shocking and deplorable. What do fads, crazes, manias, urban legends, moral panics, riots, stampedes, and other mass expressions of emotion have in common? By creating a typology of such behavior, past and present, the authors show how common extraordinary group reactions to fear or excitement are. And they offer insights into how these sometimes dangerous mob responses can be avoided. We may not be surprised to read about the peculiarities of the European Middle Ages, when superstition was commonplace: like the meowing nuns of France, 'tarantism' (a dancing mania) in Italy, or the malicious anti-Semitic poison-well scares. But similar phenomena show up in our own era. Examples include the social-networking hysteria of 2012, which resulted in uncontrollable twitching by teenage girls in Leroy, NY; the 'phantom bus terrorist' of 2004 in Vancouver, Canada; and the itching outbreak of 2000 in South Africa. Vivid, detailed, and thoroughly researched, this is a fascinating overview of collective human behavior in its many unusual forms"-- Provided by publisher. Subjects: Collective behavior--History. Social psychology--History. Delusions--Social aspects--History. Fear--Social aspects--History. Mobs--Psychological aspects--History. Popular culture--Psychological aspects--History. HISTORY / Social History. PSYCHOLOGY / Social Psychology. Social Science / Sociology / General. Notes: Includes bibliographical references and index.

A practical guide to computer forensics investigations LCCN: 2014955541 Personal name: Hayes, Darren Richard, author. Main title: A practical guide to computer forensics investigations / Darren R. Hayes. Published/Produced: Indianapolis, Indiana Pearson, [2015] ©2015 Description: xxi, 502 pages: illustrations; 24 cm. ISBN: 9780789741158 (paperback) 0789741156 (paperback) LC classification: HV8079.C65 H39 2015 Contents: Machine generated contents note: Introduction -- Popular Myths about Computer Forensics -- Types of Computer Forensics Evidence Recovered -- Electronic Mail (Email) -- Images -- Video -- Websites Visited and Internet Searches -- Cellphone Forensics -- What Skills Must a Computer Forensics Investigator Possess? -- Computer Science Knowledge -- Legal Expertise -- Communication Skills -- Linguistic Abilities -- Continuous Learning -- An Appreciation for Confidentiality -- The Importance of Computer Forensics -- Job Opportunities -- A History of Computer Forensics -- 1980's: The Advent of the Personal Computer -- 1990's: The Impact of the Internet -- Training and Education -- Law Enforcement Training -- Summary -- Introduction -- Physical and

Logical Storage -- File Storage -- File Conversion and Numbering Formats -- Conversion of Binary to Decimal -- Hexadecimal Numbering -- Conversion of Hexadecimal to Decimal -- Contents note continued: Conversion of Hexadecimal to ASCII (American Standard Code for Information Interchange) -- Unicode -- Operating Systems -- The Boot Process -- Windows File Systems -- Windows Registry -- Registry Data Types -- FTK Registry Viewer -- Microsoft Windows Features -- Windows Vista -- Windows 7 -- Windows 8.1 -- Summary -- Introduction -- Hard Disk Drives -- Small Computer System Interface (SCSI) -- Integrated Drive Electronics (IDE) -- Serial ATA (SATA) -- Cloning a PATA or SATA Hard Disk -- Cloning Devices -- Removable Memory -- FireWire -- USB Flash Drives -- External Hard Drives -- MultiMedia Cards (MMCs) -- Summary -- References -- Introduction -- Lab Requirements -- American Society of Crime Laboratory Directors -- American Society of Crime Laboratory Directors/Lab Accreditation Board (ASCLD/LAB) -- ASCLD/LAB Guidelines for Forensic Laboratory Management Practices -- Scientific Working Group on Digital Evidence (SWGDE) -- Contents note continued: Private Sector Computer Forensics Laboratories -- Evidence Acquisition Laboratory -- Email Preparation Laboratory -- Inventory Control -- Web Hosting -- Computer Forensics Laboratory Requirements -- Laboratory Layout -- Laboratory Management -- Laboratory Access -- Extracting Evidence from a Device -- Using the dd Utility -- Using Global Regular Expressions Print (GREP) -- Skimmers -- Summary -- Introduction -- Working Undercover -- Generate an Identity -- Generate an Email Account -- Mask Your Identity -- Website Evidence -- Website Archives -- Website Statistics -- Background Searches on a Suspect -- Personal Information: Mailing Address, Email Address, Telephone Number, and Assets -- Personal Interests and Membership of User Groups -- Searching for Stolen Property -- Online Crime -- Identity Theft -- Credit Cards for Sale -- Electronic Medical Records -- Cyberbullying -- Social Networking -- Capturing Online Communications -- Using Screen Captures -- Contents note continued: Using Video -- Viewing Cookies -- Using Windows Registry -- Summary -- Introduction -- Obtaining Evidence from a Service Provider -- Documenting a Crime Scene -- Seizing Evidence -- Crime Scene Examinations -- Documenting the Evidence -- Completing a Chain of Custody Form -- Completing a Computer Worksheet -- Completing a Hard Disk Drive Worksheet -- Completing a Server Worksheet -- Using Tools to Document an Investigation -- CaseNotes -- FragView -- Helpful Mobile Applications (Apps) -- Network Analyzer -- System Status -- The Cop App -- Lock and Code -- Digital Forensics Reference -- Federal Rules of Civil Procedure (FRCP) -- Federal Rules of Evidence (FREvidence) -- Writing Reports -- Time Zones and Daylight Saving Time (DST) -- Creating a Comprehensive Report -- Using Expert Witnesses at Trial -- The Expert Witness -- The Goals of the Expert Witness -- Preparing an Expert Witness for Trial -- Summary -- Introduction -- Contents note continued: History and Structure of the United States Legal System -- Origins of the U.S. Legal System -- Overview of the U.S. Court System -- In the Courtroom -- Evidence Admissibility -- Constitutional Law -- First Amendment -- First Amendment and the Internet -- Fourth Amendment -- Fifth Amendment -- Sixth Amendment -- Congressional Legislation -- Rules for Evidence Admissibility -- Criminal Defense -- When Computer Forensics Goes Wrong -- Pornography in the Classroom -- Structure of the Legal System in the European Union (E.U.) -- Origins of European Law -- Structure of European Union Law -- Structure of the Legal System in Asia -- China -- India -- Summary -- Introduction -- The Tools of the Trade -- Networking Devices -- Proxy Servers -- Web Servers -- DHCP Servers -- SMTP Servers -- DNS Servers -- Routers -- IDS -- Firewalls -- Ports -- Understanding the OSI Model -- The Physical Layer -- The Data Link Layer -- The Network Layer -- The Transport Layer -- Contents note continued: The Session Layer -- The Presentation Layer -- The Application Layer -- Advanced Persistent Threats -- Cyber Kill Chain -- Indicators of Compromise (IOC) -- Investigating a Network Attack -- Summary -- Introduction --

The Cellular Network -- Base Transceiver Station -- Mobile Station -- Cellular Network Types -- SIM Card Forensics -- Types of Evidence -- Handset Specifications -- Memory and Processing -- Battery -- Other Hardware -- Mobile Operating Systems -- Android OS -- Windows Phone -- Standard Operating Procedures for Handling Handset Evidence -- National Institute of Standards and Technology -- Preparation and Containment -- Wireless Capabilities -- Documenting the Investigation -- Handset Forensics -- Cellphone Forensic Software -- Cellphone Forensics Hardware -- Logical versus Physical Examination -- Manual Cellphone Examinations -- Flasher Box -- Global Satellite Service Providers -- Satellite Communication Services -- Legal Considerations -- Contents note continued: Carrier Records -- Other Mobile Devices -- Tablets -- GPS Devices -- Summary -- Introduction -- Understanding Digital Photography -- File Systems -- Digital Photography Applications and Services -- Examining Picture Files -- Exchangeable Image File Format (EXIF) -- Evidence Admissibility -- Federal Rules of Evidence (FRE) -- Analog vs. Digital Photographs -- Case Studies -- Worldwide Manhunt -- NYPD Facial Recognition Unit -- Summary -- Introduction -- A Brief History -- Macintosh -- Mac Mini with OS X Server -- iPod -- iPhone -- iPad -- Apple Wi-Fi Devices -- Macintosh File Systems -- Forensic Examinations of a Mac -- 10Reg Info -- PMAP Info -- Epoch Time -- Recovering Deleted Files -- Journaling -- DMG File System -- PList Files -- SQLite Databases -- Macintosh Operating Systems -- Mac OS X -- Target Disk Mode -- Apple Mobile Devices -- iOS -- iOS 7 -- iOS 8 -- Security and Encryption -- iPod -- iPhone -- Contents note continued: Enterprise Deployment of iPhone and iOS Devices -- Case Studies -- Find My iPhone -- Wanted Hactevist -- Michael Jackson -- Stolen iPhone -- Drug Bust -- Summary -- Introduction -- Zacharias Moussaoui -- Background -- Digital Evidence -- Standby Counsel Objections -- Prosecution Affidavit -- Exhibits -- Email Evidence -- BTK (Bind Torture Kill) Killer -- Profile of a Killer -- Evidence -- Cyberbullying -- Federal Anti-harassment Legislation -- State Anti-harassment Legislation -- Warning Signs of Cyberbullying -- What Is Cyberbullying? --

Phoebe Prince -- Ryan Halligan -- Megan Meier -- Tyler Clementi -- Sports -- Summary. Subjects: Forensic sciences. Computer crimes--Investigation. Computer security. Evidence, Criminal. Computer crimes--Investigation. Computer security. Evidence, Criminal. Forensic sciences. Notes: Includes index.

After the American century: the ends of U.S. culture in the Middle East LCCN: 2015020790 Personal name: Edwards, Brian T., 1968- Main title: After the American century: the ends of U.S. culture in the Middle East / Brian T. Edwards. Published/Produced: New York: Columbia University Press, [2016] Description: pages cm ISBN: 9780231174008 (cloth: acid-free paper) LC classification: DS63.2.U5 E38 2016 Scope and content: "When Henry Luce announced in 1941 that we were living in thc 'American century,' he believed that the international popularity of American culture made the world favorable to U.S. interests. Now, in the digital twenty-first century, the American century has been superseded, as American movies, music, video games, and television shows are received, understood, and transformed in unexpected ways. How do we make sense of this shift? Building on a decade of fieldwork in Cairo, Casablanca, and Tehran, Brian T. Edwards maps new routes of cultural exchange that are innovative, accelerated, and full of diversions. Shaped by the digital revolution, these paths are entwined with the growing fragility of American 'soft' power. They indicate an era after the American century, in which popular American products and phenomena--such as comic books, teen romances, social-networking sites, and ways of expressing sexuality--are stripped of their associations with the United States and recast in very different forms. Arguing against those who talk about a world in which American culture is merely replicated or appropriated, Edwards focuses on creative moments of uptake, in which Arabs and Iranians make something unpredicted. He argues that these products do more than extend the reach of the original. They reflect a world in which culture endlessly circulates and gathers new meanings"--From publisher's website. Contents: After the American century: ends of circulation -- Jumping publics: Egyptian fictions of the digital age -- Argo fuck yourself: Iranian cinema and the curious logics of circulation -- Coming out in Casablanca: Shrek, sex, and the teen pic in contemporary Morocco -- Epilogue: Embracing orientalism in the homeland. Subjects: Popular culture--United States. Popular culture--Middle East. Orientalism--United States. Ethnic attitudes--Middle East. Culture diffusion--Middle East. Globalization--Social aspects--Middle East. United States--Relations--Middle East. Middle East--Relations--United States. Middle East--Civilization--21st century. Notes: Includes bibliographical references and index.

American documentary filmmaking in the digital age: depictions of war in Burns, Moore, and Morris LCCN: 2014029233 Personal name: Ricciardelli, Lucia, author. Main title: American documentary filmmaking in the digital age: depictions of war in Burns, Moore, and Morris / Lucia Ricciardelli. Published/Produced: New York; London: Routledge, 2015. ©2015 Description: xi, 162 pages: illustrations; 24 cm. ISBN: 9780415840125 (hbk) LC classification: PN1995.9.D6 R4955 2015 Contents: The realist documentary tradition in the postmodern age. Introduction: the postmodern attack on historicism, nationalism, rationalism, and realism -- Realist documentary: who, what, when, where, why, and how? -- The demise of the academic critique of realism: phenomenological approaches in documentary studies scholarship -- Audiovisual historical narration in the age of digitization. The impact of digital technology on documentary filmmaking -- From "Nanook of the north" to social-networking websites: shaping historical consciousness in the digital age -- American documentary filmmaking in the postmodern age. Ken Burns: the master of consensus in the age of dissent -- Michael Moore: the subjective/objective dichotomy -- Errol Morris: "Interrotroning" the past for the present -- Conclusion: the demise of American realist documentary filmmaking in the digital age? Subjects: Burns, Ken, 1953---Criticism and interpretation. Moore, Michael, 1954 April 23---Criticism and interpretation. Documentary films--United States--History and criticism. War films--United States--History and criticism. Historical films--United States--History and criticism. Documentary television programs--United States--History and criticism. Digital media--Influence. Morris, Errol--Criticism and interpretation. Notes: Includes bibliographical references (pages 149-158) and index. Series: Routledge advances in film studies; 35

Are social networking sites harmful? LCCN: 2014019508 Main title: Are social networking sites harmful? / Noah Berlatsky, book editor. Published/Produced: Farmington Hills, Mich.: Greenhaven Press, A part of Gale, Cengage Learning, [2015] Description: 94 pages; 24 cm. ISBN: 9780737771510 (hardcover) 9780737771527 (pbk.) LC classification: HM742 .A742 2015 Related names: Berlatsky, Noah. Subjects: Online social networks. Notes: Includes bibliographical references (pages 85 - 89) and index. Series: At issue

Asian perspectives on digital culture: emerging phenomena, enduring concepts LCCN: 2015046751 Main title: Asian perspectives on digital culture: emerging phenomena, enduring concepts / edited by Sun Sun Lim and Cheryll Ruth R. Soriano. Published/Produced: New York: Routledge, 2016. Description: pages cm. ISBN: 9781138842328 LC classification: HN655.2.I56 A77 2016 Related names: Lim, Sun Sun, 1972- editor. Soriano, Cheryll Ruth R., 1977- editor. Lim, Sun Sun, 1972- Digital giant awakens. Container of (work): Contents: A (digital) giant awakens: invigorating media studies with Asian perspectives / Sun Sun Lim and Cheryll Ruth R. Soriano -- Face and online social networking / Sun Sun Lim and Iccha Basnyat -- My letter to heaven via email: translocal piety and mediated selves in urban Marian piety in the Philippines / Manuel Victor J. Sapitula and Cheryll Ruth R. Soriano -- Exploring Confucianism in understanding face-ism in online dating sites of eastern and western cultures / Michael Prieler -- Credibility, reliability, and reciprocity: mobile communication, guanxi, and protcst mobilization in contemporary China / Jun Liu -- The local sociality and emotion of jeong in Koreans' media practices / Kyong Yoon -- Ritual and communal connection in mobile phone communication: representations of kapwa, bayanihan and people power in the Philippines / Cheryll Soriano and Sun Sun Lim -- What is corporate social responsibility (CSR) in India?: discursive constructions of CSR as sarva loka hitam in online narratives of companies in India / Ganga S. Dhanesh -- Shadow and soul: stereoscopic phantasmagoria and holographic immortalization in transnational Chinese pop / Liew Kai Khiun -- Tweets in the limelight: the contested relationship between (dis)harmony and newsworthiness / Yeon-Ok Lee -- Asian modernity and the post human future: some reflections / T.T. Sreekumar -- Re-orienting global digital cultures / Gerard Goggin. Subjects: Information society--Asia. Digital media--Social aspects--Asia. Social media--Asia. Notes: Includes bibliographical references and index. Series: Routledge advances in internationalizing media studies; 15

Business writing today: a practical guide LCCN: 2015473309 Personal name: Canavor, Natalie, 1942- author. Main title: Business writing today: a practical guide / Natalie Canavor. Edition: Second edition. Published/Produced: Los Angeles: Sage Publications, [2016] ©2016 Description: xvi, 366 pages; 23 cm ISBN: 1483358666 9781483358666 LC classification: HF5718.3 .C3655 2016 Summary: The text instructs business students how to write for the 21st century business environment in the style it demands: clearly, concisely, powerfully, and with individuality. It also addresses explicitly the digital realm of email, social networking, and social media strategies. Subjects: Business writing. Business writing. Notes: Includes bibliographical references and index. Text in English.

Cases on strategic social media utilization in the nonprofit sector LCCN: 2014050231 Main title: Cases on strategic social media utilization in the nonprofit sector / Hugo Asencio, California State University -Dominquez Hills, USA and Rui Sun, CaliforniaState University -Dominquez Hills, USA. Published/Produced: Hershey, PA: Information Science Reference, An Imprint of IGI Global, [2015] Description: lvii, 375 pages; 26 cm ISBN: 9781466681880 (hardcover: alk. paper) LC classification: HD62.6 .C375 2015 Related names: Asencio, Hugo, 1983- Sun, Rui, 1975- Summary: "This book brings together cases and chapters in order to examine both the practical and theoretical components of creating an online social community for nonprofit organizations"--Provided by publisher. Subjects: Nonprofit organizations--Management. Nonprofit organizations--Marketing. Communication in organizations. Social media. Notes: Includes bibliographical references and index. Series: Advances in social networking and online communities (ASNOC) Book Series

Claiming place: on the agency of Hmong women LCCN: 2015022458 Main title: Claiming place: on the agency of Hmong women / Chia Youyee Vang, Faith Nibbs, and Ma Vang, editors. Published/Produced: Minneapolis: University of Minnesota Press, 2016. Description: pages cm ISBN: 9780816697762 (hbk.: alk. paper) 9780816697786 (pbk.: alk. paper) LC classification: DS509.5.H66 C53 2016 Related names: Vang, Chia Youyee, 1971- editor. Nibbs, Faith G., editor. Vang, Ma, 1982- editor. Contents: Introduction: Hmong women, gender, and power / Chia Youyee Vang, Faith Nibbs, and Ma Vang -- History and knowledge production -- Rewriting hmong women in western texts / Leena N. Her -- Rechronicling histories: toward a hmong feminist perspective / Ma Vang -- Rethinking hmong women's wartime sacrifices: on gender and sexuality / Chia Youyee Vang -- Social organization and kinship -- The women of "dragon capital": marriage alliances and the rise of Vang Pao / Mai Na Lee -- Hmong women, family assets, and community cultural wealth / Julie Keown-Bomar and Ka Vang -- Divorced hmong women in Thailand: negotiating cultural space / Prasit Leepreecha -- Art and media -- Hmong women on the web: transforming power through social networking / Faith Nibbs -- Stitching hmongness into cloth: pliable identity and cultural agency / Geraldine Craig -- Reel women: diasporic cinema and female collectivity in Abel Vang's Nyab Siab zoo / Aline Lo -- Gender and sexuality -- Thinking diasporic sex: cultures, erotics, and media across Hmong worlds / Louisa Schein -- Dangerous questions: queering gender in the Hmong diaspora / Bruce Thao -- Finding queer Hmong America: gender, sexuality, culture, and happiness among Hmong LGBTQ / Kong Pha -- Afterword -- Cathy schlund-vials --

Acknowledgments -- Contributors -- Index. Subjects: Women, Hmong--Social life and customs. Women, Hmong--Social conditions. Notes: Includes bibliographical references and index.

Competitive social media marketing strategies LCCN: 2015041982 Main title: Competitive social media marketing strategies / Gordon Bowen and Wilson Ozuem, editors. Published/Produced: Hershey, PA: Business Science Reference, [2016] Description: pages cm ISBN: 9781466697768 (hardcover) LC classification: HF5415.1265 .C6544 2016 Related names: Bowen, Gordon, 1950- editor. Ozuem, Wilson, 1974- editor. Summary: "This book presents a critical examination on the integration of social networking platforms into business tactics and the challenges presented by consumers' use of these online communities, highlighting pivotal issues such as brand management, customer loyalty, and online services"-- Provided by publisher. Subjects: Internet marketing--Social aspects. Online social networks. Social media. Marketing--Social aspects. Notes: Includes bibliographical references and index.

Computer-mediated marketing strategies: social media and online brand communities LCCN: 2014034186 Main title: Computer-mediated marketing strategies: social media and online brand communities / Gordon Bowen and Wilson Ozuem, editor. Published/Produced: Hershey, PA: Business Science Reference, [2015] Description: xx, 406 pages: illustrations; 29 cm ISBN: 9781466665958 (hardcover: alk. paper) LC classification: HF5415.1265 .C655 2015 Related names: Bowen, Gordon, 1950- Ozuem, Wilson, 1974- Summary: "This book brings together marketing approaches and the application of current technology, such as social networking arenas, to show how this interaction creates a successful competitive advantage"-- Provided by publisher. Subjects: Internet marketing--Social aspects. Online social networks. Social media. Marketing--Social aspects. Notes: Includes bibliographical references and index.

Contexts of the dark side of communication: a reader LCCN:

2015040631 Main title: Contexts of the dark side of communication: a reader / edited by Eletra S. Gilchrist-Petty, Shawn D. Long. Published/Produced: New York: Peter Lang, 2016. Description: pages cm. ISBN: 9781433127502 (hardcover: alk. paper) 9781433127496 (pbk.: alk. paper) LC classification: HM1166 .C696 2016 Related names: Gilchrist-Petty, Eletra S., editor. Long, Shawn, editor. Contents: Foreword / Mark Orbe -- Acknowledgments -- Introduction: a contextual perspective of the dark side of human communication / Eletra S. Gilchrist-Petty -- Context 1: The dark side of interpersonal communication -- Unlimited: ostracism's potential to awaken us to possibility and mystery / Katie M. Striley -- "They don't get it, and I don't want to try to explain IT to them": perceptions of support messages for individuals bereaved by the death of a parent or sibling / Erin Basinger and Erin Wehrman -- On sexualization and attraction: a communication "dark" side / D. L. Stephenson -- Didn't expect you to hurt me this way: a typology of hurtful events in dating and marital relationships / Eletra S. Gilchrist-Petty -- Student-sourced verbal aggression on teaching evaluations / Felecia F. Jordan-Jackson -- Context 2: The dark side of organizational communication -- Workplace bullying: U.S. academic managers' intervention strategies / Susan L. Theiss and Lynne M. Webb -- Defamation, public persecution, and death threats: characterizing retaliation against whistle-blowers / Brian K. Richardson and Dianne Gravely -- "A cat fight in the office": the use of gossip as a means of resource control / Falon Kartch and Kathleen S. Valde -- Dispelling darkness through dialogue in discrimination crises: learning diversity lessons the hard way / Donyale R. Griffin Padgett, Melvin Gupton, and Idrissa N. Snider -- Microaggressive communication in organizational settings / Shawn D. Long, Haley Wonznyj, Marcus J. Coleman, Amin Makkawy, and Calvin Spivey -- Hazing as a tool of destructive organizational identification and loyalty / Creshema R. Murray and Kenon A. Brown -- Context 3: The dark side of health communication -- Exploring the dark side of social support among african americans with prostate cancer / Jason Thompson, Rockell Brown-Burton, and Devlon

Jackson -- "My doctor ruined my entire birthing experience": a qualitative analysis of Mexican-American women's birth struggles with health care providers / Leandra H. Hernandez -- Body politics' strategies for inclusiveness: a case study of the national breast cancer coalition / Annette Madlock Gatison -- Being detained: time, space, and intersubjectivity in long-term solitary confinement / Michael P. Vicaro -- Context 4: The dark side of computer mediated communication -- Catfished: disenfranchised grief of the never-existed / Trisha K. Hoffman and Jocelyn M. Degroot -- I heard it through the grapevine: how organizational rumors impact interpersonal relationships via traditional and CMC channels / Stacie W. Mumpower and Megan Bassick -- "I regret nothing": cyberbullying and prosocial influence in the first-person shooter game / Kimberly L. Kulovitz and Edward A. Mabry -- Past abuse, cyberstalking, and help-seeking behavior / Elaine L. Davies -- How do computer-mediated channels negatively impact existing interpersonal relationships? / Amy J. Johnson, Eryn Bostwick, and Chris Anderson -- Context 5: the dark side of blended communication contexts -- "The more things change": technologically-mediated abuse of intimate partner violence victims / Jessica J. Eckstein -- Turbulence, turmoil, and termination: the dark side of social networking sites for romantic relationships / Jesse Fox and Courtney Anderegg -- Shedding light on dark structures constraining work/family balance: a structurational approach / Jenny Dixon and Corey J. Liberman -- "The serial-killer application": email overload and the dark side of communication technology in the workplace / Ashley Barrett -- Epilogue -- Shawn d. long -- Biographies -- Index. Subjects: Interpersonal communication. Communication in organizations. Cyberbullying. Gossip in the workplace. Notes: Includes bibliographical references and index. Additional formats: Online version: Contexts of the dark side of communication New York: Peter Lang, 2016 9781453918012 (DLC) 2016006603 Series: Lifespan communication: children, families, and aging, 2166-6466; Vol. 10

Creative education, teaching, and learning: creativity, engagement, and the student experience

LCCN: 2015013206 Main title: Creative education, teaching, and learning: creativity, engagement, and the student experience / [edited by] Gayle Brewer, Senior Lecturer, University of Central Lancashire, UK, Russell Hogarth, Associate Lecturer and Honorary Fellow, University of Central Lancashire, UK. Published/Produced: New York: Palgrave Macmillan, [2015] Description: pages cm ISBN: 9781137402134 (hardback) LC classification: LB1062 .C6819 2015 Related names: Brewer, Gayle, 1978- editor of compilation. Hogarth, Russell, 1954- editor of compilation. Summary: "Educators and education policy has increasingly acknowledged the value of creativity and creative approaches to education in particular. However, despite the recommendation that teachers adopt creative teaching techniques, few guidelines for the application of creative methods are available. Therefore, sharing practice is essential for creative education to become more widespread. Creative Education, Teaching and Learning highlights a range of innovative teaching techniques successfully employed by teachers from a range of disciplines and education levels. For example, chapters highlight the use of social networking sites, virtual games, film, book groups, board games, story telling, teddy bears, archival data, comedy, and art within education. The book also considers the extent to which students can extend their traditional role through the provision of peer support or employment as Research Interns or Teaching Assistants and is intended to support teachers from all disciplines, working with students at all levels"--Provided by publisher. Contents: Machine generated contents note: -- PART I: DIGITAL TECHNOLOGY 1. Introduction to Digital Technology; Gayle Brewer 2. Twitter in the Classroom: Harnessing Social Media to Enhance Second Language Acquisition; Judith Broadbridge and Ve;ronique Charriau 3. From Cinema to the Classroom: A Critical Engagement with Madness in the Movies; The Comensus Writing Collective 4. Using Poll Everywhere to Improve the Student Experience: Increasing Confidence and Encouraging Participation; Craig Laverick 5. Video Assisted Feedback; Gayle Brewer 6. Social Media in Education and the Community;

Rory McDonald and Nicky Danino 7. Learning in Virtual Worlds; Russell Gurbutt and Dawne Gurbutt 8. Sockwashing, Service Use and Making Movies; Hannah Chamberlain 9. From the Horse's Mouth: Working as a Digital Artist on Research Projects; Steve Pool PART II: NARRATIVE 10. Introduction to Narratives; Gayle Brewer 11. Reading the World: Developing Communities through Arts and Asset-Based Education; Lynn Shorter 12. Somerstown Stories: Can Exploring a Narrative, Change a Community?; Sharon Court 13. Digital Storytelling: Media That Makes a Difference; Liz Hardwick 14. Paper, Pictures and Song: Learning Disabilities and Inclusion; Lucille Kennedy 15. Telling Tales: Creating A Space For Stories In Practitioner Education; Dawne Gurbutt and Russell Gurbutt 16. Fiction, Book Groups and Social Work Education; Amanda M.L. Taylor 17. The Power of Storytelling as a Teaching Tool; Rona Barbour PART III: ART, GAMES AND STUDENT PARTNERS 18. Introduction to Art, Games, and Student Partners; Gayle Brewer 19. Art By Design: Projects in Culture and Identity; David Knight 20. Developing a Teddy Bear Clinic: A Framework for Involving Child Service Users in a Nursing Curriculum; Linda Sanderson 21. Telling Lives: The Drama of Asylum Archives; Eric Northey 22. The Game as a Talking Tool: Using a Board Game for Creative Consultation, Engagement and Inclusion; Bev Lamey and Carol Bristow 23. What Did the Romans Ever Do For Us! The Role of Comedy in Learning, Development and Education; Jim Thomas 24. Undergraduate Research Internships: Engaging Students in the Co-Creation of Research; Helen Hewertson 25. Inspired Students, Inspiring Students: The Value of Peer Assisted Learning; Vikki Cook and Christy Evans 26. Can Arts-Based Education Help Re-Engage Excluded Learners? A Case Study of an Arts-Based Programme Aimed At Enhancing Educational Engagement; Claire Kinsella, Linda K. Kaye, and Dave Putwain 27. Learning Partnership and Teaching Partnership: Work-Related Learning in Higher Education; Rachel Cunliffe and Michael Wysocki 28. Democratic Learning for Democratic Practice: Co-Operation and Deliberation; Mick McKeown, Lynda Carey, Christine Rhodes and Fiona JonesConcluding Comments; Gayle Brewer and Russell Hogarth. Subjects: Creative thinking--Study and teaching. Creative teaching. Creative activities and seat work. Education / Educational Psychology. Education / Experimental Methods. Education / Non-Formal Education. Education / Teaching Methods and Materials / General.

Critical views on teaching and learning English around the globe: qualitative research approaches LCCN: 2015038828 Main title: Critical views on teaching and learning English around the globe: qualitative research approaches / edited by José Aldemar Álvarez V., Universidad del Valle, Colombia; Cathy Amanti, Georgia State University; Shireen Keyl, Utah State University; Erin Mackinney, Roosevelt University. Published/Produced: Charlotte, NC: Information Age Publishing, Inc., 2016. Description: pages cm. ISBN: 9781681233420 (pbk.) 9781681233437 (hardcover) LC classification: PE1128.A2 C764 2016 Related names: Alvarez V., Jose Aldemar, editor. Contents: English around the globe and translocal flows / José Aldemar Álvarez V. -- Framing learners?: identity through semiotic designs on social networking sites for language learning / Jose Aldemar Alvarez V. -- "I translate everything in my head": maintaining bilingualism in a U.S. middle school / Erin Mackinney -- The role of the EFL classroom in maintaining multilingual identities: issues and considerations in Sør-Trøndelag public schools / Anna Krulatz and Eivind Nessa Torgersen -- Language learning perspectives and experiences of Black English speaking stakeholders in the community of Flowers Bay, Roatan, Honduras / Carla McNelly -- "What! you don't speak English?": producing, reproducing, and resisting dominant English ideologies in a Mexican high school / Cathy Amanti -- "They just have the 'foreigner face'": ideologies of ethnicity, nationality, native-speakerism, and English in Taiwan / Charles Brown -- Legacies of language ideology in Alaska / Jennifer Stone -- English, Arabic, and "good teaching": how language ideologies shape l2 teachers' discourses about teaching and learning / Thomas Deus -- Learning English in the margins:

migrant worker knowledge production in Beirut's NGO spaces / Shireen Keyl -- "I cannot stay idle in this community": translocal investments in ELT for refugee resettlement / Katherine Silvester -- A pedagogy of enthusiasm: a critical view of English-language voluntourism / Cora Jakubiak. Subjects: English language--Study and teaching--Foreign countries. English language--Study and teaching--Foreign speakers. Series: Research in second language learning

Cyber poser LCCN: 2014937417 Personal name: Kesselring, Mari. Main title: Cyber poser / written by Mari Kesselring; illustrated by Mariano Epelbaum. Published/Created: North Mankato, MN: 12 Story Library, c2015. Description: 64 p.: ill.; 20 cm. ISBN: 9781632350367 (hbk.) 163235036X (hbk.) LC classification: PZ7.K4823 Cy 2015 Related names: Epelbaum, Mariano, 1975- ill. Summary: "A former classmate, Olivia Bates, reconnects with Bridget on her favorite social networking site. But Bridget's not quite sure she remembers Olivia from way back in first grade. Using some online tricks and a new app that her dad's company designed, Bridget set out to discover whether Olivia is a real friend or just a cyber poster"--P. [4] of cover. Subjects: Social media--Juvenile fiction. Social networks--Juvenile fiction. Series: Bridget gadget Kesselring, Mari. Bridget gadget.

Cybercrime risks and responses: eastern and western perspectives LCCN: 2015018338 Main title: Cybercrime risks and responses: eastern and western perspectives / [edited by] Russell G. Smith, Australian Institute of Criminology, Ray Chak-Chung Cheung, City University of Hong Kong, Hong Kong SAR, Laurie Yiu-Chung Lau, Asia Pacific Association of Technology and Society, Hong Kong SAR. Published/Produced: New York: Palgrave Macmillan, 2015. Description: pages cm. Links: Contributor biographical information http://www.loc.gov/catdir/enhancements/fy1608/2015018338-b.html Publisher description http://www.loc.gov/catdir/enhancements/fy1608/2015018338-d.html ISBN: 9781137474155 LC classification: HV6773 .C9243 2015 Related names: Smith, Russell G., editor. Cheung, Ray Chak-Chung, editor. Lau, Laurie Yiu-Chung, editor. Contents: Foreword / The Hon. Charles Mok -- Acknowledgements -- Notes on contributors -- Introduction: cybercrime risks and responses: eastern and western perspectives / Russell G Smith, Ray Chak-Chung Cheung and Laurie Yiu-Chung Lau -- Part a. understanding cybercrime through research -- Trajectories of cybercrime / Russell G. Smith -- Ethical, legal and methodological considerations in cyber-research: conducting a cyber-ethnography of www.bullying.org / Barry E. Cartwright -- That cyber-routines, that cybervictimization: profiling victimes of cybercrime / Fernando Miró -- Part b. contemporary cybercrime risks -- Organized cybercrime and national security / Peter Grabosky -- Internet fraud in hong kong: an analysis of a sample of court cases / Laurie Yiu Chung Lau -- The role of spam in cybercrime: data from the australian cybercrime pilot observatory / Mamoun Alazab and Roderic Broadhurst -- Quantifying sexually explicit language / George Weir -- Spreading the message digitally: a look into extremist organizations' use of the internet / Richard Frank, Martin Bouchard, Garth Davies and Joseph Mei -- Criminals in the cloud: crime, security threats and prevention measures / Alice Hutchings, Russell G. Smith and Lachlan James -- Industry, criminal justice and forensic responses to cybercrime -- Hong kong's experience in strengthening the security measures of retail payment services / Shu-Pui Li -- Banking security: a hong kong perspective / Tak Shing and Paul Liu -- Complicity in cyberspace: applying doctrines of accessorial liability to online groups / Gregor Urbas -- Profiling cybercrime perpetrators in china and its policy countermeasures / Darrell Chan and Dawei Wang -- Privacy and freedom online -- When privacy meets social networking sites: with special reference to facebook / Yachi Chiang -- An introduction of cyber-crowdsourcing (human flesh searching) in the greater china region / Lennon Y.C. Chang and Andy K.H. Leung -- Hacktivism and whistleblowing in the era of forced transparency? / Alana Maurushat. Subjects: Computer crimes. Internet--Law and legislation. Internet--Security measures. Notes: Includes bibliographical references.

Series: Palgrave studies in cybercrime and cybersecurity

Deadly injustice: Trayvon Martin, race, and the criminal justice system LCCN: 2015024532 Main title: Deadly injustice: Trayvon Martin, race, and the criminal justice system / edited by Devon Johnson, Patricia Y. Warren, and Amy Farrell; with a foreword by Lawrence D. Bobo. Published/Produced: New York: New York University, 2015. Description: pages cm. ISBN: 9781479873456 (hbk.: alk. paper) 9781479894291 (pbk.: alk. paper) LC classification: HV9950 .D425 2015 Related names: Johnson, Devon, editor. Contents: Acknowledgments -- Foreword: the racial double homicide of Trayvon Martin / Lawrence D. Bobo -- Introduction: race, criminal justice, and the death of Trayvon Martin / Devon Johnson, Patricia Y. Warren, and Amy Farrell -- Who is in danger? -- Profiling Trayvon: young black males, suspicion, and surveillance / Jacinta M. Gau and Kareem L. Jordan -- Presumed danger: race, bias, stigma, and perceptions of crime and criminals / Kevin M. Drakulich and Laura Siller -- Policed, punished, dehumanized: the reality for young men of color living in America / Victor M. Rios -- Threat, danger, and vulnerability: Trayvon Martin and Gwen Araujo / Toya Like, Lori Sexton, and Savannah Porter -- Where do you stand? -- Go ahead and shoot: the law might have your back: history, race, implicit bias, and justice in Florida's stand your ground law / Katheryn Russell-Brown -- The dangers of racialized perceptions and thinking by law enforcement / David A. Harris -- The acquittal of George Zimmerman: race and judges' perceptions about the accuracy of not guilty verdicts / Amy Farrell, Patricia Y. Warren, Devon Johnson, Jordyn L. Rosario, and Daniel Givelber -- Up to no good: the context of adolescent discrimination in neighborhoods / Bryan L. Sykes, Alex R. Piquero, Jason Gioviano, and Nicolas Pittman -- Which voices count? -- From Simpson to Zimmerman: examining the effects of race, class, and gender in the failed prosecution of two highly publicized, racially divisive cases / Delores Jones-Brown and Henry F. Fradella -- Divided by race: differences in the perception of injustice / Isaac Unah and Valerie Wright -- The Zimmerman verdict: media, political reaction, and public response in the age of social networking / Chenelle A. Jones and Mia Ortiz -- Read between the lines: what determines media coverage of youth homicide? / Heather M. Washington and Valerie Wright -- Afterword: reducing racialized violence and deracializing justice / Doris Marie Provine and Ruth D. Peterson -- About the contributors -- Index. Subjects: Martin, Trayvon, 1995-2012. Zimmerman, George, 1983- Discrimination in criminal justice administration--United States--History. Racial profiling in law enforcement--United States. African American men--Social conditions--21st century. United States--Race relations--History. Notes: Includes bibliographical references and index. Series: New perspectives in crime, deviance, and law

Digital solutions for contemporary democracy and government LCCN: 2015009657 Main title: Digital solutions for contemporary democracy and government / [edited by] Kelvin Joseph Bwalya, University of Botswana, Botswana; Stephen Mutula, University of Kwa Zulu Natal, South Africa. Published/Produced: Hershey, PA: Information Science Reference, an Imprint of IGI Global, 2015. Description: xxii, 426 pages: illustrations; 29 cm. ISBN: 9781466684300 (hardcover) LC classification: JF1525.A8 D554 2015 Related names: Bwalya, Kelvin Joseph, 1979- editor of compilation. Mutula, Stephen M., editor of compilation. Summary: "This book touches on several key issues and challenges surrounding the recent e-government boom and offers practical solutions from those who have been a part of implementing e-government programs internationally"--Provided by publisher. Contents: The Gamut of e-Government Research, Design and Implementation: Key Issues / Bwalya Kelvin Joseph, Stephen Mutula -- Realigning Governance: From e-Government to e-Democracy for Social and Economic Development / Bongani Ngwenya -- Revisiting Local Governments and Social Networking: Do You Speak Our Language? / Gerald A. Merwin Jr., J. Scott McDonald, Keith A. Merwin, Maureen McDonald, John R. Bennett Jr. -- Social Media Use in the Public Sector / Anteneh Ayanso, Darryl Moyers -- Increasing Voter Turn-up Using Mobile Phones as a Voting Tool / Emmanuel Eilu -- Smart Participaton: Enhancing Citizens' Participation via

Recommender Systems / Luis Terán -- Citizens and E-Government: Perceptions in Nigeria / Gbolahan Olasina -- Freedom of Information as a Catalyst for Responsiveness in the e-Government environment: A Closer look at Botswana / Bwalya Kelvin Joseph, Sebina Mazebe Peter, Saul C. Zulu -- E-Government Initiative: Key Functions of Electronic Records Management Requirements in the Malaysian Judiciary / Nurussobah Hussin -- Knowledge Management and Electronic Records Management in the Realm of e-Government: Case of Botswana / Kelvin Joseph Bwalya, Saul F.C. Zulu, Peter Mazebe Sebina -- E-Government Transparency and Citizen Engagement Increasing Accountability / Deborah S. Carstens, Stephen Kies and Randy Stockman -- Understanding Methodology Aspects for Measuring Multi-Dimensional e-Government: Pointers for Research and Practice / Bwalya Kelvin Joseph -- A conceptual model for the measurement of e-Government 2.0 adoption by developing countries / Yfantis Vasileios, Abel Usoro, Tseles Dimitrios -- Value Assessment in E-Government and M-Government / Shu Wen Lee, Pek Hia Lai -- Sustainable cloud computing frameworks for e-Government: best practices in Italian municipalities / Sabrina Leone, Giovanni Biancofiore -- Incentives for Inclusive e-Government: The Implementation of Contact Centers in Swedish Municipalities / Irene Bernhard -- Research and experiences in implementing e-Government endeavors in emerging countries: A literature review / Manuel Pedro Rodríguez Bolívar, Laura Alcaide Muñoz, Antonio M. López Hernández -- The ICT and the Legislation on Transparency and Freedom of Information: The Impact on Local Government Practices in the Dominican Republic / Alejandro Sáez-Martín, Arturo Haro-de-Rosario, Manuela García-Tabuyo, María Del Carmen Caba-Pérez. Subjects: Internet in public administration--Cross-cultural studies. Democracy--Cross-cultural studies. Notes: Includes bibliographical references (page 366-415) and index. Series: Advances in Electronic Government, Digital Divide, and Regional Development (AEGDDRD) Book Series.

Discourse and digital practices: doing discourse analysis in the digital age LCCN: 2014032968 Main title: Discourse and digital practices: doing discourse analysis in the digital age / Edited by Rodney H Jones, Alice Chik and Christoph A. Hafner. Published/Produced: London; New York: Routledge, Taylor and Francis Group, 2015. Description: xi, 250 pages: illustrations; 24 cm ISBN: 9781138022324 (hbk) 9781138022331 (pbk) LC classification: P302.865 .D57 2015 Related names: Jones, Rodney H., editor. Chik, Alice, editor. Hafner, Christoph A., editor. Summary: "Discourse and Digital Practices shows how tools from discourse analysis can be used to help us understand new communication practices associated with digital media, from video gaming and social networking to apps and photo sharing. This cutting-edge book:draws together fourteen eminent scholars in the field including James Paul Gee, David Barton, Ilana Snyder, Phil Benson, Victoria Carrington, Guy Merchant, Camilla Vasquez, Neil Selwyn and Rodney Jonesaddresses the central question: "How does discourse analysis enable us to understand digital practices?"demonstrates how digital practices and the associated new technologies challenge discourse analysts to adapt traditional analytic tools and formulate new theories and methodologiesanalyses a different type of digital media in each chapterexamines digital practices from a wide variety of approaches including textual analysis, conversation analysis, interactional sociolinguistics, multimodal discourse analysis, object ethnography, geosemiotics, and critical discourse analysis. Discourse and Digital Practices will be of interest to advanced students studying courses on digital literacies or language and digital practices"-- Provided by publisher. "Discourse and Digital Practices shows how tools from discourse analysis can be used to help us understand new communication practices associated with digital media, from video gaming and social networking to apps and photo sharing. Fourteen eminent scholars including James Paul Gee and Camilla Vasquez address the challenges of working with digital texts and interactions, and illustrate how different approaches to discourse analysis can be adapted in the face of these new digital practices. This cutting-edge book will be of interest to advanced students studying courses on digital literacies or language and digital practices"-- Provided by publisher. Subjects: Discourse analysis--Data processing. Technological innovations. Digital. Social media. Language Arts and Disciplines / General. Language Arts and Disciplines / Linguistics / General. Notes: Includes bibliographical references and index.

Educational psychology and the internet LCCN: 2015032422 Personal name: Glassman, Michael (Michael J.) author. Main title: Educational psychology and the internet / Michael Glassman. Published/Produced: New York, NY: Cambridge University Press, 2016. Description: pages cm Links: Cover image http://assets.cambridge.org/97811070/95441/cover/9781107095441.jpg ISBN: 9781107095441 (hardback) 9781107479302 (paperback) LC classification: LB1051 .G555 2016 Summary: "The first comprehensive, research-based textbook on Internet-infused education, Educational Psychology and the Internet offers students an accessible guide to important issues in the field. Michael Glassman begins with an overview of the history that traces the evolution of the Internet and its significance for education. He outlines the current state of research, clearly defining terms that students will need to discuss larger concepts, such as hypertext and cyberspace. The second part of the book explores the practical applications of this research, which range from the individual-oriented to the generalized, including massive open online courses (MOOCs), open educational resources, and augmented reality. Key issues that affect teachers and students today, such as Net Neutrality and Creative Commons and Open Source licenses, are explained in straightforward terms, and often-overlooked differences - for example, between course management systems and learning management systems, and between blogs, social networking sites, and short messaging systems - are highlighted"-- Provided by publisher. Subjects: Educational psychology. Internet in education. Computer-assisted instruction. Educational technology. Psychology / Applied Psychology. Notes: Includes bibliographical references and index.

Facebook marketing for dummies LCCN: 2014948540 Personal name: Haydon, John, author. Main title: Facebook marketing for dummies / by John Haydon. Edition: 5th edition. Published/Produced: Hoboken, NJ: For Dummies, [2015]. ©2015 Description: xii, 320 pages: illustrations, black and white; 24 cm Links: Contributor biographical information http://www.loc.gov/catdir/enhancements/fy1513/2014948540-b.html Table of contents only http://www.loc.gov/catdir/enhancements/fy1513/2014948540-t.html Publisher description http://www.loc.gov/catdir/enhancements/fy1606/2014948540-d.html ISBN: 1118951328 9781118951323 LC classification: HF5415.1265 .H388 2015 Summary: If you're trying to plan or refine a Facebook marketing campaign, this book will help you grasp the psychology of the Facebook user, build your fan basc, and integrate Facebook marketing with your other marketing strategies. Hayden shows you how to build a social networking presence, promote your page, and target specific audiences. Contents: Getting started with Facebook marketing -- Building your Facebook presence -- Engaging with your customers and prospects on Facebook -- Marketing beyond the Facebook page -- The part of tens. Subjects: Facebook (Electronic resource) Facebook (Electronic resource) Internet advertising. Online social networks. Viral marketing. Internet advertising. Online social networks. Viral marketing. Notes: Includes index. Series: For dummies. -- For dummies.

Fire tablets for dummies LCCN: 2014951012 Personal name: Muir, Nancy, 1954- author. Main title: Fire tablets for dummies / by Nancy Muir. Published/Produced: Hoboken, New Jersey: John Wiley and Sons, [2015] ©2015 Description: x, 276 pages: color illustrations; 24 cm. Links: Contributor biographical information http://www.loc.gov/catdir/enhancements/fy1513/2014951012-b.html Table of contents only http://www.loc.gov/catdir/cnhancements/fy1513/2014951012-t.html Publisher description http://www.loc.gov/catdir/enhancements/fy1606/2014951012-d.html ISBN: 9781119008255 1119008255 LC classification: QA76.8.K56 M845 2015 Summary: If you're the proud owner of a Fire tablet, this guide helps you make the most of its capabilities. Muir will be with you as you take the Fire tablet out of the box, find out how to use the touchscreen and settings, buy and play music and movies, and get connected with social networking sites and your email account. Contents: Getting started with Fire tablets. Getting an overview of Fire tablets; Firing up your Fire tablet; Exploring Fire tablet quick settings; Setting up your Fire; Fire tablets and your family -- Taking the leap online. Going shopping; Going online -- Having fun and getting productive. Taking advantage of the ereader extraordinaire; Playing music; Playing with video and cameras; Going social; Getting productive -- The part of tens. Ten great tips for your tablet; Ten (or so) great Fire apps. Subjects: Kindle Fire (Computer) Tablet computers. Kindle Fire (Computer) Tablet computers. Notes: Includes index. Series: For dummies -- For dummies.

Flat world navigation: collaboration and networking in the global digital economy LCCN: 2015021104 Personal name: McDonald, Kim Chandler, author. Main title: Flat world navigation: collaboration and networking in the global digital economy / Kim Chandler McDonald. Published/Produced: London; Philadelphia: Kogan Page, 2015. Description: xxx, 256 pages: illustrations; 24 cm ISBN: 9780749473938 (paperback) LC classification: HD69.S8 M32995 2015 Portion of title: Collaboration and networking in the global digital economy Summary: "The future of a company lies in its ability to make authentic connections in a global, "flattened world" economy, spanning departments, cultures, and countries. Flat World Navigation explains how network-building, collaboration, and authentic communication are essential to navigating this new business landscape. Exploring the essential skills, tools, techniques, and technologies involved in making and maintaining business relationships, author Kim Chandler McDonald integrates practical tips and advice with interviews with leading figures who are successful flat world navigators"-- Provided by publisher. "Flat World Navigation introduces the new future of work in the 'flattened world' of the new digital attention-based economy, where real connections can be made in seconds across departments, businesses, cultures and countries. Combining the best elements of networking, social media outreach and collaborative techniques, flat world navigation is an essential capability to build and maintain relationships between colleagues, customers and partners. Employees who can transform themselves into flat world navigators, experts in mediating these powerful relationships and bringing the customer into the conversation, will mean the difference between success and failure in business. Flat World Navigation includes exclusive insights and interviews with international business leaders who successfully use flat world navigation skills, such as the Emmy-winning former NBC and Wall Street Journal reporter Kare Anderson, Sandy Carter at IBM, Gordon Feller at CISCO Systems, Aria Finger at DoSomething.org, Louise Guido at ChangeCorp, Jeffrey A. Finkle at the International Economic Development Council and Carolyn Lawrence, CEO of Women of Influence. This book is grounded in real-world experience with insights and advice to build your skills base and empower the next generation of business people. Additionally, it is of great use to business owners and managers looking to effectively leverage the skills of these flat world navigators, whose critical role brings attention to ideas, products and services and, as such, must be part of a successful business strategy"-- Provided by publisher. Contents: Machine generated contents note: About the author -- Biographies -- Thanks -- Abbreviations and commonly used phrasesIntroduction -- Saskia Bruysten, Megan Kachur, Cameron Tuesley and Adrian Westaway -- DACE details -- Definitions -- Issues addressed -- Introductions -- In conclusion01 The tools and techniques of successful flat world navigation in practice -- Miki Agrawal, Sandy Carter, Mie Kajikawa, Katharina Kummer Peiry, Alan Rosenblatt, Sylvia RJ Scott, Bettina von Stamm and Erik Starck -- What are you navigating towards? -- Planning for your journey through the flat world -- Tools, techniques and tips -- In conclusion02 The foundations of the DACE (Digital, Attention and Collaboration Economies) -- Marc Dufraisse, Edmund Komar, Amelia Loye, Saundra Pelletier and Wendy Simpson -- Keeping up is easier than catching up -- Size doesn't matter in the global digital, attention and collaboration economies (DACE) -- The Majority World will have a major impact -- Use your tools widely and wisely -- In conclusion03 Demand and opportunity through business collaboration -- Mary Adams, Jeanine Esposito, David W Gray and Deanne Weir -- Definitions -- Why collaborate? -- Connect and communicate -- Added advantages -- Collaborative characteristics -- In conclusion04 Profiting from Your Return on Involvement (ROI) in the Attention Economy -- Morra Aarons-Mele, Kare Anderson, Karen Barnes, Lorraine Carrington, Gordon Feller, Sue Matthews and Blair Palese -- 'I don't want to get involved' is not an option -- Everyone needs to navigate ROI in the flat world -- Engage with your Endusers on their terms -- Flat World Navigators, the masters of real-world ROI -- In conclusion05 New business models built by flat world navigation -- Aria Finger, Donnie Maclurcan, Joan Michelson, Servane Mouazan and Clara Gaggero Westaway -- Nothing floats on digital denial -- Re-running present conventions is not the path to future successes -- Flat world navigation - building bigger, broader, better business -- In conclusion06 Changing markets and competitive advantages accessed through flat world navigation -- Miguel Reynolds Brandão, Chris Gabriel, Patricia Greene, Carolyn Hardy and Karima Mariama-Arthur -- The changing economic stage -- The 'undiscovered country' - the SME stalwarts -- The new gameplay of success - flattening your DACE -- The Flat World Navigator effect - transforming operations into opportunities -- In conclusion07 Navigating the direction of the DACE -- Peter Church, Jeff Finkle, Peter Hewkin, Philo Holland, Giorgio Prister, Robert Joachim Schiff and Liora Shechter -- The competition is global in scope for highly skilled IT/DACE resources -- Lengthening the odds when addressing the skills shortage in the DACE -- Finding new formulas to foster growth -- Mass unemployment is a possibility for those not able to gain access to, or collaborate effectively in, the DACE -- Governments leading the way in redefining service and services in the DACE -- In conclusion08 Is flat world navigation the game changer for women in the work force? -- Shala Burroughs, Anna Fa;lth, Natalie Goldman, Louise

Guido and Carolyn Lawrence -- Owning your position -- The state of play - winning the numbers game -- The skills already within reach -- In conclusionSummary: A collaborative conclusion -- Christopher Altman, Francesco CalabreseReferences -- Index. Subjects: Strategic alliances (Business) Business networks. Information technology--Management. Communication in management. Business and Economics / Management. Business and Economics / Leadership. Business and Economics / Workplace Culture. Computers / Web / Social Networking. Notes: Includes bibliographical references and index.

Genealogy online LCCN: 2014027050 Personal name: Crowe, Elizabeth Powell. Main title: Genealogy online / Elizabeth Powell Crowe. Edition: Tenth edition. Published/Produced: New York: McGraw-Hill Education, [2015] Description: xxix, 386 pages: illustrations; 24 cm ISBN: 9780071841108 (paperback) LC classification: CS21 .C67 2015 Scope and content: "In this edition, the author assumes you know most Internet technologies and programs, and that you want to know how to use them to do your genealogy. The potential for finding clues, data, and other researchers looking for your same family names has increased exponentially in the last decade. Since 2000, push technology, streaming video, blogs, podcasts, social networking, and indexed document scans have radically changed what can be found on the Internet and how we search for it. If you feel you need formal instruction in researching family history, online courses, from basic self-paced text to college-level instruction, can now make that happen. In short, online genealogy has never been better, and it's a good time to try your hand at it!"-- Provided by publisher. Contents: Introduction -- Part I. Basics -- 1. Beginning a Genealogy Project -- 2. Software You'll Need -- 3. Ethics. Privacy and Law in Genealogy -- Part II. Using the Internet for Genealogy -- 4. Genealogy Education -- 5. Revving Up Search Engines -- 6. Talk to Me: Twittrer, Skype, IM and Google -- 7. Fun with Email: Mail Lists, Newsletters and More -- 8. Social Networking -- 9. Blogging Your Genealogy: Sites, Software and More -- 10. DNA Genealogy -- Part III. The Nitty Gritty: Places to Find Names, Dates and Places

-- 11. Vital Records and Historical Documents -- The Church of Jesus Christ of Latter-Day Saints: FamilySearch.org -- 13. Ellis Island Online: The American Family Immigration History Center -- 14. Online Library Card Catalogs and Services -- 15. International Genealogy Resources -- 16. Ethnic Genealogy Resources -- 17. The National Genealogical Society -- 18. The Ancestry.com and RootsWeb -- 19. Genealogical Publishing Housees and Their Sites -- 20. A Potpourri of Genealogy -- Part IV. Appendixes -- A. Genealogical Standards from the National Genealogical Society -- B. How to find a Professional Genealogist -- Glossary. Subjects: Genealogy--Data processing. Genealogy--Computer network resources--Handbooks, manuals, etc. Internet--Handbooks, manuals, etc. Reference / Genealogy and Heraldry. Notes: Includes bibliographical references and index.

Globalised minds, roots in the city: urban upper-middle classes in Europe LCCN: 2014031689 Personal name: Andreotti, Alberta. Main title: Globalised minds, roots in the city: urban upper-middle classes in Europe / Alberta Andreotti, Patrick Le Gales and Francisco Javier Moreno-Fuentes. Published/Produced: Chichester, West Sussex, UK; Hoboken, NJ: John Wiley and Sons, Inc., 2015. Description: pages cm Links: Cover image http://catalogimages.wiley.com/images/db/jimages/9781444334845.jpg ISBN: 9781444334845 (hardback) 9781444334852 (paper) LC classification: HN380.Z9 S6135 2015 Related names: Le Galès, Patrick. Moreno Fuentes, Francisco Javier. Summary: "Globalised Minds, Roots in the City utilises empirical evidence from four European cities to explore the role of urban upper middle classes in the transformations experienced by contemporary European societies. Presents new empirical evidence collected through an original comparative research about professionals and managers in four European cities in three countries Features an innovative combination of approaches, methods, and techniques in its analyses of European post-national societies Reveals how segments of Europe's urban population are adopting "exit" or "partial exit" strategies in respect to the nation state Utilises approaches from classic urban sociology, globalization and mobility studies, and spatial class analysis Includes in depth interviews, social networking techniques, and classic questions of political representation and values "-- Provided by publisher. "Presents new empirical evidence collected through an original comparative research about professionals and managers in four European cities in three countries"-- Provided by publisher. Subjects: Upper class--Europe. Middle class--Europe. Professional employees--Europe. Executives--Europe. Political Science / Globalization. Notes: Includes bibliographical references and index. Additional formats: Online version: Andreotti, Alberta. Globalised minds, roots in the city Chichester, West Sussex, UK; Hoboken, NJ: John Wiley and Sons, Inc., 2015 9781118330777 (DLC) 2014033902 Series: Studies in urban and social changc

Handbook of research on digital media and creative technologies LCCN: 2015003296 Main title: Handbook of research on digital media and creative technologies / Dew Harrison, editor. Published/Produced: Hershey: Information Science Reference, 2015. Description: pages cm ISBN: 9781466682054 (hardcover) LC classification: HM851 .H3483 2015 Related names: Harrison, Dew, 1952- editor. Summary: "This book considers the latest research in education, communication, and creative social expression using digital technologies by exploring advances in art and culture across national and sociological borders"-- Provided by publisher. Contents: Preface -- Acknowledgment -- Artistic practice and theory -- Exploring liminal practices in art, technology and science / Dr Denise Doyle, University of Wolverhampton, UK -- Be[ing] you: in[bodi]mental a real-time body swapping video performance / Dr Lorna Moore, Independent artist-researcher, UK -- Big data - small world: materializing digital information for discourse and cognition / Prof Ian Gwilt, Sheffield-Hallam University, UK -- Digitizing the physical; physicalizing the digital / Prof Joan Truckenbrod, School of the Art Institute of Chicago, US -- The virtual, alternate spaces and the affects upon artwork / Dr Alistair Payne, Glasgow School of Art, UK -- Sound image and resonant animated space: beyond the sonic veil / Ross Winning, University of Wolverhampton,

UK -- Para-formalistic film and the digital avant garde / Ian P. Stone, University of Wolverhampton, UK -- "Emerging forth into the light": creating a digital book of the dead / Dr Maggie Parker, Teesside University, UK -- The earth sciences and creative practice: entering the anthropocene / Prof Suzette Worden, Independent, Australia -- Transposing, transforming and transcending tradition in creative digital media / Dr Phillip Prager, University of Copenhagen, Denmark, Dr Maureen Thomas, Oxford University, UK, Marianne Selsjord -- 'Virtual reality' reconsidered / Garfield Benjamin, University of Wolverhampton, UK -- Designing pervasive virtual worlds / Dr Everardo Reyes-Garcia, University of Paris 13, France -- Education -- Making it for the screen: creating digital media literacy / Paul Chilsen, Carthage College and the Rosebud Institute, US -- Using virtual environments to achieve learner outcomes in interprofessional healthcare education / Dr Michelle Aebersold, University of Michigan, US, Dr Dana Tschannen, University of Michigan, US -- Digital media in the classroom: emergent perspectives for 21st century learners / Prof Kathy Sanford, University of Victoria, Canada, Elizabeth Merkel, University of Victoria, Canada, Dr Timothy F. Hopper, University of Victoria, Canada -- Using spatial reasoning for creative design: merging engineering and mathematics practices / Dr. D. Craig Schroeder, Fayette County Public Schools, US, Dr Carl W. Lee, University of Kentucky, US, Dr Margaret J. Mohr-Schroeder, University of Kentucky, US -- The empirical study about internet use and computer games among croatian children / Sanja Tatalovic Vorkapic, University of Rijeka, Croatia, Elma Polanec, University of Rijeka, Croatia -- Communication and innovation -- Tools for the process: technology to support creativity and innovation / Dr Joshua Fairchild, Creighton University, US, Rachel Heinen, Creighton University, US, Salvatore Leone, Creighton University, US, Lily Cushenbery, Stony Brook University, US, Samuel Hunter, Pennsylvania State University, US -- Digital parrhesia 2.0: moving beyond deceptive communications strategies in the digital world / François Allard-Huver, Sorbonne University, France,

Nicholas Gilewicz, University of Pennsylvania, US -- Bold ideas for creative social networking / Prof Wei Zhang, Peking University, China -- Smart CCTV and the management of urban space / Jung Hoon Han, University of New South Wales, Australia, Dr Scott Hawken, University of New South Wales, Australia, Angelique Williams, University of New South Wales, Australia -- The role of state in crafting smart cities in the Gulf Region: Lusail City/Qatar and Masdar City/UAE / Dr Evren Tok, Hamad Bin Khalifa University, Qatar, Dr Hanaa Elghaish, Hamad Bin Khalifa University, Qatar, Maha Al Merekhi, Hamad Bin Khalifa University, Qatar, Fatema Mohamed Ali, Hamad Bin Khalifa University, Qatar -- Compilation of references -- About the contributors -- Index. Subjects: Information technology--Social aspects. Social media Research. Art and the Internet. Notes: Includes bibliographical references and index.

Handbook of research on educational technology integration and active learning LCCN: 2015008263 Main title: Handbook of research on educational technology integration and active learning / [edited by] Jared Keengwe, University of North Dakota, USA. Published/Produced: Hershey, PA: Information Science Reference, 2015. Description: xxiv, 470 pages: illustrations; 29 cm ISBN: 9781466683631 (hardcover) LC classification: LB1028.3 .H3554 2015 Related names: Keengwe, Jared, 1973- editor of compilation. Summary: "This book explores the need for new professional development opportunities for teachers and educators as they utilize emerging technologies to enhance the learning experience, highlighting the advancements of ubiquitous computing, authentic learning, and student-centered instruction"-- Provided by publisher. Contents: Enhanced student engagement through active learning and emerging technologies / Victoria M. Cardullo, Nance S. Wilson; and Vassiliki (Vicky) I. Zygouris-Coe -- Educational robotics as a learning tool for promoting rich environments for active learning (REALs) / Amy Eguchi -- Mobile devices in higher education classrooms: challenges and opportunities / Jennifer (Jenny) L. Penland -- A call for teacher preparation programs to model technology integration into the instructional process / Judi Simmons Estes -- A model for meaningful e-learning at Canadian universities / Lorraine Carter and Vince Salyers -- Technology-enhanced pedagogical models to learn critical citizenship at a South African university / Patient Rambe and Edem Agbobli -- Active learning strategies in technology integrated K-12 classrooms / Esther Ntuli -- Teaching history of mathematics through digital stories: a technology integration model / Lutfi Incikabi -- Active learning, deliberate practice, and educational technology in professional education: practice and implications / Heeyoung Han, Seung Hyun Han, Doo Hun Lim, and Seung Won Yoon -- Active learning strategies in enhancing learning among college students / Caroline C. Chemosit, John K. Rugutt, Viviline Ngeno, and Dorothy Soi -- Educational technology assessment: a model for analyzing online psychometric tests for course evaluations / James Edward Osler II and Mahmud A. Mansaray -- ELearning for persons with visual disabilities: case of low vision / Ruth N. Wambua, (Mutua) and Robert Oboko -- IPAD: integrating positive, active, digital tools and behaviors in preservice teacher education courses / Ursula Thomas -- Towards a theory of formative assessment in online higher education / Joyce W. Gikandi -- Challenges and opportunities for e-learning in education: a case study / Ayoub C Kafyulilo -- Opportunities and challenges in implementing distance learning and e-learning: a case study / Jennifer Kasanda Sesabo, Rashid Mfaume, and Dominik T. Msabila -- Active learning with technology tools in the blended/hybrid classes / Catherine Gakii Murungi and Rhoda K. Gitonga -- Appraisal theory: opportunities for social networking sites' complementation of writing centres / Patient Rambe -- Perceptions of competencies developed in an active learning course featuring the design of web-based instruction on mathematics / Hatice Sancar Tokmai and Lufti Incikabi -- Deployment and adoption strategy of cloud computing for blended learning in higher education Institutions in sub-Saharan Africa / Joel S. Mtebe and Mussa M. Kissaka. Subjects: Educational technology. Education--Effect of technological innovations on. Active learning. Notes: Includes bibliographical references and index. Series: Advances in Educational Technologies and Instructional Design (AETID) Book Series

Handbook of research on interactive information quality in expanding social network communications LCCN: 2014040317 Main title: Handbook of research on interactive information quality in expanding social network communications / Francisco V. Cipolla-Ficarra, Latin Association of Human-Computer Interaction, Spain and International Association of Interactive Communication, Italy. Published/Produced: Hershey: Information Science Reference, An Imprint of IGI Global, [2015] Description: xxxviii, 449 pages; 29 cm ISBN: 9781466673779 (hardcover) LC classification: HM742 .I55 2015 Related names: Cipolla-Ficarra, Francisco V. (Francisco Vicente), 1963- editor. Summary: "This book examines the strategic elements involved in ICT training within the context of online networks, combining scientific, theoretical, and practical perspectives on the importance of communicability in such networks"-- Provided by publisher. Subjects: Online social networks. Interactive multimedia. Information science. Notes: Includes bibliographical references (pages 383-439) and index. Series: A volume in the advances in social networking and online communities (ASNOC) book series

Handbook of research on maximizing cognitive learning through knowledge visualization LCCN: 2015000388 Main title: Handbook of research on maximizing cognitive learning through knowledge visualization / Anna Ursyn, [editor] Published/Produced: Hershey, PA: Information Science Reference, 2015. Description: xxv, 572 pages; 29 cm ISBN: 9781466681422 (hardcover) LC classification: LB1062 .H25 2015 Related names: Ursyn, Anna, 1955- editor of compilation, author. Summary: "This book focuses on the use of visualization technologies to assist in the process of better comprehending scientific concepts, data, and applications by highlighting the utilization of visual power and the roles of sensory perceptions, computer graphics, animation, and digital storytelling"-- Provided by publisher. Contents: Cognitive learning with electronic media and social networking / Anna

Ursyn -- Sensory extension as a tool for cognitive learning / Michael Eisenberg and Ann Eisenberg -- Simultaneous perception of parallel streams of visual data / Marcin Brzezicki -- Visualisation and mathematical thinking / Hervé Lehning -- Duality of natural and technological explanations / Anna Ursyn -- Random processes and visual perception: stochastic art / Jean Constant -- Science of the archives: visual learning about plants / Maura Flannery -- Visualization by coding: drawing simple shapes and forms in various programming languages / Anna Ursyn and Mehrgan Mostowfi -- Building a computer / Andrew Liccardo and Cameron Grimes -- Visual plan construct language (VPCL): visual system and method for teaching and learning programming and problem solving / Alireza Ebrahimi -- Connecting the dots: art, culture, science, and technology / Jing Zhou -- Re-visualising Giotto's 14th-century Assisi fresco: exorcism of the demons at Arezzo / Theodor G. Wyeld -- Visualization in learning: perception, aesthetics and pragmatism / Veslava Osinska, Grzegorz Osinski, and Anna Beata Kwiatkowska -- Analyzing Disney's early exhibits as installation artwork / Jonathan Lillie and Michelle Jones-Lillie -- Digitally mediated art inspired by scientific research: a personal journey / John Antoine Labadie -- On creativity of Asian and American Asian students / Joohyun Pyune -- AiryLight: ambient environmental data / Annelie Berner -- What does learning look like?: data visualization of art teaching and learning / Pamela G. Taylor -- Bringing the arts as data to visualize how knowledge works / Lihua Xu, Read Diket, and Thomas Brewer. Subjects: Cognitive learning. Information visualization. Notes: Includes bibliographical references and index. Series: Advances in knowledge acquisition, transfer, and management (AKATM) book series

Health policy and politics: a nurse's guide LCCN: 2014024733 Uniform title: Health policy and politics (Milstead) Main title: Health policy and politics: a nurse's guide / edited by Jeri A. Milstead, PhD, RN, NEA-BC, FAAN, Senior Nurse Consultant, Dublin, Ohio, Professor and Dean Emerita, University of Toledo (Ohio) College of Nursing. Edition: Fifth edition.

Published/Produced: Burlington, MA: Jones and Bartlett Learning, [2016] Description: xvi, 338 pages: illustrations; 24 cm ISBN: 9781284048865 (hbk.) 1284048861 (hbk.) LC classification: RT86.5 .M54 2016 Related names: Milstead, Jeri A., editor. Contents: Advanced practice nurses and public policy, naturally -- Agenda setting -- Government response: legislation -- Government regulation: parallel and powerful -- Policy design -- Policy implementation -- Program evaluation -- Impact of the internet and social networking on healthcare policy -- Interprofessional practice, education, research -- Applied healthcare economics and finance for the noneconomics major -- Global connections. Subjects: Legislation, Nursing--United States. Health Policy--United States. Politics--United States. Notes: Includes bibliographical references and index.

How do I use social networking? LCCN: 2015007456 Personal name: Yearling, Tricia. Main title: How do I use social networking? / Tricia Yearling. Published/Produced: New York, NY: Enslow Publishing, 2016. Description: 32 pages: illustrations, color; 23 cm. ISBN: 9780766068582 LC classification: HM742 .Y43 2016 Summary: "Discusses how kids can safely use social networking"-- Provided by publisher. Contents: Words to know -- Connecting online -- Learning your way around -- Follow the rules -- Online bullies -- Signing off -- Learn more. Subjects: Online social networks--Juvenile literature. Online etiquette--Juvenile literature. Notes: Includes bibliographical references (page 30) and index. 8-up. Grade 4 to 6. Series: Online smarts

How to do just about anything on the Internet LCCN: 2015004934 Main title: How to do just about anything on the Internet / by the editors of Reader's Digest. Edition: 1st [edition]. Published/Produced: New York: Readers Digest Association, 2015. Description: pages cm ISBN: 9781621452652 (alk. paper) LC classification: TK5105.875.I57 H68 2015 Related names: Reader's Digest Association Contents: Getting set up -- Browsing the internet -- Keep in touch -- Social networking -- News and knowledge -- The practical web -- Consuming media online -- Buying and selling. Subjects:

Internet--Miscellanea. World Wide Web--Miscellanea. Notes: Includes index.

Human behavior, psychology, and social interaction in the digital era LCCN: 2015009643 Main title: Human behavior, psychology, and social interaction in the digital era / Anabela Mesquita, Chia-Wen Tsai. Published/Produced: Hershey, PA: Information Science Reference, [2015] Description: xxiii, 372 pages; 29 cm ISBN: 9781466684508 (hardcover) LC classification: QA76.9.H85 H843 2015 Related names: Sarmento, Anabela. Tsai, Chia-Wen, 1977- Summary: "This book combines best practices and empirical research on social networking and other related technologies, emphasizing creative and innovative implementation across various disciplines"--Provided by publisher. Subjects: Human-computer interaction. Cognitive science. Online social networks. Technology--Social aspects. Notes: Includes bibliographical references and index. Series: Advances in human and social aspects of technology book series

Identity, intertextuality, and performance in early modern song culture LCCN: 2015050258 Main title: Identity, intertextuality, and performance in early modern song culture / edited by Dieuwke van der Poel, Louis Peter Grijp and Wim van Anrooij. Published/Produced: Leiden; Boston: Brill, [2016] Description: pages cm ISBN: 9789004314979 (hardback: alk. paper) LC classification: ML1420 .I34 2016 Related names: Poel, D. E. van der. Grijp, Louis Peter. Anrooij, W. van. Contents: Local and religious identity in Swedish popular hymn singing during the seventeenth and eighteenth centuries / Ingrid Akesson -- Performing pietism in the peatlands: songs in the manuscript miscellany of a village schoolmaster in the Dutch republic between 1750 and 1800 / Nelleke Moser -- Guilielmus Bolognino's Den gheestelijcken leeuwercker: the collected songs of a counter-reformation champion / Hubert Meeus and Tine de Koninck -- Songs and identities: handwritten secular songbooks in German-speaking areas of the fifteenth and sixteenth centuries / Franz-Josef Holznagel -- 'Social networking is in our DNA': women's alba amicorum as places to build and affirm group identities / Sophie

Reinders -- The many shades of love: possessors and inscribers of sixteenth-century women's alba / Clara Strijbosch -- Exploring love's options: song and youth culture in the sixteenth century Netherlands / Dieuwke van der Poel -- Oppositional political identity in the song culture of the Vormarz and the 1848 revolution in Germany / David Robb -- The perils of performance: from political songs to national airs in romantic-era Wales (1790-1820) / Mary-Ann Constantine -- Folksongs, conflicts and social protest in early modern France / Eva Guillorel -- "Fortune my foe": the circulation of an English super-tune / Christopher Marsh -- Samuel Pepys and the making of ballad publics / Patricia Fumerton -- Slave orchestras and rainbow balls: colonial culture and creolisation at the Cape of Good Hope, 1750-1838 / Anne Marieke van der Wal. Subjects: Vocal music -Europe--16th century--History and criticism. Vocal music--Europe--17th century--History and criticism. Vocal music--Europe--18th century--History and criticism. Vocal music--Europe--19th century--History and criticism. Music--Social aspects--Europe--History--16th century. Music--Social aspects--Europe--History--17th century. Music--Social aspects--Europe--History--18th century. Music--Social aspects--Europe--History--19th century. Autograph albums--Netherlands--History--16th century. Notes: Includes bibliographical references and index. Additional formats: Online version: Identity, intertextuality, and performance in early modern song culture Leiden; Boston: Brill, [2016] 9789004314986 (DLC) 2016000606 Series: Intersections, 1568-1181; 43

Implications of social media use in personal and professional settings LCCN: 2014040312 Main title: Implications of social media use in personal and professional settings / Vladlena Benson and Stephanie Morgan, editors. Published/Produced: Hershey, PA: Information Science Reference, [2015] Description: xx, 362 pages: illustrations; 28 cm ISBN: 9781466674011 (hardcover) 9781466674042 (print and perpetual access) LC classification: HM742 .I47 2015 Related names: Benson, Vladlena, 1976- Morgan, Stephanie J. Summary: "This book investigates the paradoxical nature of social networking in our personal lives and in the workplace, highlighting emergent research and psychological impacts"-- Provided by publisher. Subjects: Online social networks. Social media. Education, Higher-- Effect of technological innovations on. Notes: Includes bibliographical references (pages 310-349) and index.

Informal learning in organizations: how to create a continuous learning culture LCCN: 2015021106 Personal name: Hoyle, Robin, author. Main title: Informal learning in organizations: how to create a continuous learning culture / Robin Hoyle. Published/Produced: London: Kogan Page, [2015]. ©2015 Description: xi, 224 pages: illustrations; 24 cm ISBN: 9780749474591 (paperback) 0749474599 (paperback) LC classification: HD58.8 .H697 2015 Summary: "New ways of learning, whether they are planned, accidental, or unexpected, happen all the time outside of formal training. For those in charge of learning and development in organizations, understanding how this kind of informal learning can be utilized and measured is key to providing efficient and cost-effective ways of improving professional development. Author Robin Hoyle offers practical tools (including checklists and action plan questions) to guide the L&D practitioner in designing and implementing an informal learning strategy personalized to their organization's needs. Combining the latest technology and practices with established theory and research, this book provides an evidence-based review of informal learning. It explains how and why (or why not) informal learning resonates with people and offers an action plan to put the concepts into practice. "-- Provided by publisher. "As the pace of change in the workplace speeds up and training budgets are challenged, it becomes essential for employees to learn as they go along. In this connected world, new ways of learning are emerging all of the time, whether the learning is planned, unexpected or self-directed. For those responsible for learning and development in organizations, understanding how this kind of informal learning can be utilised and measured is key to providing efficient and cost-effective ways of delivering on organizational objectives around people development. Informal Learning in Organizations offers practical tools, including checklists and action plan questions, to guide the Learning and Development practitioner in how to design and implement an informal learning strategy that is personalised to the needs of their own organization. It combines the latest thinking on new technology and practices with established theory and research to provide an evidence-based review of informal learning and its true impact. It offers an overview of how and why informal learning resonates with people, how it works and when and why it doesn't. This book will assist the reader in making sense of their connected environments and creating a continuous learning culture in their organizations"-- Provided by publisher. Contents: Table of Contents: Acknowledgements -- Introduction -- SECTION ONE Making sense of informal learning at work01 What is informal learning? -- Informal Learning is about doing different things and doing things differently -- The independence of the informal learning -- A short history lesson -- Apprentices and more structured preparation for work -- The work difference -- The role of the organization in informal learning 02 A model of informal learning -- What do we mean by learning? -- A definition of informal learning -- Informal: guided discovery and learning through work -- Informal = better? 03 The capability contract -- Continuing professional development -- Vocational qualifications -- Knowledge or skills? -- Learning together -- Conclusions – Notes 04 Formal training and the budget paradox -- The budget paradox -- The role of the subject matter expert – Notes 05 Informal doesn't mean unmanaged -- The dilemma -- Belief number 1: Informal learning cannot be managed -- Belief 2: Informal learning is difficult to measure -- The checklist – Notes 06 Informal learning and culture -- How important is culture to informal learning? -- Can an informal learning culture be defined? -- More localized culture -- Growing a more local, team-based culture -- Informal learning and the dominant culture -- Winterbourne View and other scandals -- Other scandals and the learned culture of the organization -- Is better initial training the answer? -- Combatting culture – Notes SECTION TWO Liking ain't learning: the rise of social and the impact of technology 07 Liking, learning and looking up the answers -- The rise of the Mavens -- I'm a bit anti-social -- Learning or just copying? -- The brighter side of social media – Notes 08 Is there hope beyond the social media hype? -- Beyond the L&D bubble -- You had to be there -- Where's the sense in seek-sense-share? -- An uncomfortable pat on the back -- A flock of twits -- Conclusion – Notes 09 Smarter social tools -- Beware the crowd -- The limitations of algorithms -- Skilled information seekers -- The threat of like-mindedness -- Learning from IT companies -- Application beyond applications? – Notes 10 Social networking skills for learning and collaboration -- Personal knowledge management: a daily job -- Gaining the benefits of user-generated content -- Smile -- you're on TV – Notes 11 Learning from academia: MOOCs and the flipped classroom -- Flipping the classroom -- The implications for learners -- Who uses MOOCs, how and why? -- Can you build your own MOOC (and would you want to)? -- Conclusion – Notes SECTION THREE Learning as you work, working as you learn 12 Integrating learning into work -- Blended learning comes of age -- The new blend -- Moving to the workplace -- 70:20:10 -- The informality within 70:20:10 -- Stretch or challenge -- Challenge vs threat -- Collaboration -- Professional development -- Multi-tasked learning -- Conclusion – Notes 13 Measuring and evaluating -- Performance indicators -- Example 1: the sales team -- Example 2: the accident and emergency department of a hospital -- The performance director -- What are you measuring and why? -- Softer measures -- Badges? We don't need your stinking badges -- What sort of technology platform do you need? -- Artefacts of learning -- Analysing performance -- Preparing the organization for change -- the real requirement for measurement – Notes 14 The informal learning action plan -- Part 1: the questions to ask -- Part 2: strategy on one page (SOOP) -- Part 3: the recipe -- Part 4: dos and don'ts – Notes Index. Subjects: Organizational change. Employees--Training of. Non-formal education. Employees--Training of. Non-formal education. Organizational change. Notes: Includes bibliographical references and index.

Intellectual property and general legal principles: is IP a lex specialis? LCCN: 2014952156 Main title: Intellectual property and general legal principles: is IP a lex specialis? / edited by Graeme B. Dinwoodie, Professor of Intellectual Property and Information Technology Law, University of Oxford, UK. Published/Produced: Cheltenham, UK: Edward Elgar Publishing, 2015. Description: viii, 258 pages; 25 cm. ISBN: 9781784714949 (cased) 1784714941 (cased) LC classification: K1401 .I553315 2015 Related names: Dinwoodie, Graeme B., editor. Contents: 1. Contract lex rex: towards copyright contract's lex specialis / Giuseppina D'Agostino -- 2. The enforceability of mass-market e-commerce licenses and social networking agreements: is copyright or contract law the new lex specialis? / Charles R. McManis and Brett Garrison -- 3. Fair is as fair does: contractual normative regulation of copyright user contracts in South Africa / Caroline B. Ncube -- 4. Compelling disclosure of software interoperablility information: a risk for innovation or a balanced solution? / Begoña G. Otero -- 5. Is IP law a lex specialis?: a dual test / Gustavo Ghidini -- 6. Inclusivity in intellectual property / Severine Dusollier -- 7. Private ordering and consumers' rights in copyright law: a view of Japanese consumers / Branislav Hazucha, Hsiao-Chien Liu and Toshihide Watabe -- 8. Intellectual property protection for fame, luxury, wines and spirits: lex specialis for a corporate "dolce vita" or a "good quality life"? / Irene Calboli -- 9. Provocations and challenges concerning enforcement and civil procedure in IP / Kimberlee Weatherall -- 10. A "bundle" of national patents v European patent with unitary effect: a jurisdictional comparison / Torsten Bjørn Larsen -- 11. IP, disability, culture and exceptionalism: does copyright law deal with difference? / Abbe Brown and Charlotte Waelde. Subjects: Intellectual property. Notes: Includes bibliographical references and index. Series: ATRIP intellectual property series ATRIP intellectual property.

Intellectual property and private international law LCCN: 2015938365 Main title: Intellectual property and private international law / edited by Paul

Torremans, Professor of Intellectual Property Law School of Law, University of Nottingham, UK. Published/Produced: Cheltenham, UK: Edward Elgar Limited, [2015] Description: xxv, 853 pages; 25 cm. ISBN: 9781783471423 (hbk.) 1783471425 (hbk.) LC classification: K7550 .I577 2015 Related names: Torremans, Paul, editor. Contents: 1. Sophie Neumann (2011), Intellectual Property Rights Infringements in European Private International Law: Meeting the Requirements of Territoriality and Private International Law -- 2. Teruo Doi (2002), The Territoriality Principle of Patent Protection and Conflict of Laws: A Review of Japanese Court Decisions -- 3. Lydia Lundstedt (2001), Jurisdiction and the Principle of Territoriality in Intellectual Property Law: Has the Pendulum Swung Too Far in the Other Direction? -- 4. Benedetta Ubertazzi (2011), Intellectual Property Rights and Exclusive (Subject Matter) Jurisdiction: Between Private and Public International Law -- 5. Mario Franzosi (1997), Worldwide Patent Litigation and the Italian Torpedo -- 6. Paul Torremans (2011), The Sense or Nonsense of Subject Matter Jurisdiction Over Foreign Copyright -- 7. Paul L.C. Torremans (2011), Star Wars Rids Us of Subject-Matter Jurisdiction: The Supreme Court Does Not Like Kafka Either When It Comes to Copyright -- 8. Annette Kur (2006), A Farewell to Cross-Border Injunctions? The ECJ Decisions GAT v. LuK and Roche Nederland v. Primus and Goldenberg -- 9. Mario Franzosi (2009), GAT and Roche: Idola Fori, Teatri, Specus: Regulation 864/2007 Makes Cross-Border Patent Litigation Possible -- 10. Benedetta Ubertazzi (2009), Licence Agreements Relating to IP Rights and the EC Regulation on Jurisdiction -- 11. Matthias Rössler (2007), The Court of Jurisdiction for Joint Parties in International Patent Disputes -- 12. Christian Heinze (2011), Choice of Court Agreements, Coordination of Proceedings and Provisional Measures in the Reform of the Brussels I Regulation -- 13. Pedro A. de Miguel Asensio (2007), Cross-Border Adjudication of Intellectual Property Rights and Competition Between Jurisdictions -- 14. Anna Tydniouk (2004), From Itar-Tass to Films by Jove: The Conflict of Laws Revolution in International Copyright -- 15. Paul Torremans and Carmen

Otero García Castrillón (2012), Reversionary Copyright: A Ghost of the Past or a Current Trap to Assignments of Copyright? -- 16. Guido Westkamp (2006), Research Agreements and Joint Ownership of Intellectual Property Rights in Private International Law -- 17. Paul Torremans (2010), Copyright: Which Law Applies? Some Thoughts on Issues of Authorship, (First) Ownership of Rights and Works Created by Employees -- 18. Jane C. Ginsburg and Pierre Sirinelli (1991), Authors and Exploitations in International Private Law: The French Supreme Court and the Huston Film Colorization Controversy -- 19. Paul Torremans (2008), Licenses and Assignments of Intellectual Property Rights Under the Rome I Regulation -- 20. Christopher Wadlow (2009), The New Private International Law of Unfair Competition and the "Rome II" Regulation -- 21. Toshiyuki Kono (2005), Intellectual Property Rights, Conflict of Laws and International Jurisdiction: Applicability of ALI Principles in Japan? -- 22. Stefania Bariatti (2010), The Law Applicable to Security Interests in Intellectual Property Rights -- 23. Torsten Bettinger and Dorothee Thum (2000), Territorial Trademark Rights in the Global Village: International Jurisdiction, Choice of Law and Substantive Law for Trade Mark Disputes on the Internet -- 24. Axel Metzger (2012), Transnational Law for Transnational Communities: The Emergence of a Lex Mercatoria (or Lex Informatica) for International Creative Communities -- 25. Graeme B. Dinwoodie, Rochelle C. Dreyfuss and Annette Kur, (2009), The Law Applicable to Secondary Liability in Intellectual Property Cases -- 26. Pedro A. de Miguel Asensio (2011), Social Networking Sites, An Overview of Applicable Law Issues -- 27. Rita Matulionyte (2011), The Law Applicable to Online Copyright Infringements in the ALI and CLIP Proposals: A Rebalance of Interests Needed? -- 28. Pedro A. de Miguel Asensio (2012), Internet Intermediaries and the Law Applicable to Intellectual Property Infringements -- 29. Rita Matulionyte (2013), Calling for Party Autonomy in Intellectual Property Infringement Cases -- 30. Graeme B. Dinwoodie (2009), Developing a Private International Intellectual Property Law The Demise of

Territoriality? -- 31. Marketa Trimble (2009), Cross-Border Injunctions in U.S. Patent Cases and Their Enforcement Abroad -- 32. Marketa Trimble Landova (2009), Public Policy Exception to Recognition and Enforcement of Judgments in Cases of Copyright Infringement --33. Marketa Trimble (2011), Extraterritorial Intellectual Property Enforcement in the European Union. Subjects: Conflict of laws--Intellectual property. Notes: "An Elgar research collection" Series: Critical concepts in intellectual property law series; 12

Internet addiction LCCN: 2014932573 Personal name: Perdew, Laura, author. Main title: Internet addiction / by Laura Perdew; content consultant, Dr. Keith W. Beard, Marshall University, Department of Psychology. Published/Produced: Minneapolis, Minnesota: Essential Library, an imprint of Abdo Publishing, [2015] Description: 112 pages: color illustrations; 24 cm. ISBN: 9781624034213 1624034217 LC classification: RC569.5.I54 P47 2015 Summary: Discusses the issues surrounding Internet addiction, including the history of the Internet, why Internet addiction is hard to diagnose, and how people can recover from this addiction. Contents: Lost in the digital world -- Origins of the Internet -- Internet addiction emerges -- Gaming -- Communicating -- Social networking -- Shopping and gambling -- Media multitasking -- Seeking help. Subjects: Internet addiction--Juvenile literature. Compulsive behavior--Juvenile literature. Internet addiction. Compulsive behavior. Compulsive behavior. Internet addiction. Form/Genre: Juvenile works. Notes: Includes bibliographical references (pages 104-109) and index. Series: Essential issues Essential issues.

Internet security: how to defend against attackers on the web LCCN: 2015019892 Personal name: Harwood, Mike. Uniform title: Security strategies in Web applications and social networking. Main title: Internet security: how to defend against attackers on the web / Mike Harwood, MCT, MCSE, A+, Network+, Server+, Linux+, Writer and Editor for the yoursecondfifty.com/magazine. Edition: Second Edition. Published/Produced: Burlington, MA: Jones and Bartlett Learning, [2016] Description:

xvii, 438 pages; 24 cm ISBN: 9781284090550 (pbk.: alk. paper) LC classification: HM742 .H38 2016 Related names: Harwood, Mike. Security strategies in Web applications and social networking. Summary: "Internet Security: How to Defend Against Attackers on the Web, Second Edition provides a comprehensive explanation of the evolutionary changes that have occurred in computing, communications, and social networking and discusses how to secure systems against all the risks, threats, and vulnerabilities associated with Web-enabled applications accessible via the internet"-- Provided by publisher. Contents: From mainframe to client-server to world wide web -- Security considerations for smb's -- Security considerations for home and personal online use -- Securing mobile communications -- Mitigating risk when connecting to the internet -- Mitigating web site risks, threats, and vulnerabilities -- Introducing the web application security consortium (WASC) -- Securing web applications -- Mitigating web application vulnerabilities -- Maintaining pci dss compliance for e-commerce web sites -- Testing and quality assurance for production web sites -- Performing a web site vulnerability and security assessment -- Securing end-point device communications -- Securing personal and business communications -- Web application security organizations, education, training, and certification. Subjects: Online social networks--Security measures. Application software--Security measures. Internet--Security measures. World Wide Web--Security measures. Notes: Includes bibliographical references (pages 415-422) and index. Series: Jones and Bartlett learning, information systems security and assurance series

Management and the arts LCCN: 2014021213 Personal name: Byrnes, William J. Main title: Management and the arts / William J. Byrnes. Edition: Fifth edition. Published/Produced: New York: Focal Press, Taylor and Francis Group, 2015. Description: xxiii, 575 pages: Illustrations; 24 cm ISBN: 9780415663298 (paperback) LC classification: NX765 .B87 2015 Summary: "The fifth edition of Management and the Arts provides you with theory and practical applications from all arts management perspectives including planning, marketing, finance, economics, organization, staffing, and group dynamics. Regardless of whether you are a manager in a theatre, museum, dance company, or opera, you will gain useful insights into strategic planning, organization, and integrated management theories. Case studies, statistics, and real-world examples will allow you get a handle on all aspects of arts managements, from budgeting and fundraising, to e-marketing and social networking, to working effectively with boards and staff members. Revised to reflect the latest thinking and trends in managing organizations and people, this fifth edition features class-tested questions in each chapter, which help you to integrate the material and develop ideas about how the situations and problems could have been handled. Case studies focus on the challenges facing managers and organizations every day, and "In the News" quotes give you real-world examples of principles and theories. NEW TO THIS EDITION: - Sections on grant research and writing, social networking, and fundraising - Resources for developing career skills, graduate, and postgraduate training opportunities, and information on professional organizations and conferences - Expanded material on volunteers in the arts, more coverage of international perspectives, and more information on integrated software solutions and on budgeting - A companion website at www.managementandthearts.com with a sample syllabus, additional project assignments, suggested resources, and chapter-by-chapter PowerPoint slides"-- Provided by publisher. Subjects: Arts--United States--Management. Performing Arts / Theater / General.

Mobile social networking and computing: a multidisciplinary integrated perspective LCCN: 2014009746 Personal name: Wang, Yufeng (Computer scientist) Main title: Mobile social networking and computing: a multidisciplinary integrated perspective / Yufeng Wang and Jianhua Ma. Published/Produced: Boca Raton: CRC Press, Taylor and Francis Group, [2015] ©2015 Description: xxii, 394 pages: illustrations; 24 cm ISBN: 9781466552753 (hardback) 1466552751 (hardback) LC classification: QA76.59 .W36

2015 Related names: Ma, Jianhua, 1962- Summary: "This book introduces mobile social networking (MSN) and computing from a multi-disciplinary perspective. It covers fundamental theory and key problems in MSN, including characteristics, inner structural relationship, incentive mechanisms, resource allocating, information diffusion, search, ranking, privacy, trust and reputation in MSN. It reviews various applications and includes analysis on related platforms"--Provided by publisher. Subjects: Mobile computing. Online social networks. Computers / Internet / General. Technology and Engineering / Telecommunications. Technology and Engineering / Mobile and Wireless Communications. Notes: Includes bibliographical references and index.

Need LCCN: 2014034512 Personal name: Charbonneau, Joelle. Main title: Need / Joelle Charbonneau. Published/Produced: Boston; New York: Houghton Mifflin Harcourt, [2015] Description: pages cm ISBN: 9780544416697 LC classification: PZ7.C37354 Ne 2015 Summary: "In this exploration of the dark side of social media, and government control and manipulation, the teenagers in a small town are drawn deeper and deeper into a social networking site that promises to grant their every need--regardless of the consequences"-- Provided by publisher. Subjects: Social media--Fiction.

New opportunities for artistic practice in virtual worlds LCCN: 2015008171 Main title: New opportunities for artistic practice in virtual worlds / Denise Doyle, University of Wolverhampton, UK, [editor]. Published/Produced: Hershey, PA: Information Science Reference, an imprint of IGI Global [2015] Description: xxiv, 322 pages: illustrations (mostly color); 29 cm. ISBN: 9781466683846 (hardcover) LC classification: TR897.74 .N49 2015 Related names: Doyle, Denise, 1964- editor. Summary: "This book provides a coherent account of artistic practices in virtual worlds and considers the contribution the Second Life platform has made in a historical, theoretical, and critical context within the fields of art and technology"--Provided by publisher. Subjects:

Machinima films. Computer animation. Virtual reality. Computer art. Video games. Second Life (Game) Notes: Includes bibliographical references (pages 290-315) and index. Series: A volume in the advances in social networking and online communities (ASNOC) book series, 2328-1405

Online marketing for busy authors: a step-by-step guide LCCN: 2015049358 Personal name: Burke, Fauzia, author. Main title: Online marketing for busy authors: a step-by-step guide / Fauzia Burke. Published/Produced: San Francisco: Berrett-Koehler Publishers, [2016] Description: pages cm ISBN: 9781626567856 (pbk.) LC classification: Z285.6 .B87 2016 Contents: Personal branding 101 -- You gotta dream big -- Know thy reader -- Get real with your goals -- Best advice in the business -- Your priority list -- Your online marketing plan -- Building your website -- Mailing list of fans -- To blog or not to blog -- Social media and social networking -- DIY online book publicity -- Promote without being promotional -- Monitor and adjust. Subjects: Books--Internet marketing. Authorship--Internet marketing. Notes: Includes index.

Perspectives on social media: a yearbook LCCN: 2014004051 Main title: Perspectives on social media: a yearbook / edited by Piet A.M. Kommers, University of Twente, The Netherlands, Pedro Isaias, Universidade Aberta (Portuguese Open University), Portugal, Tomayess Issa, Curtin University, Australia. Published/Produced: New York: Routledge, Taylor and Francis Group, 2015. Description: xv, 192 pages; 24 cm ISBN: 9780415854153 (hardback) 9780415854160 (pbk) LC classification: HM742 .P48 2015 Related names: Kommers, Piet A. M., editor. Isaias, Pedro, editor. Issa, Tomayess, editor. Summary: "Perspectives on Social Media presents the most current research on the effectiveness of social media across sectors. Progress in finding better applications for social media relies on the difficult task of integrating media technologies into fields such as engineering, marketing, health, learning, art, tourism, and the service industry. This book is based on cutting-edge creative work among top international researchers and renowned designers and provides readers with a preview of the most visionary outcomes in the field of social media. Some of the major topics that the book discusses are: New social media design Sense of community in web applications App design and development for mobile devices. Perspectives on Social Media uniquely builds on recent disputes among the top scholars around the world, thus including the dynamics of knowledge-sharing and cross-fertilization that one would expect to happen on the web but that are rarely found in a book"-- Provided by publisher. Contents: Analysis of Computing Platforms as a Tool for Collaborative Learning of Secondary School Students in the Municipality of Guimarães in Portugal: New Perspectives / Dalila Alves Durães, Francisco Javier Hinojo -- Knowledge exchange in social networking sites / Oriol Miralbell -- Social Networking as an Enabler to Recruit and Retain Students at the University of Pretoria (UP) / Karen Lazenby, Petrus Lombard -- Toward Realizing Meta Social Media Contents Management System in Big Data / Takafumi Nakanishi, Kiyotaka Uchimoto, Yutaka Kidawara -- Social media for, with, and by professionals¿participatory design through reflexive engagement / Suvi Pihkala, Helena Karasti -- Cyberpsychology and Social Media: Online Social Support in Mental Health / Kyriaki G. Giota, George Kleftaras -- Challenges in Promoting Digital Communities in Rural Coopetitive Settings / Federico Cabitza, Carla Simone -- Non-users of ICT and Social Media: Marginal Voices / Noora Talsi -- The Use of a Social Media Community by Multicultural Information Systems Development Teams to Improve Communication / Roelien Goede, Moleboge Emma Nhlapo -- Using Social Media to Improve the Work-Integrated Learning Experience of ICT Students: A Critical Systems Approach / Roelien Goede, Anneke Harmse -- Higher Education: The Incorporation of Web 2.0 / Paula Miranda, Pedro Isaías, Sara Pífano -- Factors that influence acceptance of social Web technologies for learning / Razep Echeng, Abel Usoro, Grzegorz Majewski -- Smart Media in Higher Education: Spread of Smart Campus / JeongWon Choi, SangJin An, YoungJun Le -- An Investigation into Japanese University Students' Online

Privacy Concerns / Yukiko Maruyama -- Connecting and communicating with the near field: How NFC-services for smartphones may benefit consumers/citizens through social media integration and augmentation / Dag Slettemeås, Bente Evjemo, Sigmund Akselsen -- Biasomic Future / Esad Širbegović -- Mobile Solutions for the New Ways of Working Era / Mari Ylikauppila, Antti Väätänen, Jari Laarni, Pasi Välkkynen -- The role of interactive technology in prosocial mobile games for young children / Lynne Humphries --Location-Enabled Stamp-Rally System for Local Revitalization / Akira Hattori, Haruo Hayami, Tasuku Kobayashi -- Technology Enhanced Literacy Learning In Multilingual Sub-Saharan Africa: The Case of Graphogame Kiswahili and Kikuyu Adaptations in Kenya / Carol Suzanne Adhiambo Puhakka, Heikki Lyytinen, Ulla Richardson. Subjects: Social media--Research. Social media--Cross-cultural studies. Education / General. Notes: Includes bibliographical references and index.

Poetry: a survivor's guide LCCN: 2015018669 Personal name: Yakich, Mark, author. Main title: Poetry: a survivor's guide / Mark Yakich. Published/Produced: New York: Bloomsbury Academic, An imprint of Bloomsbury Publishing Inc, 2016. ©2016 Description: ix, 222 pages: illustrations; 20 cm Links: Cover image http://www.netread.com/jcusers2/bk1388/502/9781501309502/image/lgcover.9781501309502.jpg ISBN: 9781501309502 (HB) 9781501309502 (PB) LC classification: PN1031 .Y35 2016 Summary: "Playful and serious, unforgiving and compassionate, Poetry: A Survivor's Guide offers an original take on a subject both loved and feared. In a series of provocative and inspiring propositions, the act of reading a poem is made new, and the act of writing one is made over. Questions of poetry's difficulty, pretension, and relevance are explored with insight and daring. In an age of new media and social networking, this handbook-cum-manifesto provides fresh reverence for one of our oldest forms of art"--Provided by publisher. "A provocative and practical guide, written for students of creative writing as well as literary studies, to an art form that is both loved and feared"-- Provided by publisher. Contents: Machine generated contents note: -- I. Introduction: What Is a Poem? -- II. Reading Poetry -- III. Writing Poetry -- IV. Poetic Practices: How To Live with Poetry -- Bibliography -- Index. Subjects: Poetry. Creative writing. Literary Criticism / Poetry. Language Arts and Disciplines / Composition and Creative Writing. Notes: Includes index.

Policing and social media: social control in an era of new media LCCN: 2016000115 Personal name: Schneider, Christopher J., author. Main title: Policing and social media: social control in an era of new media / by Christopher J. Schneider. Published/Produced: Lanham: Lexington Books, [2016] Description: pages cm ISBN: 9781498533713 (cloth: alk. paper) 9781498533737 (pbk.: alk. paper) LC classification: HV7936.P8 S38 2016 Contents: Introduction: media logic, policing, and social media -- Media formats and police social control practices -- Crime and society 2.0: police and social networking -- Facebook and the 2011 Vancouver riot -- Police presentational strategies on Twitter -- Police caught on camera: framing the death of Sammy Yatim -- Conclusion: policing on social media. Subjects: Police-community relations--Canada. Police misconduct--Canada. Social media--Canada. Police and mass media--Canada. Mass media and criminal justice--Canada. Notes: Includes bibliographical references and index. Additional formats: Online version: Schneider, Christopher J., author. Policing and social media Lanham: Lexington Books, [2016] 9781498533720 (DLC) 2016008835

Privacy in the information society LCCN: 2014946839 Main title: Privacy in the information society / edited by Philip Leith, Queen's University of Belfast, UK. Published/Produced: Farnham, Surrey, England: Ashgate, [2015] Description: xxvi, 548 pages: illustrations (black and white); 26 cm. Links: Table of contents only http://www.loc.gov/catdir/toc/fy16pdf02/2014946839.html ISBN: 9781409441281 (hardback: alk. paper) 1409441288 LC classification: K3560 .P75 2015 Related names: Leith, Philip, 1954- editor. Contents: An examination of the concern for information privacy in the New

Zealand regulatory context / Ellen A. Rose -- Property rights in personal information: an economic defense of privacy / Richard S. Murphy -- Privacy and security concerns as major barriers for e-commerce: a survey study / Godwin J. Udo -- Privacy by design: principles of privacy-aware ubiquitous systems / Marc Langheinrich -- The problem of anonymous vanity searches / Christopher Soghoian -- EU data protection policy, the privacy fallacy: adverse effects of Europe's data protection policy in an information-driven economy / Lucas Bergkamp -- Information technology, marketing practice, and consumer privacy: ethical issues / Ellen R. Foxman and Paula Kilcoyne -- Consent in data protection law: privacy, fair processing and confidentiality / Roger Brownsword -- The Data Protection Directive 95/46/EC: idealisms and realisms / Rebecca Wong -- Behavioral advertising: the cryptic hunter and gatherer of the internet / Joanna Penn -- Privacy and confidentiality in an e-commerce world: data mining, data warehousing, matching and disclosure limitation / Stephen E. Fienberg -- Safe harbor: a framework that works / Damon Greer -- The "final" privacy frontier?: regulating trans-border data flows / Gehan Gunasekara -- To track or not to track: recent legislative proposals to protect consumer privacy / Molly Jennings -- Biometrics: privacy's foe or privacy's friend? / John D. Woodward -- Privacy issues in the application of biometrics: a European perspective / Marek Rejman-Greene -- Biometrics and privacy: a note on the politics of theorizing technology / Irma van der Ploeg -- Biometric technologies in support of identity and privacy assurance / Colin Soutar -- Privacy law: biometrics and privacy / Jan Grijpink -- Security and privacy implications of cloud computing: lost in the cloud / Vassilka Tchifilionova -- Privacy and consumer risks in cloud computing / Dan Svantesson and Roger Clarke -- Digital evidence in cloud computing systems / M. Taylor, J. Haggerty, D. Gresty and R. Hegarty -- Caught in the clouds: the web 2.0, cloud computing, and privacy? / Paul Lanois -- Re-mapping privacy law: how the Google Maps scandal requires tort law reform / Lindsey A. Strachan -- E-commerce tax: how the taxman brought geography to the 'borderless' internet / Dan Jerker B. Svantesson -- Tweets from Justin Bieber's heart: the dynamics of the 'location' field in user profiles / Brent Hecht, Lichan Hong, Bongwon Suh and Ed H. Chi -- Teens, privacy and online social networks: how teens manage their online identities and personal information in the age of MySpace / Amanda Lenhart and Mary Madden -- Publicly private and privately public: social networking on YouTube / Patricia G. Lange -- Employer's use of social networking sites: a socially irresponsible practice / Leigh A. Clark and Sherry J. Roberts -- Social networking websites: a concatenation of impersonation, denigration, sexual aggressive solicitation, cyber-bullying or happy slapping videos / Bruce L. Mann -- Impact of news of celebrity illness on breast cancer screening: Kylie Minogue's breast cancer diagnosis / Simon Chapman, Kim McLeod, Melanie Wakefield and Simon Holding -- Privacy, information technology, and health care / Thomas C. Rindfleisch -- "Iceland Inc."?: on the ethics of commercial population genomics / Jon F. Merz, Glenn E. McGee and Pamela Sankar -- Geocoding in cancer research: a review / Gerard Rushton, Marc P. Armstrong, Josephine Gittler, Barry R. Greene, Claire E. Pavlik, Michele M. West and Dale L. Zimmerman. Subjects: Data protection--Law and legislation. Internet--Law and legislation. Privacy, Right of. Notes: Includes bibliographical references and index. Series: The library of essays on law and privacy; volume 2

Product innovation through knowledge management and social media strategies LCCN: 2015037481 Main title: Product innovation through knowledge management and social media strategies / Alok Kumar Goel and Puja Singhal, editors. Published/Produced: Hershey: Business Science Reference, 2016. Description: pages cm ISBN: 9781466696075 (hardcover) LC classification: HD30.2 .P756156 2016 Related names: Goel, Alok Kumar, 1971- editor. Singhal, Puja, 1978- editor. Summary: "This book is an authoritative reference source for scholarly research on the application of social networking platforms to enhance knowledge sharing and innovative practice within organizations, highlighting pertinent theories and techniques for improving communication and ensuring successful product development"-- Provided by publisher. Contents: Foreword --

Preface -- Acknowledgment -- Social media strategies and knowledge management -- Best practices in social media for knowledge management: with special reference to communities / M K Prasanna Iyer, PromptKPO, India -- Cultural barriers to organizational social media adoption / Amir Manzoor, Bahria University, Pakistan -- Social media as elements of shared workspaces: the multifactory case study / Giulio Focardi, Osun Solutions, Italy, Dr. Lorenza Victoria Salati, Bigmagma, Italy -- Social aspects of reverse logistics and knowledge management / Prof. José G. Hernández R., Universidad Metropolitana, Venezuela, Prof. María J. García G., Minimax Consultores,, Venezuela, Prof. Gilberto J. Hernández G., Minimax Consultores, Venezuela -- Graph mining and its applications in studying community based graph under the preview of social network / Dr. Anirban Mitra, VITAM Berhampur, India, Prof. Bapuji Rao, V.I.T.A.M, India -- Knowledge management approaches and innovation process -- Implementing KM lessons from the frontline / Dr. Rusnita Saleh, University of Indonesia,Indonesia -- How to improve knowledge exchange by using internet technologies: an empirical study in small and medium-sized enterprises / Mrs. Simona Popa, University of Murcia, Spain, Prof. Pedro Soto-Acosta, University of Murcia, Spain -- Mapping the enterprise social network (ESN) spectrum in knowledge management and product innovations / Ms. Aparna Venugopal, Indian Institute of Management Kozhikode, India, Prof. Krishnan T.N, Indian Institute of Management Kozhikode, India -- Digital technologies as media to transfer knowledge in IT firms / Dr. Laura Zapata-Cantú, EGADE Business School, Tecnológico de Monterrey, Mexico, Mrs. Teresa Treviño, EGADE Business School, Tecnológico de Monterrey, Mexico, Mrs. Flor Morton, EGADE Business School, Tecnológico de Monterrey, Mexico -- Orientism management (om): a new framework to manage decisions and hyper dynamic knowledge process in a multi-user network / Dr. luisa Dall'Acqua, Univ.of Education Schwäbisch Gmünd PHSG, Scientific Lyceum (ITA-EU), Germany -- Relationship between knowledge management and academic integrity in a middle eastern university / Dr. Judith Mavodza, Zayed University,UAE -- New product development and managing innovation -- Managing innovation within organizations / Achilleas Boukis, Sussex University, UK -- Start-up - a new conceptual approach of innovation process / Joana Coutinho Sousa, Brainiac, Lisbon, Mr. Jorge Gaspar, Unlimited-Hashtag, Lisbon -- Learning, using and retaining deep domain expertise: working in smart r&d organizations / Mr. Anders Hemre, interKnowledge Technologies, Sweden -- Creating product innovation strategies through knowledge management in global business / Dr. Kijpokin Kasemsap, Suan Sunandha Rajabhat University, Bangkok -- Innovation landscape idea to product development / Dr. Alok Kumar Goel, Human Resource Development Centre, India, Dr. Puja Singhal, Amity University, India Compilation of references -- About the contributors. Subjects: Knowledge management. Social media. Technology transfer. New products--Management. Notes: Includes bibliographical references and index.

Rails crash course: a no-nonsense guide to Rails development LCCN: 2014034816 Personal name: Lewis, Anthony, 1975- author. Main title: Rails crash course: a no-nonsense guide to Rails development / by Anthony Lewis. Published/Produced: San Francisco: No Starch Press, [2015] Description: xxiv, 271 pages: illustrations; 24 cm ISBN: 9781593275723 (pbk.) 1593275722 (pbk.) LC classification: TK5105.8885.R83 L49 2015 Contents: Ruby fundamentals -- Building a social networking App. Subjects: Ruby on rails (Electronic resource) Ruby (Computer program language) Notes: Includes index.

Regulating speech in cyberspace: gatekeepers, human rights and corporate responsibility LCCN: 2015001683 Personal name: Laidlaw, Emily B., author. Main title: Regulating speech in cyberspace: gatekeepers, human rights and corporate responsibility / Emily B. Laidlaw. Published/Produced: Cambridge, United Kingdom: Cambridge University Press, 2015. Description: pages cm ISBN: 9781107049130 (hardback) LC classification: K4305 .L35 2015 Summary: "Private companies exert considerable control over the flow of information on the internet. Whether users are finding information with a search engine, communicating on a social networking site or accessing the internet through an ISP, access to participation can be blocked, channelled, edited or personalised. Such gatekeepers are powerful forces in facilitating or hindering freedom of expression online. This is problematic for a human rights system which has historically treated human rights as a government responsibility, and this is compounded by the largely light-touch regulatory approach to the internet in the west. Regulating Speech in Cyberspace explores how these gatekeepers operate at the intersection of three fields of study: regulation (more broadly, law), corporate social responsibility and human rights. It proposes an alternative corporate governance model for speech regulation, one that acts as a template for the increasingly common use of non-state-based models of governance for human rights"-- Provided by publisher. Contents: Machine generated contents note: 1. The internet as democratising force; 2. A framework for identifying internet information gatekeepers; 3. Corporate social responsibility in cyberspace; 4. Direct mechanisms of information control: ISPs; 5. Indirect mechanisms of information control: search engines; 6. A corporate governance model for the digital age. Subjects: Internet service providers--Law and legislation. Freedom of expression. Freedom of information. LAW / General. Notes: Based on author's thesis (doctoral -- London School of Economics, 2012) issued under title: 'Information Gatekeepers, Human Rights and Corporate Social Responsibilities.

Routledge handbook of Southeast Asian democratization LCCN: 2015013826 Main title: Routledge handbook of Southeast Asian democratization / edited by William Case. Published/Produced: London; New York: Routledge, 2015. ©2015 Description: xii, 464 pages; 25 cm ISBN: 9781138939042 (hardback) LC classification: JQ750.A91 R68 2015b Related names: Case, William, editor. Case, William. Democracy's mixed fortunes in Southeast Asia Container of (work): Summary: "Southeast Asia, an economically dynamic and strategically vital region, seemed until recently to be transiting to more democratic politics. This progress has suddenly stalled or even gone into reverse, requiring that analysts seriously rethink their expectations and theorizing. The Routledge Handbook of Southeast Asian Democratization provides the first book-length account of the reasons for democracy's declining fortunes in the region today. Combining theory and case studies, it is structured in four major sections: - Stunted Trajectories and Unhelpful Milieus - Wavering Social Forces - Uncertain Institutions - Country cases and democratic guises. This interdisciplinary reference work addresses topics including the impact of belief systems, historical records, regional and global contexts, civil society, ethnicity, women, Islam, and social media. The performance of political institutions is also assessed, and the volume offers a series of in-depth case studies, evaluating the country records of particular democratic, hybrid, and authoritarian regimes from a democratization perspective"--Provided by publisher. Contents: Democracy's mixed fortunes in Southeast Asia: torpor, change, and tradeoffs / William Case -- Dead idea (still) walking: the legacy of the Asian democracy and values debate / Mark R. Thompson -- Democratization and human rights in Southeast Asia / Sorpong Peou -- ASEAN, regionalism and democracy / Mark Beeson and Kelly Gerard -- The global context of regime change / Thomas B. Pepinsky -- Demystifying people power: an elite interpretation of democratization in Southeast Asia / Yuki Fukuoka -- The middle class and democracy in Southeast Asia / Aim Sinpeng and Aries A. Arugay -- Conflict, oppositional spaces and political representation in Southeast Asia / Garry Rodan -- Civil society and democratisation in Southeast Asia: what is the connection? / Meredith L. Weiss -- Ethnicity and democracy / Joel Sawat Selway -- Islam and political democracy / Robert W. Hefner -- Women and democracy in Southeast Asia / Susan Blackburn -- Hype or hubris? the political impact of the internet and social networking in Southeast Asia / Jason Abbott -- Electoral systems in Southeast Asia / Benjamin Reilly -- Rethinking party system institutionalization in Southeast Asia and beyond / Allen Hicken and Erik Martinez Kuhonta -- Democracy, hybridity, and accountability in Southeast Asia's legislatures / William Case -- Courts and judicialization in Southeast Asia / Bjoern Dressel -- Democracy, the rule of law and governance in Southeast Asia / Natasha Hamilton-Hart -- Money politics: patronage and clientelism in Southeast Asia / Edward Aspinall -- Southeast Asian militaries in the age of democratization: from ruler to servant / Aurel Croissant -- Can the Philippines' wild oligarchy be tamed? / Nathan Gilbert Quimpo -- Democracy in Thailand: theory and practice / Federico Ferrara -- Indonesia: democratic consolidation and stagnation under Yudhoyono, 2004-2014 / Marcus Mietzner -- Singapore: from hegemonic to competitive authoritarianism / Stephan Ortmann -- Malaysia: pseudo-democracy and the making of a Malay-Islamic state / James Chin -- Myanmar: transition, praetorian politics, and the prospects for democratic change / Renaud Egreteau -- Democracy and Vietnam / Benedict J. Tria Kerkvliet. Subjects: Democracy--Southeast Asia. Southeast Asia--Politics and government. Notes: Includes bibliographical references and index.

Social media and the good life: do they connect? LCCN: 2015017992 Personal name: Herring, Mark Y., 1952- Main title: Social media and the good life: do they connect? / Mark Y. Herring. Published/Produced: Jefferson, North Carolina: McFarland and Company, Inc., Publishers, [2015] Description: vii, 208 pages; 23 cm ISBN: 9780786479368 (softcover: alk. paper) LC classification: HM742 .H475 2015 Summary: "Social media has accelerated communication, expanded business horizons and connected millions of individuals. Social networking sites are used by scammers, criminals and sexual predators, and many people now self-diagnose illness. This book examines some of the legal and ethical issues surrounding social media, its impact on civil discourse and its role in suicides, murders and criminal enterprise"-- Provided by publisher. Subjects: Online social networks. Social media. Information technology--Social aspects. Notes: Includes bibliographical references (pages 183-204) and index.

Social media and the transformation of interaction in society LCCN: 2015012012 Main title: Social media and the transformation of interaction in society / John P. Sahlin, editor. Published/Produced: Hershey,

PA: Information Science Reference, [2015] Description: xxii, 300 pages: illustrations; 29 cm ISBN: 9781466685567 (hardcover) LC classification: HM742 .S628194 2015 Related names: Sahlin, John P., 1971- Summary: "This book is a definitive reference source for timely scholarly research evaluating the impact of social networking platforms on a variety of relationships by featuring expansive coverage on a range of topics relating to social media applications and uses across industries"-- Provided by publisher. Subjects: Online social networks. Social media. Communication and technology. Notes: Includes bibliographical references (pages 228-292) and index.

Social media communication: concepts, practices, data, law and ethics LCCN: 2014007455 Personal name: Lipschultz, Jeremy Harris, 1958- Main title: Social media communication: concepts, practices, data, law and ethics / Jeremy Harris Lipschultz. Published/Produced: New York, NY: Routledge, 2015. Description: xvi, 251 pages; 26 cm ISBN: 9781138776449 (hardback) 9781138776456 (paperback) LC classification: HM741 .L563 2015 Summary: "In Social Media Communication: Concepts, Practices, Data, Law and Ethics, Jeremy Harris Lipschultz presents a wide-scale, interdisciplinary analysis and guide to social media. Examining platforms such as Twitter, Facebook, LinkedIn, Pinterest, Youtube and Vine, the book explores and analyzes journalism, broadcasting, public relations, advertising and marketing. Lipschultz focuses on key concepts, best practices, data analyses, law and ethics--all promoting the critical thinking professionals and students need to use new networking tools effectively and to navigate social and mobile media spaces. Featuring contemporary case studies, essays from some of the industry's leading social media innovators, and a comprehensive glossary, this practical, multipurpose textbook gives readers the resources they'll need to both evaluate and utilize current and future forms of social media"-- Provided by publisher. Subjects: Social media. Social networks. Online social networks. Social media--Law and legislation. Social media--Moral and ethical aspects. Social Science / Media Studies. Computers / Web / Social Networking. Language

Arts and Disciplines / Journalism. Notes: Includes bibliographical references and index.

Social media recruitment: how to successfully integrate social media into recruitment strategy LCCN: 2015008795 Personal name: Headworth, Andy. Main title: Social media recruitment: how to successfully integrate social media into recruitment strategy / Andy Headworth. Published/Produced: London; Philadelphia: Kogan Page, 2015. Description: vii, 209 pages: illustrations, map; 24 cm ISBN: 9780749473709 (paperback) LC classification: HF5549.5.R44 H43 2015 Summary: "As the landscape of recruiting changes, different methods are needed to reach talent, and social media is a key channel. However, many HR and recruiting professionals are not equipped with the expertise to create a social media recruiting strategy.In a series of easy to follow chapters and manageable steps, Social Media Recruitment covers the essentials from the beginning to the end of the process, including: how to implement a social media strategy; the crossover between HR, recruitment and marketing; measuring ROI; HR policies and procedures needed; big data and HR; using technology in recruiting, such as video interviewing; social media as an internal collaboration and communication tool across companies; how social media will impact recruitment and HR in the future. "-- Provided by publisher. "In order to attract the right people into your organization despite a global shortfall of talented candidates, new methods are now needed to reach future talent. Social media needs to become a vital part of any recruitment strategy. Social Media Recruitment combines practical guidance with case studies and insights from industry thought leaders to provide a full understanding of what social media means for HR and recruitment and how to successfully integrate and use it. It covers the essentials from the beginning to the end of the process, including employer branding, interviewing and onboarding, and how to assess the ROI of the social media recruitment strategy. Ideal for all HR and recruitment professionals, and anyone responsible for talent strategy, this practical guide focuses on devising and implementing a social media recruitment strategy that works for your organization and is aligned with your recruitment objectives"-- Provided by publisher. Subjects: Employees--Recruiting. Social media. Personnel management. Business and Economics / Human Resources and Personnel Management. Computers / Web / Social Networking. Notes: Includes bibliographical references and index.

Social media risk and governance: managing enterprise risk LCCN: 2015027327 Personal name: Mennie, Phil. Main title: Social media risk and governance: managing enterprise risk / Phil Mennie. Edition: 1st Edition. Published/Produced: Philadelphia, PA: Kogan Page, 2015. Description: vii, 220 pages: illustrations; 23 cm ISBN: 9780749474577 (paperback) LC classification: HD61 .M4596 2015 Summary: "In a recent survey, 71 percent of executives polled said their company was concerned about the possible risks posed by social media, but 59 percent do not perform a social media risk assessment. This book is a comprehensive, practical guide to the components and considerations that make up a social media governance strategy, spanning both external communications channels such as Facebook, Twitter and LinkedIn, as well as enterprise social networks within an organization. Phil Mennie, PwC's Global Social Media Risk and Governance leader, addresses key issues such as policy evaluation and planning, information security and fraud risks, how to respond to a crisis and how to archive data. The book empowers professional users of social networks to collaborate with their compliance and risk management counterparts, and to harness the power of social media safely and successfully for their organization"-- Provided by publisher. "Few topics are as pressing to policy makers, business leaders and the risk management community as the secure and compliant management of social media. Social Media Risk and Governance is a practical guide to the components and considerations which make up a good social media governance strategy, spanning both external communications channels such as Facebook, Twitter and LinkedIn, as well as enterprise social networks within an organization. Written by social media risk and governance expert Phil Mennie, Social Media Risk and Governance addresses the concepts professionals in information security, marketing, compliance and risk management need to take into account in their daily practice, guiding us through policy evaluation, planning on social media, information security and fraud risks, how to respond to a crisis or to archive data and more. Featuring examples from companies such as BP, MasterCard, Netflix, PwC, Silk Road UBS and Yelp, the book is designed to promote cross-functional working between professional users of social media, acknowledging the impact of these technologies across the business and the interaction of the various stakeholders when planning new activities to effectively harness the power of social media safely and successfully for their organization"-- Provided by publisher. Contents: Machine generated contents note: Part 1 - IntroductionPart 2 - RiskPart 3 - StrategyPart 4 - Data privacy and controlPart 5 - GovernancePart 6 - Policy, training and awarenessPart 7 - Crisis managementPart 8 - SecurityPart 9 - Regulatory response. Subjects: Risk management. Business enterprises--Computer networks. Personnel management--Computer programs. Internet--Security measures. Business and Economics / Insurance / Risk Assessment and Management. Computers / Web / Social Networking. Computers / Internet / Security. Business and Economics / Human Resources and Personnel Management. Computers / Internet / General. Notes: Includes bibliographical references (page 214) and index.

Social media strategies for dynamic library service development LCCN: 2014040420 Main title: Social media strategies for dynamic library service development / Adeyinka Tella, editor. Published/Produced: Hershey, PA: Information Science Reference, [2015] Description: xxv, 388 pages: illustrations; 30 cm. ISBN: 9781466674158 (hardcover) LC classification: Z674.75.S63 S64 2015 Related names: Tella, Adeyinka, 1972- Summary: "This book discusses the integration of digital social networking into library practices, highlighting the advantages and challenges faced by libraries in the application of social media"-- Provided by publisher. Subjects: Online social networks--Library applications. Online social networks--Library applications--

Africa. Social media. Social media--Africa. Libraries and the Internet. Libraries and the Internet--Africa. Libraries--Marketing. Libraries--Marketing--Africa. Notes: Includes bibliographical references (pages 351-380) and index. Series: Advances in library and information science (ALIS) book series

Social networking LCCN: 2014040689 Main title: Social networking / Daniel Gaetán-Beltrán, book editor. Published/Produced: Farmington Hills, Mich.: Greenhaven Press, A part of Gale, Cengage Learning, [2015] Description: 103 pages: illustrations (chiefly color); 24 cm ISBN: 9780737772401 (hardcover) LC classification: HM742 .S6295 2015 Related names: Gaetán-Beltrán, Daniel. Subjects: Online social networks. Social networks. Social media. Notes: Includes bibliographical references (pages 94-96) and index. Series: Issues that concern you

Social networking: redefining communication in the digital age LCCN: 2015047556 Main title: Social networking: redefining communication in the digital age / edited by Anastacia Kurylo and Tatyana Dumova. Published/Produced: Lanham: Fairleigh Dickinson University Press, 2016. ©2015 Description: pages cm. ISBN: 9781611477382 (cloth: alk. paper) 9781611477405 (pbk.: alk. paper) LC classification: HM742 .S6297 2016 Related names: Kurylo, Anastacia, editor. Dumova, Tatyana, 1962- editor. Contents: Acknowledgments -- Foreword / Robert Shuter -- Introduction: social networking without walls / Anastacia Kurylo and Tatyana Dumova -- Together and apart: social and technical networks / Guy Merchant -- The application of traditional social network theory to socially interactive technologies / Corey Jay Liberman -- Social networking sites, self-disclosure, and personal engagement / Pamela J. Kalbfleisch -- Mobile social networking / Giuseppe Lugano -- Students, the ivory tower, and educational uses of social networking sites / Anastacia Kurylo and Yifeng Hu -- The illusion of control: a historiographical examination of social media, bookmarking, and perceived control in the digital sphere / Pamela E. Walck and Hans K. Meyer -- Social networking in times of crisis / Hayley Watson, Kush Wadhwa,

Lemi Baruh, and Salvatore Scifo -- Social networking technologies and social movements / Zeynep Günel and Lemi Baruh -- Networked activism in china / Zixue Tai -- Social network research methods: approaches and key issues / Tatyana Dumova -- Index -- About the contributors. Subjects: Online social networks. Social media. Social movements--Technological innovations. Social networks--Research--Methodology. Notes: Includes bibliographical references and index. Additional formats: Online version: Social networking Lanham: Fairleigh Dickinson University Press, 2016 9781611477399 (DLC) 2016006594 Series: Fairleigh Dickinson University Press series

Strategic infrastructure development for economic growth and social change LCCN: 2014045048 Main title: Strategic infrastructure development for economic growth and social change / Nilanjan Ray, Royal Thimphu College, Bhutan, Dillip Kumar Das, Sikkim Central University, India, Somnath Chaudhuri, Royal Thimphu College, Bhutan, Arindam Ghosh, Royal Thimphu College, Bhutan. Published/Produced: Hershey: Business Science Reference, An Imprint of IGI Global, [2015] Description: xxix, 404 pages; 29 cm. ISBN: 9781466674707 (hardcover: alk. paper) LC classification: HD2741 .S83 2015 Related names: Ray, Nilanjan, 1984- editor. Summary: "This book explores different avenues of research in the areas of corporate governance, socioeconomic conditions, modern business infrastructure, business automation, strategic financial management, and financial aspects of modern businesses"--Provided by publisher. Contents: Corporate governance: the catalyst for economic growth and social change / Sandeep Goel, Finance, Management Development Institute, Gurgaon. INDIA -- Development strategy in the Northern State of Jalisco from the institutional perspective / José G. Vargas-Hernández, LEC.Mónica Isabel García Mora -- University center for economic and managerial sciences, university of Guadalajara -- The effectiveness of non-profit organisations in society through marketing practices / Irene Samanta, Department of Business Administration -- Graduate Technological Education Institute of Piraeus (TEI) --

Financial development and economic growth / Dimitrios Nikolaou Koumparoulis, Fellow FInstAM, Institute of Administrative Management, United Kingdom -- Impact of intellectual capital on the organizational performance of airline industry in Malaysia / Muhammad Khalique, University Malaysia, Sarawak, Malaysia, Abu Hassan Md. Isa, University Malaysia Sarawak, Malaysia -- The role of e-business adoption in the business world / Kijpokin Kasemsap, Suan Sunandha Rajabhat University, Thailand -- Measuring performance of hotels in Kolkata: an empirical study through vaictm method / Debasish Batabyal, IIASSOM, Siliguri, India -- Growth theory: a primer / Atanu Sengupta, The University of Burdwan, Burdwan, West Bengal, India, Anirban Hazra, The University of Burdwan, Burdwan, West Bengal, India -- Infrastructure development in developing countries: issues of tourism, cultural configuration, and service alignment / Raj Kumar Bhattarai, Tribhuvan University, Kathmandu, Nepal -- A novel technique for securing e-commerce transaction / Arnab K. Maji -- North eastern hill university, india -- Ppps in road infrastructure: the indian experience / Manisha Verma, India -- Business process offshoring services in India: addressing untapped opportunities and policy implications / Falendra Kumar Sudan, University of Jammu, India -- Bhutan tourism: issues and challenges / Nilanjan Ray, Royal Thimphu College, Dillip Kumar Das, Sikkim Central University, India -- Relationships among information technology, service quality and overall satisfaction of the customers in life insurance corporation of India / Partha Sarathi Choudhuri, The University of Burdwan, West Bengal, India -- An empirical analysis of FII movement and currency value in India / Saurav Sen, Ruchi Sen, Sunbeam College for Women, Varanasi, India -- Internet use and destination preferences: evidence from crete and Cyprus / Nikolaos Pappas, Leeds Metropolitan University, U.K -- Issues and prospects of sugar industry: an evidence from India / Ajit Dhar Dubey, DDU Gorakhpur University, Gorakhpur, India -- Financial performance of selected FMCG companies in india during post-reform era: a comprehensive analysis / Kaushik Chakraborty,

Netaji Mahavidyalaya, India, Subhasis Sarkar, The University of Burdwan, India -- Targeting a new tourism market: is barbados ready for the Brazilian market? / Nicola Harrison, Cristina Jönsson, The University of the West Indies, West Indies -- Surplus labour in the unorganised sector of India: the case of female labour / Atanu Sengupta, The University of Burdwan, India, Ujjwal Seth, Govt.College of Engineering and Textile Technology,Berhampore -- Work-value orientation: perspective to analyze employee responses -- Anshuman bhattacharya / Sunbeam College for Women, Varanasi, India -- Measuring service quality dimensions in nationalized and private banks / Upendra Singh Panwar, DOMS, SGSITS, Indore, India -- Social networking-an effective tool of virtual marketing? / Shivani Arora, SBS College, Delhi University, India -- Application of supply chain management through sap in agriculture of SAARC nations / Somnath Chaudhuri, Royal Thimphu College, Kingdom of Bhutan. Subjects: Corporate governance. Industrial management. Strategic planning. Electronic commerce. Corporations--Finance. Notes: Includes bibliographical references (pages 360-392) and index. Series: A volume in the Advances in Business Strategy and Competitive Advantage (ABSCA) Book Series

Success secrets of the online marketing superstars LCCN: 2014039154 Personal name: Meyerson, Mitch. Main title: Success secrets of the online marketing superstars / by Mitch Meyerson. Published/Produced: [Irvine, California]: Entrepreneur Press, [2015] Description: x, 324 pages: illustrations; 23 cm ISBN: 9781599185583 (paperback) 159918558X (paperback) LC classification: HF5415.1265 .M47 2015 Summary: "Eager business owners gain access to the playbooks of 24 of today's most respected and well-known online marketers, who reveal their most valuable online strategies and tactics for capturing new customers and influencing ongoing purchases from current ones. Each chapter is a coaching session designed to help business owners avoid the pitfalls and mistakes by the experts who have been there and done that. Readers learn how to develop a personal media brand, build a total online presence, and create a social media strategy that increases traffic. They also discover how to develop and use content that converts visitors into buyers and ultimately loyal customers, succeed with SEO, pay-per-click, and linking strategies that get websites ranked. Also included is information on leveraging social networking apps, including Facebook, online video, and Instagram, and avoiding the mistakes made by new online businesses"-- Provided by publisher. "Successful online marketer and consultant Mitch Meyerson presents an unmatched advantage into the world of internet marketing--the secrets, strategies, tactics, and insights of 24 of today's top online influencers. Each well-known digital marketer delivers a chapter sharing their best practices in creating online discovery, engagement, and sales"-- Provided by publisher. Subjects: Internet marketing. Internet advertising. Business and Economics / E-Commerce / Internet Marketing. Business and Economics / Marketing / General. Computers / Web / Social Networking. Computers / Web / Podcasting and Webcasting. Notes: Revised edition of the author's Success secrets of the online marketing superstars, published in 2005. Includes index.

Teach yourself visually iPhone LCCN: 2014943274 Personal name: Hart-Davis, Guy, author. Main title: Teach yourself visually iPhone / by Guy Hart-Davis. Edition: 2nd edition. Published/Produced: Indianapolis, IN: Visual, John Wiley and Sons, [2015] ©2015 Description: 337 pages: color illustrations; 25 cm. Links: Publisher description http://www.loc.gov/catdir/enhancements/fy1607/2014943274-d.html ISBN: 9781118932223 1118932226 LC classification: QA76.8.I64 H3725 2015 Summary: A visual guide to the world's most popular mobile device, "Teach Yourself VISUALLY iPhone" is your practical and accessible guide to mastering the powerful features and functionality of Apple's iPhone. For new iPhone users and long-time customers alike, this excellent resource features visually rich tutorials and step-by-step instructions that will help you understand all of your iPhone's capabilities--from the most basic to the most advanced. Most consumers gravitate toward the iPhone and Apple products in general because they "just work." But you may not have been getting the most out of your iPhone, until now. With "Teach Yourself VISUALLY iPhone," you'll learn how to access and download books, apps, music, and video content as well as send photos and e-mails, edit movies, sync with Apple devices and services, and effectively use the current OS. All the new features and capabilities of the latest, cutting edge iPhone are covered. This practical guide will help you: Learn the features of iOS visually with 500 full-color screen shots Master the basic functions of your iPhone and customize your settings to ensure you are getting optimal performance from your smartphone, understand how to find the best apps and services to fit your personal and business needs. Written for visual learners and anyone who is interested in either starting out with a brand new iPhone or learning about the latest features of the most recent revolutionary device from Apple, "Teach Yourself VISUALLY iPhone" is the ultimate visual guide to the world's favorite smartphone. Contents: Getting started with your iPhone -- Personalizing your phone -- Working with voice and accessibility -- Setting up communications -- Making calls -- Networking and social networking -- Working with apps -- Browsing the web and e-mailing -- Keeping your life organized -- Playing music and videos -- Working with photos and books -- Using the built-in apps -- Taking photos and videos -- Troubleshooting your iPhone. Subjects: iPhone (Smartphone) iPhone (Smartphone) Notes: "Covers iPhone 5s, 5c, 6 and 6 Plus"--Cover. Includes index. Series: Teach yourself visually Teach yourself visually.

Television, social media, and fan culture LCCN: 2015034009 Main title: Television, social media, and fan culture / edited by Alison F. Slade, Amber J. Narro, and Dedria Givens-Carroll. Published/Produced: Lanham: Lexington Books, 2016. Description: pages cm ISBN: 9781498506168 (cloth: alk. paper) 9781498506182 (pbk.: alk. paper) LC classification: PN1992.55 T46 2016 Related names: Slade, Alison, 1977- editor. Narro, Amber J., editor. Givens-Carroll, Dedria, 1960- editor. Contents: The new network: how social media is changing and saving television / Ryan Cassella -- Spoiler alert: understanding television enjoyment in the social media era / Benjamin Brojakowski -- Rhetorical strengths and limitations of interactivity for activism in the Stewart and Colbert universe / Christopher A. Medjesky -- Fandom communication in a mediated age: the use of Twitter and blogs for dissent practices among National Basketball Association (NBA) fans / Corey Jay Liberman, Michael Plugh and Brian Geltzeiler -- What types of #sportsfans use social media? the role of team identity formation and spectatorship motivation on self-disclosure during a live sport broadcast / Shaughan A. Keaton, Nicholas M. Watanabe and Brody J. Ruihley -- The online community: fan response of community's unlikely fifth season / Matthew Collins and Danielle M. Stern -- Game(s) of fandom: the hyperlink labyrinths that paratextualize Game of thrones fandom / Garret Castleberry -- Be original: examining fan comments on A&E's Duck dynasty facebook page after the Robertson suspension / Michel M. Haigh -- The parents have the dream, but the kids are in the nightmare: digital interactivity, toddlers and tiaras viewers, and social networking sites / Leandra H. Hernandez -- Zombie fans, second screen, and television audiences: redefining parasociality as technoprosociality in AMC's #talkingdead / Sabrina Pasztor and Jenny Ungbha Korn -- Memes, tweets, and props: how fans cope when shows go off the air / Alane Presswood and Steve Granelli -- So are the days of our tweets: an examination of Twitter use by American daytime serials and their fans / Marsha Ducey -- Army wives connect: Lifetime viewers' everyday lives and fandom converge in online communities / Darcey Morris -- Butter, Facebook, and Paula Deen: examining fans use of social media in crisis / Michel M. Haigh and Shelley Wigley -- Fans can be journalists too: a look at fan interaction with HBO's The newsroom / Julia E. Largent and Jason Roy Burnett -- It's bigger on the inside: fandom, social media, and Doctor Who / Krystal Fogle -- Television-inspired cosplay and social media / Laura Kane and William E. Loges -- Who killed @thelaurapalmer? Twitter as a performance space for Twin peaks fan fiction / Kathryn L. Lookadoo and Ted M. Dickinson -- Fifty years of The man from U.N.C.L.E.: how the ever-changing media sustained and shaped one of the oldest fan communities / Cynthia W. Walker -- Managing multiscreen / Daniel Faltesek. Subjects: Television viewers--Social aspects. Television programs--Social aspects. Online social networks--Social aspects. Fans (Persons)--Social aspects. Notes: Includes bibliographical references and index.

Terms of service: social media and the price of constant connection LCCN: 2014035599 Personal name: Silverman, Jacob. Main title: Terms of service: social media and the price of constant connection / Jacob Silverman. Edition: First edition. Published/Produced: New York, NY: Harper, an imprint of Harper Collins Publishers, [2015] Description: xiv, 429 pages; 24 cm ISBN: 9780062282460 (hardback) LC classification: HM851 .S554 2015 Subjects: Information technology--Social aspects. Information technology--Moral and ethical aspects. Right of privacy. Electronic surveillance--Social aspects. Social Science / Media Studies. Computers / Web / Social Networking. Computers / Social Aspects / General.

The Cambridge handbook of acculturation psychology LCCN: 2015046464 Main title: The Cambridge handbook of acculturation psychology / edited by David L. Sam and John W. Berry. Edition: Second edition. Published/Produced: Cambridge, United Kingdom: Cambridge University Press, 2016. Description: pages cm. Links: Cover image http://assets.cambridge.org/97811071/03993/cover/9781107103993.jpg ISBN: 9781107103993 (hardback) LC classification: GN502 .C36 2016 Portion of title: Handbook of acculturation psychology Acculturation psychology Related names: Sam, David L., editor. Berry, John W., 1939- editor. Summary: "Research and practice in the field of acculturation psychology is continually on the rise. Featuring contributions from over fifty leading experts in the field, this handbook compiles and systemizes the current state of the art by exploring the broad international scope of acculturation. The collection introduces readers to the concepts and issues; examines various acculturating groups (immigrants, ethnic minorities, indigenous peoples, expatriates, tourists, refugees and asylum seekers); highlights the global contexts for acculturation in a variety of societies; and focuses on acculturation of a number of special groups, such as young people, the workplace, and outcomes for health and well-being. This comprehensive new edition addresses major world changes over the last decade, including the increase in global migration, religious clashes, and social networking, and provides updated theories and models so that beginners and advanced readers can keep abreast of new developments in the study of acculturation"-- Provided by publisher. "The collection introduces readers to the concepts and issues; examines various acculturating groups (immigrants, ethnic minorities, indigenous peoples, expatriates, tourists, refugees and asylum seekers); highlights the global contexts for acculturation in a variety of societies; and focuses on acculturation of a number of special groups, such as young people, the workplace, and outcomes for health and well-being. This comprehensive new edition addresses major world changes over the last decade, including the increase in global migration, religious clashes, and social networking, and provides updated theories and models so that beginners and advanced readers can keep abreast of new developments in the study of acculturation"-- Provided by publisher. Contents: Machine generated contents note: 1. Introduction John W. Berry and David L. Sam; Part I. Theories, Concepts and Methods: 2. Theoretical perspectives John W. Berry and David L. Sam; 3. Acculturation and identity Karmela Liebkind, Tuuli Anna Mähönen, Sirkku Varjonen and Inga Jasinskaja-Lahti; 4. Personality and acculturation Karen van der Zee, Veronica Benet-Martinez and Jan Pieter van Oudenhoven; 5. Acculturation development and the acquisition of culture competence Brit Oppedal and Claudio O. Toppelberg; 6. Assessment Fons J. R. van de Vijver, John W. Berry and Ozgur Celenk; Part II. Research with Specific Acculturating Groups: 7. Changing the acculturation conversation: indigenous cultural reclamation in Australia and Aotearoa/New Zealand Pat Dudgeon, Dawn Darlaston-Jones, Linda Waimarie Nikora, Waikaremoana Waitoki, Rogelia Pe-Pua, Le Nhat Tran and Lobna Rouhani; 8. Immigrants and ethnocultural groups Jan Pieter van Oudenhoven, Jaimee Stuart and Linda K. Tip; 9. Refugees and forced migrants Giorgia Don... and Marta Young; 10. Sojourners Saba Safdar and Tracy Berno; Part III. Acculturating Contexts: Societies of Settlement: 11. Acculturation in Canada Kimberly A. Noels and John W. Berry; 12. Acculturation in Central and South America Alejandra del Carmen Dominguez Espinosa and Sylvia Dantas; 13. Acculturation in East and Southeast Asia Adam Komisarof and Chan-Hoong Leong; 14. Acculturation in Eastern Europe Radosveta Dimitrova and Nadezhda Lebedeva; 15. Israel Gabriel Horenczyk and Yoav S. Bergman; 16. Acculturation theory and research in New Zealand and Australia Colleen Ward and Anita S. Mak; 17. South Asia R. C. Tripathi and R. C. Mishra; 18. Acculturation in Sub-Sahara Africa Byron G. Adams and Amina Abubakar; 19. The United Kingdom Rupert Brown, Hanna Zagefka and Linda K. Tip; 20. The United States of America Gail M. Ferguson and Dina Birman; 21. Acculturation in Western Europe Colette Sabatier, Karen Phalet and Peter F. Titzmann; 22. Multiculturalism John W. Berry and Colleen Ward; Part IV. Applications: 23. Children, families and schools Paul Vedder and Frosso Motti-Stefanidi; 24. Cultural diversity in the workplace Karen van der Zee and Gro Mjeldheim Sandal; 25. Health David L. Sam, Inga Jasinskaja-Lahti, Andrew G. Ryder and Ghayda Hassan; 26. Conclusions: where are we and where are we headed? David L. Sam and John W. Berry. Subjects: Ethnopsychology. Acculturation. Series: Cambridge handbooks in psychology

The concise new Partridge dictionary of slang and unconventional English LCCN: 2014010953 Personal name: Partridge, Eric, 1894-1979. Uniform title: New Partridge dictionary of slang and unconventional English Main title: The concise new Partridge dictionary of slang and unconventional English / edited by Tom Dalzell and Terry Victor. Edition: Second Edition. Published/Produced: London; New York: Routledge, 2015. Description: xvi, 864 pages; 26 cm ISBN: 9780415527200 (hardback) LC classification: PE3721 .P3 2015 Portion of title: Dictionary of slang and unconventional English Related names: Dalzell, Tom, 1951- Victor, Terry. Summary: "The

Concise New Partridge Dictionary of Slang presents all the slang terms from The New Partridge Dictionary of Slang and Unconventional English in a single volume. Containing over 60,000 entries from around the English-speaking world, this concise new edition of the authoritative work on slang details the slang and unconventional English of the English-speaking world since 1945, and through the first decade of the new millennium, with the same thorough, intense, and lively scholarship that characterized Partridge's own work. Unique, exciting and, at times, hilariously shocking, key features include: unprecedented coverage of World English, with equal prominence given to American and British English slang, and entries included from Australia, New Zealand, Canada, India, South Africa, Ireland, and the Caribbean - emphasis on post World War II slang and unconventional English - dating information for each headword New to this second edition: A new preface noting slang trends of the last five years - Over 1,000 new entries from the US, UK and Australia, reflecting important developments in language and culture - New terms from the language of social networking from a range of digital communities including texting, blogs, Facebook, Twitter and online forums Many entries now revised to include new dating, ensuring maximum accuracy of content"-- Provided by publisher. Subjects: English language--Slang--Dictionaries. Foreign Language Study / General. Language Arts and Disciplines / General. Language Arts and Disciplines / Library and Information Science / General.

The cybrarian's web 2: an A-Z guide to free social media tools, apps, and other resources LCCN: 2015000244 Personal name: Peltier-Davis, Cheryl Ann. Main title: The cybrarian's web 2: an A-Z guide to free social media tools, apps, and other resources / Cheryl Ann Peltier-Davis; foreword by David Lee King. Published/Produced: Medford, New Jersey: Information Today, Inc, [2015] Description: pages cm ISBN: 9781573875127 LC classification: ZA4225 .P44 2015 Contents: Adobe: productivity and creativity tools -- Amazon CreateSpace: self-publishing platform -- Aurasma: augmented reality service -- BrandYourself: online reputation management service -

- Camtasia: screen recording and video editing software -- Codecademy: online education platform (programming) -- Coursera: massive open online courses (MOOCs) platform -- Digital public library of America: digital library -- Diigo: social bookmarking service -- Dropbox: cloud storage/file hosting/sharing service -- Ebooks: ebook collections and services -- Ebook readers: ebook reading devices -- Evernote: note-taking software -- Flipboard: social news aggregator -- Google drive: cloud storage/file hosting/sharing service -- Google glass: augmented reality/wearable technology -- Google hangouts: video conferencing service -- GoToMeeting: video conferencing service -- Hootsuite: social media management service -- Infogr.am: infographics creator -- Instagram: photo and video sharing service -- Issuu: digital publishing service -- Jumpshare: cloud storage/file hosting/sharing service -- Kaywa: qr code scanner and generator -- Kickstarter: crowdfunding platform -- Learnist: digital learning board -- LiveBinders: social bookmarking service -- Makerspaces: DIY collaborative workspaces -- Mendeley: reference management and collaboration service -- Microsoft Office online: productivity tool -- Mobile apps for libraries: mobile applications -- Netvibes: social media management service -- OneDrive: cloud storage/file hosting/sharing service -- Paper.li: social news aggregator -- Pinterest: social bookmarking service -- Poll everywhere: audience response/polling service -- Popplet: visualization service -- Project Gutenberg self-publishing press: self-publishing platform -- Quick response (QR) codes: barcode scanning and generator software -- Readability: Web and mobile reading application -- Scoop.it: social news aggregator -- Scribd: digital library/self-publishing platform -- Smashwords: digital library/self-publishing platform -- Snapchat: photo and video sharing service -- Storify: social news aggregator -- Technology, entertainment, design (TED): global conference/ideas sharing platform -- Text 2 mind map: visualization service -- TodaysMeet: microblogging service -- Tumblr: microblogging/social networking service -- Tweetdeck: social media management service -- Udutu: course management system -- Unglue.it: crowdfunding platform -- Vine: video sharing service -- Voki: avatar creation service -- Wattpad: social networking service -- Weebly: web hosting service -- WhatsApp: instant messaging service -- Wikispaces: wiki hosting service -- XPRIZE: philanthropic competition -- Yammer: social networking service -- Zinio: digital publishing service -- Appendix I. Tips and teaching tools for keeping up-to-date with emerging technologies and discovering new resources -- Appendix II. Social media tools, apps and other resources - annotated summaries -- Appendix III. Referenced websites -- Appendix IV. Tools by type of service -- Appendix V. Tools availability by mobile device. Subjects: Web sites--Directories. Free computer software--Computer network resources. Libraries and the Internet. Notes: Includes bibliographical references and index.

The digital difference: media technology and the theory of communication effects LCCN: 2015039005 Personal name: Neuman, W. Russell, author. Main title: The digital difference: media technology and the theory of communication effects / W. Russell Neuman. Published/Produced: Cambridge, Massachusetts: Harvard University Press, 2016. Description: pages cm ISBN: 9780674504936 (alk. paper) LC classification: HM1206 .N477 2016 Summary: "Although the shift from one-way to two-way mass communication - from broadcasting to social networking - represents a revolutionary restructuring, it does not necessarily mean the public is better informed, more culturally or politically polarized, or more engaged in public life. Practices, institutions, and norms are in mid-transition and potentially subject to our individual and collective choice. The book is designed to connect the best of recent scholarship with these pressing policy questions"--Provided by publisher. Subjects: Information society. Information networks. Technology and civilization. Information technology--Social aspects. Information technology--Political aspects. Mass media--Social aspects. Mass media--Political aspects. Notes: Includes bibliographical references and index.

The discourse of digital civic engagement: perspectives from the developing world LCCN: 2015040999 Main title: The discourse of digital civic engagement: perspectives from the developing world / editors, Rotimi Taiwo and Tunde Opeibi (Department of English, Obafemi Awolowo University, Nigeria, and University of Lagos, Nigeria). Published/Produced: Hauppauge, New York: Nova Science Publisher's, Inc., 2016. Description: pages cm. ISBN: 9781634841207 (hardcover) LC classification: JF799.5 .D57 2016 Related names: Taiwo, Rotimi (Dr.), editor. Opeibi, Babatunde Olusola, editor. Contents: Digital media and civic engagement in Nigeria: a corpus-assisted discourse study of president Goodluck Ebele Jonathan's Facebook / Tunde Opeibi -- Language use in crisis situations: a discourse analysis of online reactions to digital news reports of the Washington Navy Yard shooting and the Nairobi Westgate attack / Innocent Chiluwa and Esther Ajiboye -- A multimodal analysis of the public discourse of the 2013 university lecturers' strike in Nigeria / Mohammed Ademilokun -- Sentence typologies and civic engagement in Nairaland forum / Yetunde Idehen and Rotimi Taiwo -- The "eboliticization" of discourse: online legitimations on the outbreak of Ebola virus disease (EVD) in West Africa / Ikenna Kamalu -- Finding their feet: digital immigrants in a "natives" generation contrasting the use of SMS and IM in everyday communication / Ayo Onanuga and Emmanuel Taiwo Babalola -- Visual representation of power in selected online Nigerian newspapers' political cartoons / Felicia Oamen and Micheal Olusegun Fajuyigbe -- Personal branding styles on some social networking sites / Olaosun Ibrahim Esan and Oyebamiji Mojirayo Patricia -- Discourse of online preaching: a stylo-linguistic analysis of pastor Tunde Bakare's sermons on religion, politics and poverty in Nigeria / Adegboye Adeyanju -- The discursive features of Nigerian online political cartoons / Oludele, E. Omobola. Subjects: Political participation--Technological innovations--Developing countries--Case studies. Political participation--Technological innovations--Nigeria--Case studies. Digital media--Political aspects--

Developing countries--Case studies. Digital media--Political aspects--Nigeria--Case studies. Notes: Includes index. Additional formats: Online version: Discourse of digital civic engagement Hauppauge, New York: Nova Science Publisher's, Inc., 2016 9781634841214 (DLC) 2016000832 Series: Electronics and telecommunications research

The evolution of the internet in the business sector: Web 1.0 to Web 3.0 LCCN: 2014036396 Main title: The evolution of the internet in the business sector: Web 1.0 to Web 3.0 / Pedro Isaias, Piet Kommers, Tomayess Issa, editors. Published/Produced: Hershey: Business Science Reference, 2015. Description: xxi, 407 pages: illustrations; 29 cm. ISBN: 9781466672628 (hardcover: alk. paper) LC classification: HD30.37 .E96 2015 Related names: Isaias, Pedro, editor. Kommers, Piet A. M., editor. Summary: "This book takes a historical look at the policy, implementation, management, and governance of productivity enhancing technologies, sharing best practices with public and private universities, IS developers and researchers, education managers, and business and web professionals interested in implementing the latest technologies to improve organizational productivity and communication"-- Provided by publisher. Contents: Preface -- Web and business models -- Are signals a solution to perceived risk and opportunism in mobile shopping?: gender differences and similarities -- Models and approaches for web information extraction and web page understanding -- Web applications -- A roadmap on awareness of others in accessible collaborative rich internet applications -- An usability evaluation of facebook's privacy features based on the perspectives of experts and users -- HTML segmentation for different types of web pages -- Social networking sites -- Understanding employee attitudes to sns implementation in the australian banking sector -- Teacher-student relationship in the facebook-era -- Examining the opportunities of social networking adoption in the health care systems -- Web, technology and social influence -- We have good information for you: cognitive authority and information retrieval on the web -- A web-based method for ontology population -- User engagement in feedback sharing through social influence -- Web and education -- Creating a community of practice in learning -- Influence of perceived quality of official university websites to perceived quality of university education and enrollment intention -- Students as customers: participatory design for adaptive web 3.0 -- The open innovation paradigm: can digital storytelling generate value for the educational field?. Subjects: Business enterprises--Computer network resources. Information technology--Economic aspects. Notes: Includes bibliographical references (pages 354-395) and index.

The performing subject in the space of technology: through the virtual, toward the real LCCN: 2015002381 Main title: The performing subject in the space of technology: through the virtual, toward the real / Matthew Causey, Emma Meehan and Néill O'Dwyer. Published/Produced: New York: Palgrave Macmillan, 2015. Description: pages cm. ISBN: 9781137438157 (hardback) LC classification: NX180.T4 P48 2015 Related names: Causey, Matthew. Meehan, Emma, 1981- O'Dwyer, Néill, 1979- Summary: "Now that the shock of the virtual has subsided toward a 'new-normal' of computational interference in all areas of life, it is an advantageous moment to reflect on the passage through the virtual and back to the real. Digital culture has developed into a bio-virtual environment in which the categories of the biological and the virtual no longer stand as separate. The contributors to this volume respond to the questions raised by the 'after-event' of the digital through practice-led research analyses of performance processes, philosophical readings of the work of art and technology, and performance studies investigations of the subject in the spaces of technology. The volume examines a wide range of activities, from bio-art to internet child pornography, gaming and social networking technologies to the use of motion-tracking in developing choreography and documentation. The authors draw from diverse perspectives in dance, theatre, performance, film and music studies, digital arts and culture. "-- Provided by publisher. Contents: Machine generated contents note: --

Introduction: 'In the after-event of the virtual'; Matthew Causey, Emma Meehan, Néill O'Dwyer -- PART I: PROVOCATIONS: SUBJECTIVITY AND TECHNOLOGY -- Introduction to Part I; Matthew Causey, Emma Meehan and Néill O'Dwyer -- 1. 'Into the body of another: strange couplings and unnatural alliances of Harlequin Coat'; Burcu Baykan -- 2. 'The Cultural Critique of Bernard Stiegler: Reflecting on the Computational Performances of Klaus Obermaier; Néill O'Dwyer -- 3. 'The Flicker at the threshold of societies of control'; Sharon Phelan -- 4. 'The Right to Be Forgotten and The Image-Crimes of Digital Culture'; Matthew Causey -- 5. 'Materiality, immateriality and the dancing body; the challenge of the inter in the preservation of intangible cultural heritage'; Sarah Whatley -- 6. 'Performing (the Subject of) Exteriority: Virtuality, Mimesis, and the Gratuitous 'One Must"; Riku Roihankorpi -- PART II: PRACTICES: EMBODIED NOTIONS OF ART AND TECHNOLOGY -- 7. Introduction to Part II; Matthew Causey, Emma Meehan and Néill O'Dwyer -- 8. 'Not Waving But Drowning: The Affect Of Random Programming On The Creation Of A Digital Performance Work'; Mary Oliver -- 9. 'BrainExplode! Audiences and agency through the appropriation of Videogame structures'; Dan Bergin -- 10. 'Relational Works-In-Movement Using The Body Response System'; Maria Coleman -- 11. 'Dancing With Dirt And Wires; Reconciling The Embodied And The Digital In Site Responsive Collaborative Practice'; Natalie Garrett Brown, Christian Kipp And Amy Voris -- 12. 'Jeanette Doyle: Fifteen Days And Factory Direct At The Andy Warhol Museum: The Relationship Between The 'Immaterial', 'Dematerial' And 'Material' In Contemporary Art Practice'; Jeanette Doyle -- 13. 'Inscribing Work And Process: The Ontological Implications Of Virtual Scoring Practices For Dance'; Hetty Blades -- 14. 'Traces And Artifacts Of Physical Intelligence'; Scott Delahunta -- Index. Subjects: Technology and the arts. Performing arts. Performance art. Performing Arts / Theater / History and Criticism. Series: Palgrave studies in performance and technology

The promiscuity of network culture: queer theory and digital media LCCN: 2014031934 Personal name: Payne, Robert, 1973- Main title: The promiscuity of network culture: queer theory and digital media / Robert Payne. Published/Produced: New York: Routledge, Taylor and Francis Group, 2015. Description: xii, 156 pages; 24 cm. ISBN: 9781138816510 (hardback) LC classification: HM742 .P38 2015 Summary: "Liking, sharing, friending, going viral: what would it mean to recognize these current modes of media interaction as promiscuous? In a contemporary network culture characterized by a proliferation of new forms of intimate mediated sociality, this book argues that promiscuity is a new standard of user engagement. Intimate relations among media users and between users and their media are increasingly structured by an entrepreneurial logic and put to work for the economic interests of media corporations. But these multiple intimacies can also be understood as technologies of promiscuous desire serving both to liberalize mediated social connection and to contain it within normative frames of value. Payne brings crucial questions of gender, sexuality, intimacy, and attention back into conversation with recent thinking on network culture and social media, identifying the queer undercurrents of these current media dynamics"-- Provided by publisher. Subjects: Online social networks. Promiscuity. Intimacy (Psychology) Digital media-- Social aspects. Sex in mass media. Queer theory. Social Science / Media Studies. Computers / Web / Social Networking. Social Science / Gender Studies. Notes: Includes bibliographical references and index. Series: Routledge studies in new media and cyberculture; 26

The smart revolution towards the sustainable digital society: beyond the era of convergence LCCN: 2015933352 Main title: The smart revolution towards the sustainable digital society: beyond the era of convergence / edited by Hitoshi Mitomo, Erik Bohlin, Hidenori Fuke. Published/Produced: Cheltenham: Edward Elgar Publishing, [2015] Description: 1 volume ISBN: 9781784710033 (hbk.) 1784710032 (hbk.) Related names: Mitomo, Hitoshi, editor. Bohlin, Erik, 1961- editor. Fuke, Hidenori, 1946- editor. Summary: The objective of this book is to present a comprehensive evaluation of the smart revolution, including its social and economic impacts. It proposes a modern framework to help assess how recent Information and Communication Technologies (ICTs) can contribute to societies as a whole. The authors offer a guide to how advanced network technologies have led to a greater variety of applications and social networking services. These allow people to connect with each other both at a more personal and global level, and will ultimately herald a new era of ICTs that will shape the 'digital society'. This essential resource will appeal to academics, government officials and practitioners in telecommunications and media -- Book jacket. Contents: The dominance of the IT industry in a converging ICT ecosystem / Anders Henten and Reza Tadayoni -- Model analysis of the two-sided market of the mobile broadband business: in Japan and worldwide / Keisuke Takachi and Toshiya Jitsuzumi -- Digital power shift from network to smart devices: how will regulators cope with digital power? / Minoru Sugaya -- Empirical analysis of the relationship between social media use and product innovation: focusing on SNS use and social capital / Hiroki Idota, Teruyuki Bunno, and Masatsugu Tsuji -- Efficiency of transport infrastructure and ICT development / Kyoung-Youn Na and Chang-Ho Yoon -- Telecommunication service countermeasures against disasters: Japanese people's willingness to pay for telecommunication services / Akihiro Nakamura -- The role of media and ICT to motivate people to take post-quake recovery action: an evidence of the 'Pythagorean effect' / Hitoshi Mitomo, Tokio Otsuka, and Mikio Kimura -- Customer service quality and incomplete information in mobile telecommunications: a game theoretical approach to consumer protection / Rafaele López, Teodosio Pérez-Amaral, Teresa Garin-Muñoz, and Covadonga Gijón -- Industry-specific patterns inherent in personal information leakage incidents in Japan: analyses of an incident database / Naoko Sakurai -- Smart devices, fixed/mobile convergence and the cloud: some medium-term regulatory challenges / Martin Cave and Keiko Hatta -- Problems with international mobile roaming: excessive deregulation works against users' interests / Hidenori Fuke -- An estimation of marginal WTP for variety in the broadcasting platform / Manabu Shishikura and Norihiro Kasuga -- The impact of newly emerging media on traditional media platforms in Taiwan: a co-opetition perspective / Yu-Li Liu -- The Australian digital market: opportunities and challenges / Gary Madden and Hasnat Ahmad -- NGA networks as basis for a sustainable digital society: European country studies (Germany, the UK, the Netherlands and Switzerland) / Ernst-Olav Ruhle, Matthias Ehrler, Natascha Freund, and Martin Lundborg -- Understanding market definition, relevant market and significant market power (SMP) frameworks in the EU / Chatchai Kongaut and Erik Bohlin. Subjects: Digital media--Social aspects. Digital media--Economic aspects. Digital communications--Social aspects. Digital communications--Economic aspects. Information society.

The story of Twitter LCCN: 2013029614 Personal name: Gilbert, Sara. Main title: The story of Twitter / Sara Gilbert. Published/Produced: Mankato, MN: Creative Education, [2015] Description: 46 pages: color illustrations; 28 cm ISBN: 9781608183982 (hardcover: alk. paper) LC classification: HM743.T95 G56 2015 Summary: "A look at the origins, leaders, and innovations of Twitter, the online social networking and microblogging service founded in 2006, which has hundreds of millions of users worldwide"-- Provided by publisher. Subjects: Twitter (Firm)--Juvenile literature. Twitter--Juvenile literature. Microblogs--United States--Juvenile literature. Notes: Includes bibliographical references and index. Additional formats: Online version: Gilbert, Sara. Story of Twitter Mankato, MN: Creative Education, [2014] 9781566604260 (DLC) 2013030414 Series: Built for success

Trends and innovations in marketing information systems LCCN: 2015009416 Main title: Trends and innovations in marketing information systems / Theodosios Tsiakis, [editor]. Published/Produced: Hershey: Business Science Reference, [2015]. Description: xviii, 454 pages: illustrations; 29 cm ISBN: 9781466684591 (hardcover: alk. paper) LC classification: HF5415.13 .T7334 2015 Related names:

Tsiakis, Theodosios, 1978- Summary: "This book features the latest prevailing technological functions and procedures necessary to promote new developments in promotional tools and methods, bringing together extensive discussions on the role of digital tools in customer relationship management, social media, and market performance"-- Provided by publisher. Contents: Preface -- Strategic use of IT/IS and technologies for marketing -- Web 2.0 technologies and marketing / Dora Simões, University of Aveiro, Portugal, Sandra Filipe, University of Aveiro, Portugal -- Information technology communication: main challenges and pitfalls to marketing and management: evidence from curitiba (in brazil) / Adriane Setti, University of Algarve, Portugal, Marisa Cesário, University of Algarve, Portugal, -- Sílvia Fernandes -- Artificial intelligence: marketing's game changer / Edward Forrest, University of Alaska-Anchorage, USA, Bogdan Hoanca, University of Alaska-Anchorage, USA -- Business management and new technologies to improve the services / Giuseppe Granata, University of Cassino and Southern Lazio, Italy -- The treacherous path of corporate social responsibility (CSR) and the role of information systems in its implementation / Tabani Ndlovu, Nottingham Business School, UK, Amon Simba, Nottingham Trent University, UK, Anastasia Mariussen, Oslo School of Management, Norway -- Managing digital bonds in the buyer-supplier relationships / Jari Salo, Oulu Business School, Finland, Giuseppe Pedeliento, University of Bergamo, Italy, Robert Wendelin, Scania, Sweden -- Customer relationship management (CRM) -- The role of customer relationship management in the global business environments / Kijpokin Kasemsap, Suan Sunandha Rajabhat University, Thailand -- Data-driven customer centricity: crm predictive analytics / Othman Boujena, Néoma Business School, France, Kristof Coussement, IESEG School of Management; France, Koen W. De Bock, IESEG School of Management, France -- Social media and social networking -- Social media as marketing information systems: co-creation in viral video advertising / Christos Karpasitis, University of Central Lancashire, Cyprus, Antonios Kaniadakis, Queen

Mary University of London, UK -- The rise of relationship marketing with social media / Ana Margarida Barreto, New University of Lisbon, Portugal -- Social media performance measurement / Goetz Greve, Hamburg School of Business Administration, Germany -- The role of online social networking in the recruitment context / Vanessa Ratten, La Trobe University, Australia -- Improving market performance through marketing -- Online pricing and auctions / Kalender Özcan Atilgan, University of Mersin, Turkey -- Risk management, trust and repeat online shopping intentions: a south African perspective / Mercy Mpinganjira, University of Johannesburg, South Africa -- The rise of eBay: confronting the challenges of asymmetry of information and competition / Mikhail Ion Melnik, Southern Polytechnic State University, USA -- Successful new product planning / Nicholas Grigoriou, Monash University, Malaysia -- Upgrading marketing research: neuromarketing tools for understanding consumers / Anka Gorgiev, CITY College, Greece, Nikolaos Dimitriadis, CITY College, Greece -- Examining the brand communication tools that impact brand preferences of women consumer buying intentions-empirical investigation of middle east / A M Sakkthivel, Sur University College, Sultanate of Oman, B Sriram, Sur University College, Sultanate of Oman -- Compilation of references -- About the contributors -- Index. Subjects: Marketing--Management. Marketing. Management information systems. Notes: Includes bibliographical references (pages 373-442) and index.

Twitter for dummies LCCN: 2014940492 Personal name: Fitton, Laura, author. Main title: Twitter for dummies / by Laura Fitton, @pistachio, Anum Hussain, @anum, and Brittany Leaning, @bleaning; foreword by Jack Dorsey, inventor, founder and chairman, Twitter. Edition: Third edition. Published/Produced: Hoboken, New Jersey: John Wiley and Sons, Inc., [2015] ©2015 Description: xiv, 294 pages: illustrations; 24 cm. Links: Contributor biographical information http://www.loc.gov/catdir/enhancements/fy1513/2014940492-b.html Table of contents only http://www.loc.gov/catdir/enhancements/fy1513/2014940492-t.html Publisher description http://www.loc.gov/catdir/enhancements/fy1606/2014940492-d.html ISBN: 9781118954836 1118954831 LC classification: TK5105.8884 .F58 2015 Related names: Hussain, Anum, author. Leaning, Brittany, author. Summary: Overview: A fully updated guide to the how and why of using Twitter. The fastest-growing social network utility sports new features, and they're all covered in this how-to guide from a leading Twitter marketing consultant. Nearly 20 million people are tweeting on Twitter, and this book shows you how to join them and why you should. You'll learn the nuts and bolts of using Twitter, how to make good connections, and how it can benefit your life and your business. Twitter is the fastest-growing of the social networking tools; this book gets you up to speed on the basics as well as how Twitter can enrich your life and boost your business. Explains how to sign up, find friends and people you want to follow, make the most of shortcuts, use popular Twitter tools, and Twitter on the go; -- Discusses how Twitter can be used for business, fundraising, and maintaining contact with people who share common goals; -- With complete information about all the latest Twitter enhancements, Twitter For Dummies, 2nd Edition will help you get the most from this popular social networking tool. Contents: Foreword -- Introduction: -- About this book: -- New for third edition -- Motivation -- Conventions used in this book -- What you're not to read -- Foolish assumptions -- How this book is organized: -- Part 1: Twitter? Like birds do? -- Part 2: Finding your flock -- Part 3: Twittering in high gear -- Part 4: What's the point? Using twitter to your advantage -- Part 5: Part of tens -- Icons used in this book -- Beyond the book -- Where to go from here -- Part 1: Twitter? Like Birds Do?: -- Getting started with Twitter: -- Figuring out this Twitter thing -- How individuals use Twitter -- How organizations use Twitter -- How businesses use Twitter -- Twitter ecosystem -- Thinking in 140 characters -- Welcome to the world of Twitter: -- Signing up -- Picking a username -- Finding contacts: -- Using useful people-finding tools -- Searching by using Twitter search -- Inviting contacts -- Getting comfortable: just Tweet it! -- Customizing your profile: -- Changing your profile photo -- Changing your header photo -- Using your header image to expand your profile -- Changing your personal background -- Tour Of The Twitter Interface: -- Navigating your home screen: -- Your profile snapshot -- Tweet interface -- Trends -- Who to follow -- Your Twitter stream -- Viewing your notifications tab: -- Favorites -- Retweets -- @replies and @mentions -- Direct messages -- Touring your discover tab: -- Tweets -- Activity -- Who to follow -- Find friends -- Popular accounts -- Twitter search -- Checking out your me tab: -- Your tweets -- Photo/videos -- Seeing who you follow -- Figuring out who's following you -- Revisiting your favorite tweets -- Using Twitter wherever you think best: -- Desktop experience: -- Desktop clients -- Browser plug-ins -- Widgets and gadgets -- Lists that improve your desktop experience -- Leaving the nest: Twitter for mobile: -- Twitter mobile app -- Text messages (SMS delivery) -- Part 2: Finding Your Flock: -- So how do I start Twittering?: -- Finding people to follow on Twitter: -- Seeing who's talking -- Searching for people -- Doing a simple search -- Inviting people personally, through Twitter -- Checking out Twitter lists -- Following back -- Following people: -- Using the follow button -- Replying to tweets -- Retweeting: -- Retweeting a link -- Retweeting the old-fashioned way -- Sending direct messages: -- Direct-messaging shorthand -- Should I @ or DM? -- Encouraging more followers -- Who's using Twitter: -- Tweeting with regular people -- Popular accounts -- Verified accounts -- Building company relationships with Twitter -- Talking politics with actual politicians -- Following celebrities on Twitter -- Twitter directories -- Signing up for automated material -- Part 3: Twittering In High Gear: -- How to tweet like tweeps do: -- Following Twitter protocol: -- Language and abbreviations -- Engaging other on Twitter -- Tweeting frequency -- Inserting links into your Tweets -- Adding your location -- Subscribing to text-message notifications: -- fav -- stats-- get -- whois -- follow -- leave -- on/off username -- invite -- quit and stop -- Improving your Twitteracy: -- Finding interesting Twitter talk with search tools: -- Twitter search -- Topsy -- Joining the hashtag revolution: -- Conversations -- Live events -- Twitter chats -- Trending hashtags -- Expanding our Twitter world by using clients: -- Desktop clients -- Mobile clients -- Tag clouds -- Monitoring beyond Twitter-com: -- Google alerts -- Sidekick plus zapier --Social inbox -- Knowing your network: follower and following tools -- Flaunt your feathers with photos and videos: -- Exploring your uploading options: -- Attaching phots to your Tweets -- Making collages in your tweets -- Tagging users in your tweeted phots -- Sizing images for Twitter: -- Adding flavor with a header photo -- Identifying yourself with a profile photo -- Uploading photos with your tweets -- Uploading videos to Twitter: -- Vine -- YouTube -- GIFs -- Uploading other visuals on Twitter: -- Instagram -- SlideShare. Part 4: What's The Point? Using Twitter To Your Advantage: -- Finding your tweet voice: -- Finding your voice: -- Individuals on Twitter -- Businesses on Twitter -- Mixing business with pleasure -- Understanding your audience: -- Who's following you? -- Diversifying your network -- Targeting specific networks -- Measuring your influence -- Measuring your overall presence -- Measuring the reach of your tweets -- Understanding your extended network -- Keeping your tweets authentic: -- Being genuine -- Evangelizing your causes -- Keeping Twitter personal-but not too personal: -- Protecting personal details -- Maximizing privacy and safety -- Twitter for business: -- Understanding the business of Twitter -- Putting your best face forward: -- Public relations -- Customer service -- Networking on Twitter -- Building brand awareness -- Offering promotions and generating leads -- Promoting bands and artists -- Sharing company updates -- Building community -- Conducting research -- Going transparent -- Advising employees on tweeting -- Sharing knowledge -- Twitter and the evolving media landscape: -- Tweedia: understanding Twitter and the media -- Breaking news through tweets: -- Breaking news from individual users -- Breaking news from brands or organizations -- Using Twitter as your news source: -- Integrating Twitter into your news experience -- Building your newspaper -- Following news-related trends -- Being a Twitter journalist: -- Citizen journalism hits the mainstream -- Tweeting accurate info -- Gathering your journalistic tools -- Using news to grow your business: -- Fueling your efforts with adverting -- Engaging with your favorite programming -- Social side of Twitter: -- Using Twitter as a support system -- Connecting with people -- Making new connections: -- Searching for topics of interest -- Attending Twitter-based events -- To follow or not to follow? -- Getting quick answers: -- Accessing celebrities and experts -- Checking breaking news -- Getting recommendations -- Sharing information -- Changing the world, one tweet at a time: -- Twittering the globe for change: -- Tweeting for the greater good -- Tweeting in politics -- Tweeting during natural disasters -- Tweeting to help others -- Twitter to the rescue -- Using Twitter to stay alert -- Organizing people online and in real life: -- Drive to change a nation -- Organizing on a small scale -- Banding together for creative purposes -- Planning an event with Twitter -- Planning a tweetup to meet Twitter friends -- Part 5: Part Of Tens: -- Ten tweets to send today: -- Say hello -- Retweet (RT) someone -- Answer a question -- Share something great -- Say thank you -- Ask a question -- Put a # on it -- Tell us about someone -- Be human -- Don't tweet at all -- Ten cool ways to use twitter: -- Socialize and network -- Follow breaking news -- Find, follow, and fan celebrities -- Participate in live media: sports and television -- Engage with shared media: books, movies, and more -- Optimize your lifestyle -- Support charities, causes, and education -- Plan and promote events -- Find inspiration and personal and professional development -- Invent new uses of twitter -- Ten Twitter tools and services: -- TweetDeck -- Hootsuite -- Social inbox -- Twitter app -- Wefollow and justunfollow -- Twitter counter -- Bitly -- Fuffer -- Canva -- Topsy -- Ten resources for Twitter glory: -- Official Twitter blog -- #twittertips -- How to write a tweet: 8 formulas to get your stared -- Twitter chat schedule -- Twitter support -- Mashable's Twitter category -- @Twitter -- Tweetup meetup groups -- Everything you need to know to successfully live-tweet your event -- @Dummies -- Glossary -- Index. Subjects: Twitter. Blogs. Instant messaging. Online social networks. Notes: Includes index. Series: For dummies --For dummies.

Ultimate guide to Facebook advertising LCCN: 2014025082 Personal name: Marshall, Perry S. Main title: Ultimate guide to Facebook advertising / by Perry Marshall, Keith Krance, Thomas

Meloche. Edition: Second Edition. Published/Produced: Irvine: Entrepreneur Press., [2015] Description: xiv, 327 pages: illustrations; 26 cm. ISBN: 9781599185460 (paperback) 1599185466 (paperback) LC classification: HF6146.I58 M364 2015 Related names: Krance, Keith. Meloche, Thomas. Summary: "Covering the latest and breaking news in Facebook advertising, this updated edition introduces revised, expanded, and new chapters covering fundamentals, Newsfeed ads, sidebar ads, and BIG data. In addition, advertisers are taken farther than just Facebook itself. Marshall and coauthors provide priceless insight into the audience, exploring what was happening before the visitor clicked on an ad and what needs to happen after - ten seconds later, ten minutes later, and in the following days and weeks. Presented in the same step-by-step format that made Marshall's Ultimate Guide to Google AdWords a top seller, this book guides online marketers with a potential audience of 1.11 billion people via a completely different, unbelievably powerful online advertising channel. Facebook presents enhanced tools and exciting opportunities to capture clicks and create brand-loyal customers"--Provided by publisher. "Covering the latest and breaking news in Facebook advertising, the second edition introduces revised, expanded and new chapters covering Fundamentals, Newsfeed ads, Sidebar ads, and BIG data. Plus, advertisers are taken further than Facebook itself. Marshall and co-authors provide priceless insight into the audience, exploring what was happening before the visitor clicked on an ad and what needs to happen after--10 seconds later, 10 minutes later and in the following days, and weeks"--Provided by publisher. Subjects: Facebook (Electronic resource) Internet advertising. Business and Economics / Advertising and Promotion. Computers / Web / Social Networking. Business and Economics / E-Commerce / Internet Marketing. Business and Economics / Sales and Selling.

Ultimate guide to LinkedIn for business LCCN: 2014039156 Personal name: Prodromou, Ted. Main title: Ultimate guide to LinkedIn for business / Ted Prodromou. Edition: Second edition Published/Produced: Irvine, California: EP,

Entrepreneur Press, [2015] Description: xxii, 282 pages; 25 cm ISBN: 9781599185606 (paperback) 1599185601 (paperback) LC classification: HD69.S8 P75 2015 Summary: "This popular title delivers an in-depth guide to targeting, reaching, and gaining ideal customers using the latest updates on LinkedIn. LinkedIn expert Ted Prodromou offers a wealth of no- or low-cost methods for maximizing this dynamic resource. Following his lead, readers learn to link with the most effective connections for greater exposure. Updates in this edition include: staying up-to-date with LinkedIn Contacts, Pulse, and Publisher programs; expansion of premium accounts to help optimize business profiles, stand out in search results, and track impact; t how to implement new features like Showcase and Company Updates pages for extended presence in newsfeeds and with followers; smarter LinkedIn Search that saves time and money with customized, comprehensive results. Other important topics covered include: techniques and tips to easily navigate LinkedIn's interface; timesaving tips on finding and matching data from businesses and people; expert guidance on super-charging a business or individual profile; insider advice on getting found through LinkedIn and maximizing search; professional instruction on promoting a LinkedIn profile. The latest information is illustrated with current snapshots, fresh examples, and case studies, along with new techniques to easily maneuver LinkedIn's interface"-- Provided by publisher. "The increased use of LinkedIn by professionals and companies has nearly doubled since the first edition (from 150 to 300+ million users), causing LinkedIn to create, enhance, and retire several features. The second edition covers those latest advancements with revised, expanded, and new chapters"-- Provided by publisher. Subjects: LinkedIn (Electronic resource) Business networks. Online social networks. Internet marketing. Business and Economics / Small Business. Business and Economics / E-Commerce / Internet Marketing. Computers / Web / Social Networking. Business and Economics / Advertising and Promotion. Notes: Revised edition of the author's Ultimate guide to Linked in for business: how to get connected with 130 million customers in ten minutes, published in 2012. "Quickly engage with ideal customers, partners, and employees -- Use insider tips and tactics to create a steady flow of leads -- Showcase your company and attract new opportunities"--T.P.

Underground airlines LCCN: 2015041417 Personal name: Winters, Ben H., author. Main title: Underground airlines / Ben Winters. Edition: First edition. Published/Produced: New York: Mulholland Books/Little, Brown and Company, [2016] Description: pages; cm ISBN: 9780316261241 (hardcover) LC classification: PS3623.I6735 U53 2016 Summary: "It is the present-day, and the world is as we know it: smartphones, social networking and Happy Meals. Save for one thing: the Civil War never occurred. A gifted young Black man calling himself Victor has struck a bargain with federal law enforcement, working as a bounty hunter for the US Marshall Service. He's got plenty of work. In this version of America, slavery continues in four states called "the Hard Four." On the trail of a runaway known as Jackdaw, Victor arrives in Indianapolis knowing that something isn't right--with the case file, with his work, and with the country itself. A mystery to himself, Victor suppresses his memories of his childhood on a plantation, and works to infiltrate the local cell of a abolitionist movement called the Underground Airlines. Tracking Jackdaw through the back rooms of churches, empty parking garages, hotels, and medical offices, Victor believes he's hot on the trail. But his strange, increasingly uncanny pursuit is complicated by a boss who won't reveal the extraodinary stakes of Jackdaw's case, as well as by a heartbreaking young woman and her child who may be Victor's salvation. Victor himself may be the biggest obstacle of all--though his true self remains buried, it threatens to surface. Victor believes himself to be a good man doing bad work, unwilling to give up the freedom he has worked so hard to earn. But in pursuing Jackdaw, Victor discovers secrets at the core of the country's arrangement with the Hard Four, secrets the government will preserve at any cost. Underground Airlines is a ground-breaking novel, a wickedly imaginative thriller, and a story of an America that is more like our own than we'd like to believe"-- Provided by publisher. Subjects: Bounty hunters--Fiction. Slavery--United States--Fiction. Conspiracies--Fiction. Fiction / Thrillers. Fiction / Alternative History. Form/Genre: Alternative histories (Fiction) Suspense fiction.

You said what?!: the biggest communication mistakes professionals make LCCN: 2015028905 Personal name: Zoller, Kim. Main title: You said what?!: the biggest communication mistakes professionals make / by Kim Zoller and Kerry Preston. Published/Produced: Wayne, NJ: Career Press, Inc., 2015. Description: pages cm ISBN: 9781632650108 (alk. paper) LC classification: HF5718 .Z65 2015 Related names: Preston, Kerry. Contents: Introduction -- Not being on your a-game -- Not beginning with the end in mind -- Not knowing your personal brand -- Not managing perceptions -- Not connecting and building relationships -- Not making appropriate small talk -- Meltdown of communication through technology use -- Not managing your social networking -- Lack of awareness of communication stallers and stoppers -- Making assumptions -- Not focusing on the details -- Not giving and receiving precise feedback -- Not adapting to different communication styles -- Not reacting professionally -- Bloopers and blunders: saying and doing the wrong thing -- Ask Kim and Kerry: answers to sticky situations -- Not communicating value -- Your action plan for continued success -- Index -- About the authors. Subjects: Business communication. Interpersonal communication. Notes: Includes bibliographical references and index.

INDEX

D

E

L

M

S

T

U

V

W